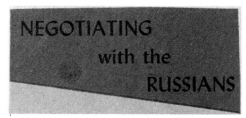

NEGOTIATING
with the
RUSSIANS

Edited by RAYMOND DENNETT
and JOSEPH E. JOHNSON

CAN we negotiate with the Russians?
What does "negotiation" mean? What
does such negotiation involve? What are
the techniques? What happens when
we do negotiate? Is it worth while?

This volume provides clues to the
answers.

These are questions which must be
faced before proposals or evaluation of
proposals for reducing the tension between the Soviet Union and the rest of
the world can be made.

The record of ten distinguished
Americans who negotiated with the Russians during and after World War II—
1940–1950 is not intended as a record of
American foreign policy, nor have the
editors attempted to draw conclusions or
to seek solutions. Nevertheless out of
the record a pattern does emerge and
from the experience of these men "both a
lesson and a warning" is conveyed to
thoughtful Americans.

NEGOTIATING

with the

RUSSIANS

Written by

JOHN R. DEANE

JOHN N. HAZARD

SIDNEY S. ALDERMAN

RAYMOND F. MIKESELL

GEORGE H. BLAKESLEE

E. F. PENROSE

MARK ETHRIDGE

C. E. BLACK

FREDERICK OSBORN

ERNEST J. SIMMONS

PHILIP E. MOSELY

NEGOTIATING WITH THE RUSSIANS

Edited by

RAYMOND DENNETT and

JOSEPH E. JOHNSON

WORLD PEACE FOUNDATION

PRINTED IN THE UNITED STATES OF AMERICA

WORLD PEACE FOUNDATION

40 Mt. Vernon Street, Boston, Massachusetts

Founded in 1910

The World Peace Foundation is a non-profit organization which was founded in 1910 by Edwin Ginn, the educational publisher, for the purpose of promoting peace, justice and goodwill among nations.

For many years the Foundation has sought to increase public understanding of international problems by an objective presentation of the facts of international relations. This purpose is accomplished principally through its publications and by the maintenance of a Reference Collection which furnishes on request information on current international problems.

Recently increased attention has been focused on the field of international affairs with particular emphasis on the field of American foreign policy through the publication of an annual series, *Documents on American Foreign Relations.*

v

162902

TABLE OF CONTENTS

EDITORS' PREFACE

The idea for this book came out of a meeting of the Trustees of the World Peace Foundation in March, 1950. During a general review of the Foundation's program—which over the years has concentrated rather heavily upon the presentation of factual and documentary material in convenient form for the use of educators, government officials and specialists—one Trustee urged that we pay more attention to the behavior of the Soviet Union, which today presents perhaps the most critical of the problems of peace; material is needed to assist the general public in understanding the nature of the task with which this behavior confronts the free world. One member then pointed out that the very first question that had to be answered about the Soviet Union was whether it was in fact possible to negotiate with the USSR at all. Thereupon the two editors of this symposium, one the Director of the Foundation and the other a member of its Board of Trustees, were requested by the Board to work out the plans for a volume on this question.

The Korean crisis of 1950, transferring the "cold war" into a hot war, has so much changed the international climate that it is worth recalling some aspects of the international political scene in March of 1950. Tension between the Soviet Union and the West was steadily mounting. There had been no meeting of the Council of Foreign Ministers for ten months. There was much talk in the United States of negotiation to ease the tension. Senator Brien McMahon of Connecticut had proposed on the floor of the Senate that the United States adopt a fifty billion dollar development program for the whole world, conditioned upon acceptance by the Kremlin of the United Nations proposals for the control of atomic energy. Others were urging that there be another meeting between President Truman and Generalissimo Stalin, similar to the Potsdam Conference.

At the time we were asked to edit this volume, we believed, and we still believe, that before any evaluation can be made of

ix

proposals for reducing the tension between the Soviet Union and
the rest of the world, the question of what negotiations with the
USSR can be expected to achieve must be squarely faced. This
involved in our minds the examination of the whole negotiating
process—the climate in which negotiation takes place, the issues
involved, the expected or hoped for results, the techniques and
tactics of the United States, Russia and other nations, the nature
of the compromises, if any, offered by participants, the reasons
for agreement or disagreement, the outcome, and the consequences. We also felt then, and believe now, that the best way
to begin searching for an answer to our questions was to find
out what had been the experience of those Americans who had
faced the practical problem of negotiating with the Russians over
the years. It was therefore to some of these men that we turned.

The purpose of this symposium is to present the record. It is
not intended to be a record of American foreign policy as such;
it is intended to be a record of how we negotiate with Russians
and what happens when we do. Even as a record, however, it
suffers from certain shortcomings of which we are fully conscious.
Originally we had hoped to be able to provide a greater historical
perspective by covering negotiations with Russia prior to the
October Revolution, during the period of American relief activities, and at the time of United States recognition of the USSR
in 1933. For a number of reasons this proved impractical, and so
we decided to concentrate on war and postwar negotiations, those
of a brief but very full decade from 1940 to 1950. Even with this
more limited goal, we have been only partially successful. We
were unable to secure chapters on the negotiations in regard to
Germany, reparations, the United Nations Charter, or the five
successful peace treaties: those who had generously agreed to
help, and were fully conversant with the very top-level negotiating, have been, since Korea, caught up in heavy official responsibilities and had to be excused.

Nevertheless, the record of ten separate negotiations independ-
ently put forward here by ten different authors who did not
consult with each other, or read any of the other chapters, is,
to our mind, a useful contribution. The new substantive information provided, although not to be overlooked, is probably of
less significance than the degree to which a pattern emerges from
the descriptions by the several authors of the actual process of

negotiation, and the rather general agreement voiced by them that negotiations with the Soviet Union are rarely useful or successful unless the international political climate is favorable. Also noteworthy is the frequent conclusion that, even though little in the way of positive results can be expected, the free world should, nevertheless, be prepared to expend the time, money and effort in additional negotiation; perhaps the authors would not, however, be prepared to agree unreservedly to the aphorism that "eternal negotiation is the price of peace." The record of the experience of these men and their informed and careful judgments convey for thoughtful Americans both a lesson and a warning.

There is no summary of conclusions nor any analysis of the meaning of this difficult decade of negotiation with the Russians. There is not meant to be. This is the story as it looks, in retrospect, to ten distinguished Americans who participated in the effort to halt Fascist aggression and rebuild a shattered world into a better one. While obviously neither we as editors nor the Trustees of the World Peace Foundation can assume responsibility for statements of fact and opinion in the several chapters, we and the Trustees are deeply appreciative of the willingness of the various authors to participate in the symposium and to give a wider public the benefit of their experience and wisdom.

Raymond Dennett, *Director*
World Peace Foundation

Joseph E. Johnson, *President*
Carnegie Endowment for
International Peace

June 15, 1951.

NEGOTIATING
with the
RUSSIANS

Major General John R. Deane was born in California, attended the University of California and entered the regular Army in October, 1917. He served at various posts and stations in the United States and had foreign service for three years in Panama and two years in China. At the outbreak of World War II, he was appointed Secretary of the War Department General Staff. In September, 1942, he was promoted to the rank of Brigadier General and made United States Secretary of the Combined Chiefs of Staff, where he served until September, 1943. At that time he was sent to the Soviet Union in command of the newly created United States Military Mission which had the function of coordinating the land, sea, and air activities of the United States with those of the Soviet Union. The Military Mission also handled the Russian end of the United States Lend-Lease Program Following World War II, General Deane retired from active service and entered the wine business. He is now President of the Italian Swiss Colony, a subsidiary of the National Distillers Products Corporation.

General Deane wrote an account of his experiences in Russia in his book, The Strange Alliance, *published by The Viking Press in 1947.*

CHAPTER ONE

Negotiating on

Military Assistance, 1943-1945

BY JOHN R. DEANE

As one very ordinary American who has sat at the conference table with present-day leaders of the Soviet Union, I
shall try to describe my experience to other Americans. If I
succeed, I shall have helped others hoist a danger signal. If we
Americans can see this signal, heed it, and do our utmost best
about it, morning, noon and night for the next two, three or
four years, there is hope. I approach my task with more temerity
than is justified, with more humility than is apparent—great opportunity, little capability—nevertheless, I shall try.

One would have thought that during the war there would have
been few issues between the United States and the Soviet Union
which would have had to be settled by negotiation. We were
allies with a common enemy, both fighting for our very existence—the success of one, the success of the other. Nevertheless,
every relationship that existed between the two nations was the
subject of protracted negotiation. Even the delivery of American supplies to the Soviet Union, realistically a donor-donee

relationship, inspired negotiations in which the United States was more than once accused of bad faith. It was the existence of lend-lease that accounts for the difference that characterized our wartime relations with the Soviet Union, as contrasted with our postwar relations. As long as lend-lease was operative, Soviet leaders were forced to indulge in international and personal good manners, sufficient, at least, to keep us sweet. During the war there was discussion that lead to agreement and decision. As soon as the end of the war was in sight and particularly when lend-lease ceased, Soviet leaders quickly divested themselves of the strain imposed by ordinary courtesy.

I

I arrived at Moscow on October 18, 1943 and remained there almost exactly two years. I went as Military Adviser to the Secretary of State, Cordell Hull, in his delegation at the Moscow Conference of Foreign Ministers. Thereafter, I was to be in command of the United States Military Mission. The function of the mission was to act as an agency through which land, sea and air activities of the United States could be coordinated with those of the Soviet Union. The mission also represented the United States lend-lease authorities.

No one could have gone to the Soviet Union under more favorable circumstances than I did. From a personal standpoint, it was a delightful assignment. I was to work under the immediate direction of the new ambassador, W. Averell Harriman. This pleased me because, aside from my affection for him as a friend, I knew that he would use the full influence of his position to promote the objectives of my mission. In addition, I was to report directly to, and receive my instructions directly from, the Joint Chiefs of Staff in Washington. This released me from miles and miles of departmental red tape—thus working conditions could not have been better.

My mental approach to the task was favorable. I thought of the Soviet Union as a country that was putting up a gallant battle against the common enemy under adverse circumstances and I was certainly prepared to like those who provided the leadership. My task was, in reality, to act as an American representative whose duty it was to see that the Soviet Union received the maximum American aid in defeating the enemy. Upon my departure, General Marshall instructed me to be frank and open in my military discussions. He had heard of "Soviet suspicion" and told me I must endeavor to overcome it, if collaboration was to be effective. The lend-lease aspect of my mission afforded an opportunity for me to obtain equipment and supplies needed by the Soviet forces. In brief, I went to the Soviet Union full of good will, ready to bubble over with honesty and frankness, and prepared to be lavish in my recommendations for the delivery of American supplies to the Soviet Union.

The Moscow Conference of Foreign Ministers accounted for the first ten days of my stay in the USSR. The delegates met each afternoon at Spirivdonivska House, the scene of all conferences and official entertainment in Moscow in which foreigners are involved. Only those meetings and functions attended by Marshal Stalin are held in the Kremlin.

The conference was the first formal gathering of high-level representatives of the United States, the United Kingdom and the Soviet Union. Flags of the three nations were clustered at the airport and in miniature on the conference table. The occasion was apparently not one which called for much decoration in a city that is plastered with fifty-foot portrait posters of Stalin and other members of the Politburo at the slightest provocation. The people were not to get the impression an alliance with foreign nations was something to be celebrated.

Nevertheless, the atmosphere within the conference room was idyllic—no serious differences developed. The great achievement of the conference was the Four Power Declaration—the brain child of Secretary Hull and the inception of the United Nations. The only acrimony that existed openly was in our insistence on, and Molotov's resistance to, China's being a signatory. In the interest of harmony, backed no doubt by a desire to receive the undelivered portion of $11 billion worth of American supplies, Molotov overcame his objections to the recognition of China and the conference ended on a happy note.

The tranquillity of the conference must have been more than the Soviet delegation could bear because at the end of it, I was singled out to be given in private the abuse that we have come to expect our representatives at such conferences to receive in public. My whipping was at the hands of Vyshinsky, with whom

I met at the conclusion of the conference to iron out points of difference as to what should be included in the minutes with reference to action taken on certain military proposals I had made. He took the occasion to berate us about our military effort in general and our attitude toward Turkey in particular.

Toward the end of the conference, Molotov had proposed that immediate steps be taken to bring Turkey into the war. Both Eden and Hull objected. We felt that the geographical importance of Turkey as a base had almost disappeared when we occupied southern Italy. The necessity of equipping Turkish units and the obligation of coming to Turkey's aid if she met with military reverses were commitments we felt should be avoided. Molotov appeared to accept the rejection of his proposal in good grace and the subject was dropped.

During the course of the conference, I had proposed that air bases in the Soviet Union be made available for American shuttle bombing, that exchange of weather information be perfected and that communications between the United States and the Soviet Union be improved, both as to signal communications and air travel. Molotov informed Secretary Hull that my proposals were approved "in principle" and that details could be worked out between Soviet representatives and me after the conclusion of the conference. Of course, I thought I had achieved a tremendous victory to win such concessions after only a few days in the Soviet Union. My elation was short-lived because Molotov refused to allow my proposals, or the action taken on them, to become a part of the minutes. Secretary Hull protested and it was arranged that Vyshinsky and I should meet in private to work out a solution.

Meeting a Soviet official in an office in Moscow is a bit on the grim side. The foreigner is met at the door by a member of the Secret Police. For some reason all public buildings have the same objectionable odor—one that is difficult to place. It may be the detergents used or it may be the lack of them; it may be cabbage being converted into borscht; it may be most anything —whatever it is it is always present and always unpleasant. There is an eerie quietness in Soviet public buildings—no clatter of typewriters, no slamming doors—rather more like the parlor of a dentist or a fortune teller where the client sits in the anteroom dreading the parting of curtains from which emerges the villain.

Well, on this particular Sunday, Vyshinsky emerged on me. Of course, the tales that I had heard of his duties at the purge trials of 1938 did nothing for my peace of mind.

After the serenity of the main conference, I was totally unprepared for the vigor of Vyshinsky's attack. "Neither the United States nor the United Kingdom were seriously opposing Hitler or Gitler," as he was called po Rooske (in Russian). If Garriman (Averell) or Dyen (*me*) believed that the Soviet Union was deluded by the false promises of a second front, we were both sadly mistaken. The Soviet Union alone was carrying the war to the Germans and the western allies objected to the USSR receiving what little help Turkey might be able to offer. What matter if Turkey were overrun by Germans—that would at least divert some German effort from the Russian front. The idea of coming to Turkey's aid was absurd. Their neutrality thus far had already made them deserving of any fate that might befall them. And, as for the United Kingdom and the United States! What were they doing to take pressure off the glorious Red Army? On and on and on—the most violent and vituperative abuse! The spleen that was let loose was all the more shocking because the events of the conference—my first few days in the Soviet Union—had made me believe that we were in fact among friends.

My private meeting with Vyshinsky was an eye-opener. We had met for one purpose—that of reaching agreement as to what should be included in the conference minutes with reference to the military proposals that I had made during the conference. I was surprised to learn that the Soviet delegation had no real objection to including my proposals or the favorable action on them as part of the conference report. (I was to learn later that one should never be surprised at agreement on the part of Soviet leaders—the surprise comes when they do what they have agreed to do.) While the heat of Vyshinsky's attack, as well as the heat of my reaction to his attack, did not permit our reaching a solution to our problem on that day, Molotov readily agreed to the inclusion of my proposals in the minutes on the following day.

The real Soviet purpose in arranging the meeting between Vyshinsky and me was to let the British and American delegations know, through me, their true feelings about Turkish participation in the war, their displeasure with regard to the delay in opening a "second front" and other matters about which they had been relatively tranquil during the conference in the interest of harmony.

The Vyshinsky incident was my personal baptism into at least two of the techniques of Soviet negotiation—one, a vigorous offensive with no regard for the truth; the blatancy of their misstatements makes rebuttal seem so absurd as to be embarrassing, hence untruth is frequently unchallenged—second, the devious approach as exemplified in the Soviet expression of displeasure with British and American actions and policies by upbraiding me, an unimportant member of the American delegation at a private and informal meeting. Of course, to me, the victim of Vyshinsky's onslaught, the sincerity, friendliness and spirit of cooperation that had characterized the Soviet delegation during the conference became doubtful indeed.

The conference over, Averell Harriman and I settled down to the task of promoting mutual cooperation and harmony with our Soviet ally on a more permanent day to day basis.

My principal objectives were two, first, to promote coordination of effort against the Germans and, second, to pave the way for the maximum Soviet help in defeating Japan, once Soviet-Japanese neutrality lost its importance.

With respect to the European war, there were innumerable opportunities for cooperative action, which, if taken, could only be mutually beneficial to the Soviet Union and her western allies. Yet I know of no action initiated by the Soviet Union that was designed to facilitate the task of her western allies. In every instance in which the efforts of the Soviet Union were coordinated with ours, the proposal was originated by the British or the Americans. Typical among the many proposals made by the United States and negotiated with the Soviet Union by my mission were:

Use of Soviet bases by American bombers.

Coordination of strategic and tactical plans of military forces.

Maintenance of liaison between Soviet and British-American forces, both ground and air.

Method of preventing clashes between Soviet and British-American air forces.

Care of liberated prisoners of war.

Improved signal communications.

Establishment of Air Transport Service between the Soviet Union and the United States.

Exchange of information on the enemy.

Soviet aid in defeating Japan was always a long-range problem. Our efforts for the most part were pointed to the day when the Soviet Union would enter the war against Japan and there were some preparatory measures which we thought might be undertaken. Among the questions negotiated in connection with the defeat of Japan were:

The coordination of strategic plans;

The use of Soviet bases for American aircraft;

The creation of a Soviet strategic bombing force;

The build-up of reserve supplies for the Red Army in the Far East;

The maintenance of Pacific sea routes.

I shall describe the negotiations that took place with respect to repatriation of prisoners of war, one project in the European theater, and with respect to the establishment of an American air force in Siberia, in connection with the war against Japan. I believe that these will suffice to illustrate the general pattern of Soviet behavior that may be expected in any international negotiations.

II

Of all the casualties of war, none elicit more sympathy from the American people than those known to be in the hands of the enemy. I felt a great personal responsibility in the matter. As the senior military officer in the Soviet Union, it was up to me to see that American war prisoners liberated by the Red Army received the sympathetic treatment and warm reception that they had earned by their valor and suffering. Conversation with officers of the Red Army had convinced me that they were skeptical about the loyalty of any prisoners of war—hence it was imperative that I arrange to have American soldiers in American hands as soon after their liberation as possible.

Even more important than the physical well-being of a few liberated American prisoners during weeks or days that they remained in Russian hands, was the opportunity to build up good will between the United States and the Soviet Union through the solicitude that we displayed for each other's liberated prisoners. My negotiations with Soviet leaders to accomplish these objectives met with complete success—on paper. The implementation of our agreement was the most dismal failure that I encountered during my stay in the USSR—so much so that the matter was the subject of a bitter exchange between President Roosevelt and Stalin just prior to the President's death.

One would have thought that the Russians had everything to gain through close adherence to reciprocal agreements concerning the treatment to be accorded liberated persons since there were so many more Russian captives to be liberated. Instead, they attempted to eat their cake and have it too. Their interpretation of agreements coincided with ours as to our treatment of Russian nationals liberated by us. They had an entirely different interpretation with regard to the treatment of Americans liberated by them.

The problems that would arise with the liberation of allied nationals could be foreseen with more certainty than victory itself. We knew that most American prisoners were in German camps in eastern Germany or western Poland. By the middle of 1944 the Red Army began to arrive within striking distance of many such camps.

I made my first approach to the Red Army General Staff on this subject on June 11, 1944, which was slightly more than six months prior to the liberation of the first prisoner of war camp by the Red Army. At that time, I gave General N. V. Slavin a list of the American prisoner of war camps known to be in the path of the Russian advance. I also gave him the names of all Americans known to be in these camps. Slavin assured me that Americans liberated by the Red Army would be well cared for. It was apparent from his manner, however, that the problem was one that had not occurred to the General Staff and that no plans had been made to meet it.

On August 30, 1944, I prepared a letter which I asked Averell Harriman to send to Molotov, and at the same time I sent a similar one to General A. E. Antonov, Chief of the Red Army General Staff. I proposed that our two governments agree, first, that when liberation of American or Soviet prisoners of war could be foreseen through the imminent recapture of territory where prisoner of war camps were known to exist, plans should be worked out as far in advance as possible for the prompt return of such prisoners to their respective homelands; second, that there should be a prompt and continued exchange of information regarding the location of prisoner of war camps in hostile territory and that Soviet and American officers should always be available to go to those which came under the control of each other's armies for the purpose of establishing the nationality of the prisoners who were liberated and assuming control of them until they were repatriated; and, third, that individuals or small groups claiming Soviet or American nationality should be reported promptly by name to the authorities of the nation in which they claimed citizenship, so that their claims could be substantiated and they could be repatriated quickly.

Neither Harriman nor I had replies to our letters for several months although we each kept pressing for one. Meanwhile, we were making detailed preparations for taking care of those Americans who might be liberated in eastern Germany or western Poland. We organized small American teams which we hoped would operate as closely as possible behind the Red Army. They were to be on the natural lines of drift to the rear—at points which liberated Americans would be certain to pass when leaving the combat zone on their way to friendly territory. Our teams were to have clothing, money, toilet articles, medical supplies, cigarettes, candy, telegraph blanks—all of the things we could think of that young Americans might need or want most, after years or months as prisoners of the Germans.

General Eisenhower's staff became concerned about the Soviet Union's unwillingness to make any commitments concerning the treatment of American prisoners liberated by the Red Army. Bedell Smith wrote me a letter, in which he stated that there was a group of Russians at General Eisenhower's headquarters in connection with the repatriation of displaced Russians and Red Army prisoners of war which was being afforded every facility for its work. Bedell proposed that its activities be curtailed if the Russians didn't show some disposition to reciprocate. I should have accepted Bedell's proposal as it would have been exactly the type of *quid pro quo* that Soviet leaders respect. However, at the time it seemed to me that we would be engaging in a competition of discourtesy in which the odds were against us, so I decided to have another go at the Red Army General Staff. This was in early November 1944.

When I tackled Slavin in an effort to get a reply to the letter I had sent to the Chief of Staff, I was told that the Red Army was doing and would continue to do everything possible for the well-being of any Americans whom they might liberate. Slavin then went on the offensive. He gave me the first of a series of complaints about how we were handling Russians liberated on the western front. It was an attack typical of Soviet leaders when they realize fully the insecurity of their own position. He was unable to tell me just how Russians were being mistreated, but promised to do so in a few days. I told him that if there was any basis for his accusations, there was all the more reason why we should reach an agreement on the measures to be taken in looking after each other's ex-prisoners of war.

Slavin's complaints were expanded upon by Colonel General Felip Golikov in the November 9 issue of Pravda. He spoke of millions of Russians who had been taken to Germany and France as forced laborers. He said that many escaped to assist the French partisans. He spoke of those who had been forced to fight for Germany, but who deserted at the first opportunity intending to fight for the allies. He complained that we were putting such prisoners into prisoner of war camps with Germans. Molotov used the diplomatic channel to add to the protests of the General Staff. Actually the Russians knew as well as we that their complaints were unfounded. They knew that the Russians to whom they were referring were those fighting as German soldiers, many of whom were taken while in the act of shooting at American soldiers. They knew as well as we that there was room for doubt as to the friendliness of these people toward either the Soviet Union or the United States. However, the situation was one perfectly adapted to Soviet negotiating technique. Under the guise of solicitude for Soviet nationals, we were accused of mistreating Russians, while at the same time urging proposals for proper care of liberated Americans. The implication was that when we mended our ways, our proposals could be considered. At the same time, we were being needled to segregate and return every Soviet national to Soviet authority, regardless of the wishes of the individual or the circumstances under which he was apprehended.

On November 25, 1944, Molotov wrote to Harriman agreeing "in principle" to the proposals made in Harriman's letter of August 30. He promised that the proper Soviet authorities would meet with me to work out the details of an agreement. Nothing happened for a month. So on December 28, 1944, Ambassador Harriman again wrote Molotov urging that the promised discussions be arranged. He received a reply on the same day stating that Lieutenant General K. D. Golubev and Major General N. V. Slavin had been selected to meet with me to work out "questions connected with the plan for the repatriation of Soviet and American Prisoners of War and civilians." The first meeting was held on January 9, 1945, just a little over six months after my first approach to the General Staff on the subject.

My meeting with Golubev and Slavin was typical of hundreds of meetings I had with Soviet officials. It was held in Golubev's office. He was the deputy administrator of the newly formed Repatriation Commission, which was headed by Colonel General Golikov. My interpreter and I were met at the door of a building that was strange to me. There was the same aforementioned eerie quietness, the same peculiar odor and the usual parlor-like reception room hiding the unknown by the usual drapes. Soon the drapes parted and there appeared Golubev! He had the largest body and the lowest I.Q. of any human being I have ever encountered.

We went into his office, in which there was quite a gathering. Slavin was present as a representative of the General Staff. As usual, there was a representative of the N.K.V.D. prepared to take notes of everything that transpired. This Soviet practice is, in itself, sufficient reason why negotiation with Soviet leaders is so difficult, if not to say futile. They dare not agree with any argument that is advanced by the other party no matter how sound it may be, if it is not in accord with the instructions received prior to the conference. Hence, it is impossible to come to an agreement at a first meeting if any differences of opinion develop. It is best not to press for agreement under such circumstances, since there is no chance of obtaining it and it evokes fantastic argument from the Soviet official, from which it is difficult and embarrassing for him to recede at a later meeting if he is permitted to do so after reporting to his superiors.

On this occasion, Golubev presented me with a completed plan for carrying out the proposals we had made the previous August. It was a reasonable plan and with a few minor changes it embodied exactly what we hoped to accomplish. The agreement was signed at Yalta a few weeks later. Colonel General Gryslov of the Red Army General Staff signed for the Soviet Union while I signed for us. The agreement was a good one, but so far as the Russians were concerned it turned out to be just another piece of paper.

Article one of the agreement provided that all Soviet citizens liberated by the United States and all United States citizens liberated by the Soviet Union would be segregated from enemy prisoners of war and maintained in separate camps until handed over to their respective military authorities at places to be *mutually* agreed upon. It provided that such separate camps would be protected from enemy bombing and artillery fire, which carried the thought that they would not be far from the combat zone and as close to the point of liberation as possible. When the agreement was being negotiated, we emphasized this point as evidence of our desire to contact our nationals as soon as possible after their liberation. As the agreement was carried out, we were not allowed to contact our liberated soldiers until they arrived at Odessa where they were to board American ships. This was after our men had made their way across Poland by hitch-hiking —living on the generosity of Polish peasants—after they had been herded like animals into vile prisoner of war camps in eastern Poland and the western USSR and shipped in box-cars to Odessa, the port of embarkation.

Article two of our agreement provided that our respective military authorities would inform each other, without delay, regarding American or Soviet citizens found or liberated, and that the repatriation representatives of each nation would have the right of immediate access to the camps or concentration points in which their citizens were located, where they would take over the internal administration and discipline of the camp. It was in the implementation of this article and in our efforts to agree on its meaning that we met with our most miserable failure.

My first information that Americans had been liberated by the Red Army came on February 14, 1945, from the Polish Minister in Moscow. He told me that there were about 1,000 American ex-prisoners of war in various Polish cities. Three days later, three of these Americans, Captain Ernest M. Gruenberg of New York City, Second Lieutenant Frank H. Colley of Washington, Georgia and Second Lieutenant John M. Dimmling, Jr., of Winston-Salem, North Carolina, arrived unescorted in Moscow.

These officers had a grim story to tell of their treatment at the hands of the Russians. They had been liberated from a German camp at Szubin in northwestern Poland on January 21 about one month prior to their arrival in Moscow. When they were first liberated, the Red Army paid no attention to them other than to tell them to "go East." They made their way to Wegheim near Exin, Poland, where the Russian repatriation authorities had established a small camp. Conditions there were intolerable and so the three officers escaped and went further east on their own. They met other Americans, all of whom agreed that detention in a Russian camp was something to be avoided. For this reason they avoided joining in large groups. They were warned in particular against the indescribable filth of the largest camp where Americans were being assembled. It was at Rembertow on the outskirts of Moscow. The American ex-prisoners made their way east by begging rides on Russian supply trains going to the rear for replenishment. At night they sought shelter from Polish peasant farmers. Eventually they were able to get aboard a troop train which fortunately was going to Moscow. Upon arrival there, a Russian soldier directed the three Americans to my office. The N.K.V.D. had failed completely. Other Americans who arrived in Moscow later were seized by the Secret Police and taken to barracks outside of the city where they were kept a few days and thoroughly interrogated before being turned over to my custody.

The experience of these officers was convincing evidence that our Yalta agreement was not being carried out. In the first place, I had never been notified of the liberation of any Americans despite the fact that thousands had been liberated at Szubin and elsewhere for at least a month. Secondly, no attention was being paid to our agreement that American officers would control camps where American ex-prisoners were detained temporarily. Captain Gruenberg and his companions had told me of a great number of Americans who were seriously ill. I was frantic with worry and hastened to my friend Golubev for a showdown.

Armed with the information given me by the three American ex-prisoners who had arrived in Moscow, I confronted Golubev with chapter and verse of Soviet violations of our pact. He denied all allegations, chapter and verse. He said that only 450 Americans had been liberated thus far and that all of them were already on their way to Odessa. He proposed that we should set up only one camp under American control and that at Odessa, nearly 2,000 miles from any possible points of prisoner of war liberation. His figure of 450 as the total number of Americans that had been liberated was not in accord with the information I had received from either the Polish Minister or from the stories of the three American officers. As it turned out, Golubev revised his figures upward every few days until a figure of about 3,000 was reached. His continued uncertainty was ample evidence of the ineffectiveness of his organization and the lack of foresight in planning to meet problems which were certain to arise.

While Golubev could not deny that our agreement called for the presence of American officers closer to the point of liberation than Odessa, he always denied permission for them to proceed to such points on the grounds that the necessity did not exist. His behavior was about as extreme a case of insisting that black is white as will ever be contrived by Soviet experts. The situation was urgent. I was frustrated, so I turned first to Averell Harriman.

Harriman went to the Foreign Office and quickly obtained approval from Vyshinsky for my sending a small group to Lublin, Poland which would serve to attract liberated Americans wandering about the Polish countryside. This was a great victory. Even prior to Vyshinsky's approval, I had the group organized under the leadership of Lieutenant Colonel J. D. Wilmeth, an officer of my mission. I was further cheered by Vyshinsky's assurance that Wilmeth would be allowed to go anywhere in Poland where American prisoners of war might be, provided the Polish Government approved and the places were not too close to the Russian front.

My elation over this turn of events was of short duration. First, there was a delay of ten days in starting, imposed by the Russians before the written documents of authorization were forthcoming. This was maddening because the situation was one calling for immediate action. When the authorization was received, Wilmeth was denied authority to use an American airplane. This was also disappointing because I had planned that the plane should be used not only to take the party in, but to take them to other localities where they might be needed and to bring in supplies from our air base at Poltava in the Ukraine as the need for them developed.

When Wilmeth's party arrived in Lublin, he was informed that they could remain only ten days. I directed him to remain there as long as there were any Americans whom he could assist, unless he was forcibly removed by the Russians. He remained three weeks under constant pressure to leave and his was the only American contact group to get within 500 miles of localities at which American prisoners were liberated.

While Wilmeth's party was in Lublin, his operations were restricted. He found 100 Americans there awaiting transportation to Odessa. Initially he was refused access to these Americans and later allowed to visit them only at stated hours, despite the fact that our agreement indicated that such a group should be under American control. Wilmeth's medical officer, Colonel C. B. Kingsbury, was denied permission to visit two seriously wounded Americans known to be a few miles from Lublin. Wilmeth was not even allowed to send messages or supplies to these two men. This, despite the fact that Vyshinsky had agreed that Wilmeth's group could travel in Poland as necessity indicated.

. The report that emanated from Poland regarding the health of American prisoners of war was alarming and contradictory. I decided that I ought to have better success with the authorities in Moscow if I could confront them with evidence gathered at firsthand. I would try to go to Poland and see for myself. Permission for a trip to Poland was a request of such magnitude as to be far beyond Golubev's authority. He suggested that I continue to go over his head and get Ambassador Harriman to submit my request to the Foreign Office. This was done and Vyshinsky informed Averell that I could go provided the Polish Government agreed. This was an effort to force us to request favors from a government which we did not recognize, but one which the Soviet Union wished us to recognize. Since this was out of the question, Averell asked President Roosevelt to send a message to

Stalin requesting that I be given permission to go to Poland for the purpose of locating Americans who might be ill or hospitalized there.

The President sent such a request to Stalin on March 18, 1945. It was indignant in tone. The President told Stalin he could not understand Stalin's reluctance to permit American contact officers to assist their own people in Poland.

On March 23, Stalin replied to President Roosevelt informing him that all Americans liberated had been evacuated except seventeen then ill in Poland. These, he said, were being well cared for and would be evacuated in a few days. He declared he could not burden his commanders by having me bothering them in or near the combat zone. He concluded by contrasting the treatment the Red Army gave liberated Americans to the treatment being received by Soviet citizens found by Americans in camps with German prisoners of war. He neglected to point out that the Soviet citizens he referred to had been captured in German uniform.

Stalin's reply killed any hope of my going to Poland. In any case, the war was fast approaching the end and the critical time when liberated American prisoners of war needed assistance had really passed. I still believe that the constant pressure that was kept on the Soviet authorities to meet their obligations served at least to have our men evacuated to the embarkation point at Odessa much more expeditiously than otherwise would have been the case.

During the entire course of our negotiations, Soviet authorities from Stalin down poured forth a continuous stream of accusations regarding the treatment of liberated Soviet citizens. All accusations were investigated and all proved to be unfounded. For example, we were accused of poisoning Soviet citizens by giving them methyl alcohol in their food. The facts showed that a tank car containing methyl alcohol was looted by Russians at a displaced persons' camp and many of them died despite all that American doctors could do for them.

No American representative could have had better support from his own people than I had in my efforts to obtain reasonably good treatment for Americans liberated by the Red Army. The President of the United States, the American ambassador, the Army, Navy and Air Forces were all eager to help me. With just a little cooperation from my Soviet friends the task would have been simple.

III

One of the principal objectives of my mission in Moscow was to arrange for the use of air bases in the Maritime Provinces of Siberia once Germany had been defeated and the Soviet Union had declared war on Japan. Such bases would enable us to utilize the thousands upon thousands of bombers of the Fortress and Liberator types that would become available following the collapse of Germany. We could thus supplement the efforts of the B-29 super-fortresses in softening Japan for the final invasion. In addition, an air attack from the north would force Japan to redeploy some of her air defenses, both aircraft and anti-aircraft, to meet such attack and thus make them weaker and thinner elsewhere. We visualized too that American aircraft could assist the Red Army's attack against the Japanese in Manchuria by strategic bombing of Japanese industrial and supply installations in Manchuria, Korea and north China. At that time the Russians had no strategic air force of their own. In brief, there seemed to be no question of the ultimate need for American air bases in Siberia. My job was to convince the Russians and I spent two years trying.

It was at the Teheran Conference that Stalin first told us of his determination to enter the war against Japan once Germany had been defeated. He felt that it was of the utmost importance to preserve his neutrality with Japan until that time. We, of course, concurred in this view because a two front war for the Soviet Union would take a very considerable amount of Soviet pressure off Germany and it would also mean that the Pacific would be closed as a supply route for the delivery of much needed American supplies to the Soviet Union. It was imperative that nothing be done that would give the least semblance of Soviet violation of neutrality. Apparently all of Soviet officialdom was indoctrinated in this respect because I could get no one even to mention Japan until some time after Stalin's pronouncement at Teheran.

Following the Teheran Conference, the question of American air bases in the Maritime Provinces blew hot and cold for nearly two years. At Ambassador Harriman's request, President Roosevelt, during the Teheran Conference, asked Stalin for facilities in Siberia for the operation of 1,000 American bombers. On February 2, 1944, Stalin agreed to the President's proposal. He said at that time that additional facilities would have to be constructed as there were bases available for only 300 at that time. Stalin told Harriman that he had sent for high-ranking air officers to come from the Far East to join me in making such plans and preparations as were possible considering the limitations imposed by their neutrality pact with Japan.

This delighted me. I felt that there was a great possibility of stock-piling supplies in the Far East that was being neglected. All of the trains that were transporting supplies from the Soviet Union's Pacific ports to the German front were returning to Vladivostok empty. They could have been used quietly to build up supplies of gasoline, oil, spare parts and all the other items of supply needed by a strategic air force. I had proposed such a venture, suggesting Chita, near Lake Baikal as the locale of an air depot.

Perhaps my proposals and my apparent impatience to get started scared the Soviet leaders because the promised conference with the Soviet far eastern air officers never materialized. It seems that they were always "en route" or "just about to start." This condition persisted until October 1944 when Churchill arrived to discuss war and postwar problems with Stalin. Because of the primary interest of the United States in the Pacific war, it was agreed that Averell Harriman and I should participate in these discussions, particularly with reference to the war with Japan. Up to that time I had accompanied Averell during many of his discussions with Stalin, but this was my first opportunity to participate in somewhat protracted negotiations with him over a period of several days.

The first meeting was held on October 14, 1944. We assembled in a conference room outside of Stalin's office at about nine o'clock in the evening, which was in reality close to the beginning of Stalin's working day. Meetings at midnight or in the small hours of the morning were much more usual.

Churchill's party included Anthony Eden, Sir Alan Brooke, then Chief of the Imperial General Staff, General Sir Hastings Ismay, who was the Prime Minister's personal Chief of Staff,

Lieutenant General M. B. Burrows, who was my British counterpart in Moscow, and Major General E. I. C. Jacob, a member of the War Cabinet Secretariat. For the Americans there were Ambassador Harriman; Edward Page from our Embassy, an expert on Soviet affairs and the Russian language; and I. Stalin's entourage was quite large. It included Molotov, Vyshinsky, General A. E. Antonov, who was the Red Army Chief of Staff, and a group of Soviet generals whom I had not met before—the long-promised high-rankers from Siberia! They looked surprisingly trim and alert considering they had been reported as being en route for almost eight months.

The room in which we met was just off Stalin's private office. It was typical of all other Soviet conference rooms that I had visited. The odor of cabbage was a bit fainter in deference to Stalin's position, but otherwise the conference room was just as drab as those of my more lowly Soviet contacts. It included a long conference table, covered with green felt, surrounded by uncomfortable straight backed chairs, a few deep leather armchairs, a small plain flat-top desk in one corner and a little stand holding a pitcher of water and a few glasses against one of the walls. The floors were of polished hardwood covered with scatter rugs. The illumination came from a chandelier with a green porcelain shade in the center of the room and from another green porcelain-shaded lamp, on the desk. It was satisfactory, but not brilliant. Such are the surroundings in which Stalin meets with his advisors and issues his instructions.

If I may, I shall digress a moment to give my impressions of Stalin. I hope that other collaborators in this book will do the same, as a composite opinion may approach a true picture of the man.

To start with, Stalin is the leader of an unlimited autocracy with power as absolute as that of Ivan the Terrible or Peter the Great. Seeing him in company with individuals of the Politburo, such as Molotov or Mikoyan, one is convinced that the power of decision is his alone. He listens to his advisors, but appears to feel no constraint in brushing aside whatever point of view they may be pressing. Stalin is isolated to a startling degree both from the Soviet Union and from the outside world. Only on rare occasions is he seen outside the Kremlin. His only contacts with the outside world—at least in so far as I have been able to learn

—consist of a brief visit to Stockholm in his youth, the war conferences of Teheran, Yalta and Potsdam, and the interviews with
foreigners, which, however, have decreased almost to the disap-
pearing point since the war. Hence, for his knowledge of the
world beyond the Kremlin walls, he is dependent on news dis-
patches and the reports of his subordinates. This emphasizes his
dependence on his advisors, which may account for the prestige
and power some attribute to the Politburo. I am certain, however, that those gentlemen realize fully that they can disappear
as promptly and totally as any other "Comrade" in the Soviet
Union.

In appearance, Stalin is unprepossessing. He is short and color-
less. It may be that it is his lack of color or desire for it that is
his greatest strength. He seems to be completely indifferent as
to what others might think of him and pays little or no attention
to any of the social graces. One gets the impression that a physical toughening of early days is giving way to a pallid paunchiness
developed by the more sedentary habits of later years. He shows
the marks of his 71 years in the deep wrinkles of his skin and
the gray thinness of what once must have been thick black hair.
He betrays little emotion and his manner is neither pleasant nor
unpleasant. It is markedly indifferent. I have seen him smile, but
I have not heard him laugh. I have never seen him unduly agi-
tated. He has all the attributes of a good poker player.

As to his character, I would say Stalin is courageous, but cautious. He can act quickly and decisively or wait with infinite patience. He can be kind or merciless as the spirit moves him. He has
a keen intellect and more than ordinary intelligence. He knows
political values—the people are seldom out of sight of his statue
or his picture, which is plastered over all of the Soviet Union most
of the time. He fawns over children in public. He can slap backs
with the same ease that he can slit throats. His blind spots result
from the narrow confines of ideological fanaticism in which his
life has run.

Returning to our conference, the first part was taken up with
discussions pertaining to the European war. The principals
at the conference, Churchill, Stalin and Ambassador Harriman,
had the deep, leather easy chairs. They faced the wall where
maps were hung and used by British and Russian speakers to
illustrate their presentation of events occurring respectively on

the western and eastern fronts. The rest of us were standing or sitting in the rear of the three principals. As usual, when Churchill and Stalin were in the same room, the air was somewhat electric. One or the other was constantly interrupting the speaker to bring out some point designed to impress on the other the magnitude of the effort of British or Soviet arms as the case might be. Churchill was always stingingly polite—Stalin was bluntly rude. Any honey that existed, and there was some, was there only as an expedient of the moment.

On the second night of the conference, it was my task to outline the progress of the Pacific war from Pearl Harbor on and to divulge our projected plans for the final defeat of Japan. I concluded my presentation by asking Stalin about Soviet intentions with respect to Japan and, among other things, how much of the capacity of the Trans-Siberian railroad could be devoted to the build-up of an American strategic air force in the Maritime Provinces once Germany had been defeated. It was implicit in my question that permission for American use of Siberian air bases had already been granted, as indeed it had. Stalin did not answer any of the direct questions that I had asked of him, nor did he give any indication when answers would be forthcoming. As we were leaving the meeting, Mr. Churchill said, "Young man! I admired your nerve in asking Stalin those questions. There was certainly no harm in trying, but I doubt that you will be given the answers." I was more optimistic, however, because the questions were asked in open meeting and any evasion on Stalin's part would have tended to destroy the illusion of cooperative effort during the closing stages of the war when Stalin wished to avoid unilateral actions by his allies, both as to Germany and Japan. As it turned out, Stalin, at the meeting on the following night, not only answered all of the questions that I had asked, but unfolded his entire plan with regard to Soviet participation in the Japanese war.

At this meeting, Stalin did practically all of the talking. He had had maps prepared, which he used to show where American air bases in Siberia would be located, where Soviet troop concentrations would be and where stock piles of supplies would have to be built up. He answered questions freely and committed the Soviet Union to a degree of cooperative effort that had never been attained in the war against Germany. At the conclusion of the meeting he said that he would like to meet again with Ambassador Harriman and me to go over some of the details of our joint effort against Japan. The British and American delegations were highly gratified at the frankness of Stalin's statements, the apparent firmness of his intentions and for the aid that the Soviet Union was prepared to give in the final defeat of Japan. The British delegation, particularly Anthony Eden, thought it would be well if some of Stalin's promises were committed to paper. Accordingly, Eden and Harriman prepared a paper outlining our understanding of the conclusion that had been reached. When the document reached Stalin, he went into a rage which he let loose on Averell at our next and final meeting of the conference. He stormed that the document not only indicated our doubt of his spoken word, but it also jeopardized security. He said, "Stenographers and secretaries are eager to exaggerate their own importance by telling news to their friends, thus military secrets no longer remain military secrets." He then proceeded to provide the perfect example of Soviet inconsistency by handing Averell a seven-page typewritten document listing the supplies needed from the United States for a two months' reserve of supplies in Siberia. I am certain that this document was not typed by Stalin!

At our final meeting our bargain was fully developed. We were to be allowed bases, but, in turn, we must agree to send the Soviet Union about 1,000,000 tons of supplies as a reserve stock pile for the Red Army in its attack against the Japanese in Manchuria. The supplies were to reach the Soviet Union not later than June 1945 and were to be in addition to the American supplies sent to the Soviet Union for use in the war against Germany.

When Stalin presented his demand to us, both Averell and I were amazed at his detailed knowledge of the supplies which he had listed and of the reasons why the supplies were needed. Many of the items, such as port and harbor machinery or railroad equipment, had a marked postwar significance, but Stalin could, in each case, justify their inclusion on his list by their immediate value in defeating Japan.

When presenting us with his bill of goods, Stalin agreed to almost every proposal we had made. We could have air bases; we could count on the same priority as to use of transportation and other facilities as was given to the build-up of the Red Army; we could have Petrokavlovsk as a naval base; we could send small parties to survey our prospective air bases; and most important of all, we could proceed at once with joint Soviet-American detailed planning. Looking back, it is difficult to see how Stalin kept a straight face because the end result of the negotiations was that the Russians got their supplies and the United States got nothing but a belated, last minute, undesirable Soviet attack against the Japanese.

Immediately following the Churchill conferences, the United States set about fulfilling the supply commitment it had undertaken. Within a month after Ambassador Harriman agreed that we would send the needed stock pile to Siberia, supplies had been started across the Pacific. The Soviet bill of goods was filled to the last item and the supplies were at their destination on time.

Immediately following the Churchill conferences, the Soviet Union set about sabotaging the commitment it had undertaken. Appointment of Soviet officers to meet with Americans for planning purposes was delayed until January 1945. When the appointments were made, planning proved to be impossible. The first meeting of planners was social in nature and involved great consumption of vodka in consonance ' of an old Russian tradition when a new association is formed". The succeeding meetings were devoted to lengthy arguments as to organization, procedure and definition of the objectives to be accomplished. When the American planners did succeed in raising matters of substance, they were always beyond the scope of the Soviet planners' authority—so much so that they could not even be discussed. It soon became evident that there was a firm Soviet intention that joint planning for the war against Japan was not to be accomplished. Soviet disregard of commitments was revealed with pristine clarity in December 1944 when Antonov, Chief of Staff, called me to his office and informed me, without embarrassment or even the suggestion of an apology, that "The Soviet Government wishes to inform the United States Government that requirements of the Red Air Force will not permit granting the use of air bases in the Maritime Provinces to the American Air Forces." This, after much of our promised 1,000,000 ton stock pile had been delivered and much of the balance was in the pipe line.

United States protests at all levels from the President on down failed to induce Stalin to live up to the promises he had made at the Churchill conference in early October. In order to keep our supplies coming, Stalin did finally agree that we might have bases far north of the Red Army and Red Air Force concentration areas. The sites offered were so far from Japan as to permit the use of B-29s only. Our supply of that type aircraft was limited and we already had sufficient bases south and east of Japan to take care of the number of aircraft that were available. Nevertheless, we thought it would be desirable to have a "look-see" at the Siberian sites that we were told we could use. Again we were to discover the ease with which our Russian allies could avoid fulfillment of unpleasant obligations. We were invited to send a reconnaissance party to look at the Siberian locations offered to us. We accepted and sent a large party of key air force personnel on their way. They got as far as Fairbanks, Alaska, where they waited for more than a month for the Soviet officers who were to meet them there. The delay was explained by excuse after excuse—each more fatuous than the one preceding. We finally gave up in despair and abandoned all hope of operating American air forces from the Maritime Provinces of Siberia.

IV

My Soviet experience with respect to caring for liberated prisoners of war and with respect to obtaining American air bases in Siberia, differed only in detail and in degree with hundreds of other problems that were negotiated during my two years in the Soviet Union. Whatever success was achieved in obtaining cooperation from Soviet leaders in the prosecution of the war was only because of their necessity to keep us in a Santa Claus mood. Never were two events more simultaneous than the cessation of lend-lease and the cessation of Soviet cooperation.

Most of us have followed postwar negotiations with the Soviet Union either in the halls of the United Nations, in the meetings of Foreign Ministers, or in the usual diplomatic exchanges. The pattern of Soviet behavior has become an evident and accepted phenomenon of the times. It is so well known that all Americans are now "experts" on the subject.

There is perhaps no more futile occupation than endeavoring

to discover what makes the Soviet negotiator what he is. Averell Harriman and I spent many a long evening before his fireplace in Moscow advancing and shattering theories on the subject. I suppose that no one, including the Soviet leaders themselves, could fully give the answer. From my experiences, however, I believe that Soviet behavior in the conduct of negotiations and in the implementation of agreements will almost invariably be marked by certain characteristics. When we recognize these characteristics as part of a technique, we discover the dog to be more a barker than a biter. Its barking is endless, but biting is attempted only when the victim is helpless.

In negotiation with foreign nations, one may be sure that Soviet representatives come to the conference table without authority to make any departures from their instructions—only one man in the Soviet Union can make "on the spot" decisions and he is Joe Stalin. The Molotovs, Vyshinskys, Gromykos and Maliks are little more than messengers. The vehemence with which they attempt to carry out instructions is no doubt inspired by the instinct of self-preservation, since failure has never been popular with Stalin. It is almost axiomatic that the vigor, vindictiveness, spleen and outright dishonesty of Soviet argument increases in direct ratio with the weakness of its position. This has been well illustrated by Malik of late in his tirade against the "American Aggressors in Korea." We may always be sure that negotiations will never be broken off entirely until the Soviet representative has had an opportunity to report back. If his instructions are changed, he will unexpectedly change his position in the middle of a conference without explanation or embarrassment. At the same time, it is evident that Soviet leaders do have concern for world opinion. When it begins to pile up against them, we may look for some oily sweetness from them or proposals designed to restore them favorably in world opinion—witness the saccharine attitude of Vyshinsky at the 1950 meeting of the General Assembly and Malik's offer to pledge that the Soviet Union "will not be the first to use the atomic bomb."

Agreements with the Soviet Union should be on a *quid pro quo* basis with the *quid* running concurrently with the *quo*. We should avoid agreements in which we pay in advance. Honesty is not a virtue of present-day Soviet leadership.

It has been said with some justification that Stalin and his crowd are masters of political science. In my opinion, it is not difficult to be the master of any game in which one reserves the right to make or break the rules as the game progresses. Soviet leaders approach their international relations without any of the inhibitions inspired by morality, integrity or any other virtue. At the same time they have none of the strength derived from the practice of such virtues.

CHAPTER TWO

NEGOTIATING UNDER LEND-LEASE

John N. Hazard has been Professor of Public Law at Colum-bia University since 1946. Educated at Yale, Harvard, the Mos-cow Juridical Institute and the University of Chicago, he was, from 1941 to 1945, Deputy Director of the USSR Branch of the Foreign Economic Administration and its predecessor agencies. He was advisor on state trading to the Department of State in 1945 and 1946, advisor on Soviet law to the United States Chief of Counsel for the Prosecution of Axis War Criminals, and has lectured on Soviet law in a number of universities and colleges. He is the author of Soviet Housing Law *(1939) and a number of articles.*

Negotiating Under Lend-Lease, 1942-1945

BY JOHN N. HAZARD

Negotiating with Soviet citizens—Russians, Ukrainians, Georgiàns, Jews and Armenians—concerning the shipment of wartime supplies provided a continuing experience over five years for a host of Americans. Many of those on the American side were in the uniform of the Army, Air Force, Navy or Marines, but the majority were civilians. Special sections were created for the purpose in the War and Navy Departments, and in the civilian agencies of the War Production Board, the Procurement Division of the Treasury Department, the Office of the Petroleum Coordinator for War, the War Shipping Administration, the Department of Agriculture and the Office of Lend-Lease Administration, later to become the Foreign Economic Administration.

Multiplication of negotiating points was inevitable with the large number of specialized activities concerned on the working level, but the task was made even more complex by the determination of Congress early in the war that the appropriations for supply of lend-lease goods would be split between Army, Navy and the civilian agencies, the latter being represented by the Office of Lend-Lease Administration. This split of appropriations created three sources of funds for procurement and hence three sources of supply financially independent of each other. The Soviet negotiators had three faucets to turn, and this fact made considerable difference to those on the working level, as will be seen shortly.

Basic policy decisions were not the concern of most of those engaged in the process of supply. The President, himself, often as advised by Harry Hopkins, set the policy. The hundreds of lesser people were concerned, at least in theory, with nothing more than determining whether a requested item of equipment fell within the confines of the policy and when it could be made available and shipped. Defined in such terms, the task of the working level sounds simple, but it was not. The policy was stated broadly, as the unforseeable nature of military successes and reverses required, and there was room for considerable administrative interpretation of the basic policy line. It is the negotiation relating to such interpretation that provides material for this chapter, as the negotiation was observed from the Division for Soviet Supply of the Office of Lend-Lease Administration and successor agencies.

I

Negotiation at the working level varied considerably depending on the personal characteristics of the parties immediately concerned. On the American side there was a range of temperaments, as might have been expected: the patient, the impatient, the skilled methodical mind and the inexperienced and sometimes confused mind, the seeker after social prestige and the self-effacing type who sought only to do his job with a minimum of fanfare so as to get home to his garden. On the Soviet side there was the same variation, conditioned, however, by the years of discipline of Soviet society, which proved to be a type of discipline obviously foreign to the experience of the Americans, even including those in uniform. The Americans felt able to make their own decisions in many cases without referring the question to higher authority. The Soviet citizens were functioning under an order from a superior, and any deviation whatever required a conference with that superior, who might or might not have to seek authority from a higher level before the proposed plan of action could be accepted.

This factor of reference to a superior, more than any other, gave rise to friction in negotiating at the working level. The Americans were generally not civil servants but outsiders brought into the war effort and planning to return to private life as soon as possible after the war. They had no careers to make in government, and they were not fearful of superiors. They made up their own minds, sometimes even out of harmony with directives from above, and they wanted quick action for efficient shipment of supplies. They expected a conference to result in a decision after which telephones could be lifted and orders given. When they learned that in almost no conference with a Soviet negotiator could a decision be made, some Americans were exasperated. The conference was usually only a means of imparting to the Soviet negotiator some information to be reported by him to his superior. Decisions had to be saved for another day.

Some of the difficulties of the conference technique lay in the questionable understanding of English on the part of the Soviet negotiators. To bridge this gap a few Russian-speaking Americans had to be supplied, but they were hard to obtain. It was general lend-lease policy not to hire as lend-lease staff persons who had been former citizens of the country to which supplies were to be shipped. This was thought to be good policy to avoid any possibility or even suspicion of a possibility that a country receiving lend-lease aid could obtain through invisible pressures or sympathies that which basic policy denied. The USSR program was, of course, under the rule, so that the large supply of Russian-Americans in the United States was not available for tapping. In consequence the few native born citizens who had learned Russian for some professional reason were busy helping where they could with interpreting. All letters to the Soviet representatives were written, however, in English, and all letters from the Soviet negotiators were received in English. If there was doubt as to whether the Soviet interpreters would put the desired tone into a communication to the chairman of the Soviet Purchasing Commission, who knew no English, a Russian speaking American from the lend-lease staff would deliver the letter personally and make an oral statement concerning its substance.

To meet the language difficulty and to be certain that the Soviet negotiators understood the American position, it became customary to write the substance of the communication which was being made in the conference in the form of a letter or memorandum. This was delivered to the Soviet official after the conference was terminated, and he was advised that it contained a restatement of what had already been said. While this would have been impossible if the conferences had been occasions on which decisions had been made, it served well under a system such as has been described where the conferences were largely for the purpose of making forceful communications to a subordinate for transmission to a superior and in answering his questions so as to make certain that he understood, and could subsequently explain to his superior, the point being made.

Not all misunderstandings arose because of the language hurdle. Some arose because of the differences in political ideology. The Soviet negotiators approached the Americans with a considerable background of political education in their own schools. They had been taught that government officials in non-Soviet states were capitalists, or the lackeys of capitalists. As such the motives of the American officials were presumed to be those of the capitalists and not those of genuine friends seeking to help the USSR as one member of a family will help another. The Soviet officials assumed that the United States must be helping the USSR only because it saw in the aid an advantage to itself. They also assumed that it was the desire of the capitalists in the United States to leave the USSR after victory with wounds which would take so long to heal that nothing could stand in the way of American policy for years to come. As a result of this attitude springing from their Marxist training, the Soviet negotiators from top to bottom approached their opposite numbers on the American side with a certain suspicion. They tended to impute motives to every suggestion of the American officials.

The imputing of motives made little difference in many cases, except in so far as it sometimes led to a lack of mutual good will in personal relationships, but in some important cases it was a real handicap to getting a quick decision. In some instances, such as the necessity of delaying or rerouting a convoy because of Germany's activity on the sea, a quick decision was imperative. The military situation of the moment required the delay, but the Soviet officials would assume that there was some other motive, and they would hesitate to concede or make the arrangements required on their side to fit in with the changed plans. It was quickly learned that matters of grave concern, such as convoy schedules, required conversations at the top levels of the White House or the Embassy in Moscow. Yet lesser decisions also suffered because of this suspicion on the part of the Soviet citizens. In these lesser decisions, it was found on occasion that it was sometimes better to express decisions in terms which a Marxist would understand so that the Soviet official might be able to say to himself that at least the American proposal was sincere and there was no concealed motive which would require time to find. The Soviet decision seemed to come more quickly, perhaps because it was made in terms of the motives given.

In most cases, however, no effort was made to imagine what motives would be comprehensible to a Marxist, but every effort was made to give the Soviet citizens sufficient background to permit them to understand why a departure from prearranged plans had to be proposed. Thus, at one time, when the Association of American Railroads required the United States Government to change its shipping procedure, with a resulting increase in costs, a most extensive discussion of the relation of the railroads to the government, even in wartime, was required. The Soviet negotiators could not understand why the government was not all powerful so that it could require the railroads to act as directed and to perform in accordance with the commitment made earlier to the Soviet Government on the basis of what had later proved to be an inadequate understanding of a railroad rule.

The question of cost was a constant plague to negotiations. Most Americans could not see why the Soviet citizens concerned themselves with it. President Roosevelt had described lend-lease as the loan of a garden hose to help put out a neighbor's fire. The Americans expected lend-lease military supplies to be purchased at the lowest price possible by skilled United States procurement officials. The cost would then be charged to an account which would be considered by the governments concerned after the war and reduced to a fraction of its total because of the contribution made by the foreign government. No United

States Government official expected that the USSR would be presented eventually with a bill for the full amount of the aid sent to it. The history of negotiations since the war has indicated that this expectation was correct.

The Soviet negotiators never approached the lend-lease account in such fashion. They always not only talked but behaved as if their government would eventually be charged with the full cost of everything shipped. This fact led to many protracted discussions, and to some hard feeling since it seemed to the Americans to be unrealistic on the Soviet part. The matter was of particular concern during the first year of the aid. Those who recall the history of wartime aid to the USSR will remember that shortly after the German crossing of the Soviet frontier, the United States Government unblocked Soviet accounts which had been blocked during the period of Soviet-German collaboration. The regular Soviet peacetime purchasing agency, the Amtorg Trading Corporation of New York City, began to buy war supplies in the United States.

Amtorg was manned by an able group of Soviet officials trained in the schools of the Soviet Commissariat of Foreign Trade and its subordinate public purchasing corporations. For years the Soviet officials had been promoted or demoted on the basis of their business ability as measured in terms of skillful negotiation to achieve low price and high quality. Even the necessities of quick supply in wartime seemed to have no influence on these Soviet business men. They persisted in struggling for low prices at a time when the war situation was driving everything up. Years of negotiation had provided them with long case histories of each American supplier, and they could negotiate with more information on past pricing policies than was possible for most Americans.

As purchasing became impossible except through agencies of the United States Government, because of the hesitancy or inability of American suppliers to sell to non-government procurement officers, a hesitancy which was accentuated by memories of the recent low position to which Soviet reputation had fallen in the United States during the Soviet-German period of collaboration, United States procurement officials were called upon to help. On November 7, 1941, the President declared that the defense of the USSR was essential to the defense of the United

States and thus qualified the USSR for the receipt of lend-lease aid under the Lend-Lease Act of March 11, 1941. A five-year credit of $1,000,000,000 was offered to and accepted by the Soviet Government. Thereafter, all purchasing, except for a few small items purchased by Amtorg itself, was conducted by procurement officers of the United States and paid for out of funds appropriated by the Congress to the lend-lease program.

American procurement officers began to buy items approved on the program of supply. There was no Soviet experience in buying tanks and machine guns and ammunition, and so there was no argument over price paid by the United States officers, but there was a vast Soviet experience in buying machine tools which were an important item on the supply programs. Soviet machine tool buyers asked to be consulted on prices paid for such items. At first the request was resisted as an interference with the United States authorities, but when Soviet experience was tested and proved to be well grounded, it became a practice to consult with the machine tool specialists from Amtorg and to draw upon their experience in making purchases.

While the matter was solved amicably in the machine tool case, it became increasingly apparent to American officials that the Amtorg's staff was a peacetime staff incapable of adapting itself to the speedy and sometimes relatively wasteful procedures required in wartime when speed may require the paying of costs which would seem excessive in peacetime. Some suggestions were made to the Soviet Government that relations between the two countries on the supply level might be aided if the military program were removed from the business men of Amtorg and placed in the hands of military supply officers. The Soviet Government responded and established a "Government Purchasing Commission of the U.S.S.R. in the U.S.A." in the spring of 1942. A major general of the Soviet air force was placed in charge with two deputies, one of whom was a rear admiral of the Soviet navy, and the other of whom was the former president of Amtorg. Thereafter the chairmanship of the purchasing commission remained in military hands, although personnel at the head was changed.

No question of price was raised thereafter on military supplies, but there were occasional flurries over the cost of steel, nickel, aluminum, copper, machine tools and foods. Even when the

USSR was placed on a lend-lease basis similar to that of the United Kingdom, and the responsibility to repay the $1,000,000,-000 credit at the end of five years was set aside in favor of post-war discussions on the whole matter, there were still comments about cost in some negotiations, followed by the statement that the USSR had to consider cost, since payment would be expected subsequently. None of the Americans knew whether there was an internal office memorandum on the subject in the Soviet Purchasing Commission or whether this was only a relic of the period of the credit and the peacetime thinking of many of the civilian staff concerned with raw materials and foods. Whatever the reason, the cost approach marred the friendliness of some discussions and frayed tempers on both sides.

The most exasperating instance concerned some hazel nuts belonging to the United States and stored in Turkish warehouses near Istanbul. The nuts had been purchased by United States agents to keep them from falling into German hands. Their oil was a prized item for delicate machinery, and their food value was important. At the time the United States had no access by ship to Turkey, and it could not remove the nuts. They were stored in Turkish warehouses in which they were expected to deteriorate in time, and in which storage costs increased under the terms of a familiar contract designed to keep warehouses open for a steady turnover of goods rather than clogged by long-term storage.

It was suggested that the nuts could be put to use, and warehouse costs eliminated if the Soviet Government would take them. The offer was made to the food man in the Soviet Government Purchasing Commission. It was explained that the cost of the nuts would be placed upon the lend-lease account of the USSR and negotiated after the war. The United States official in Istanbul received a call some time later from a Soviet inspector who said that he was instructed to determine the quality of the nuts so that value might be estimated. After seeking instructions from Washington the United States official was advised to admit the inspector, who reported that the nuts had greatly deteriorated and the original cost price was too high to be paid by the USSR. This reply came back through the Soviet Purchasing Commission in Washington.

Explanations were made that this was not a commercial operation, and if the nuts were moved to the USSR, a decision could then be made as to their value for purposes of listing it on the lend-lease account. The food man in the Soviet Purchasing Commission seemed to understand the operation fully and said that he had explained it to the Commissariat of Foreign Trade in Moscow. It was known in Washington that the Commissariat of Foreign Trade had a special section for trade with the east. Presumably this section existed because the bazaar conditions of trade in the Middle East required special negotiating skills. It appeared obvious that a Soviet agent with such skills had been sent to inspect the nuts and that his training would probably prevent him from reaching any decision on price within a reasonable time. Meanwhile the nuts continued to deteriorate in the heat of Turkey, and the warehouse charges were being advanced from time to time. Drastic measures were required, and the American Embassy in Moscow was asked to make a high-level explanation and authorize inspection of the nuts on Soviet territory after they had been moved across the Black Sea. It was explained that the United States would accept the valuation placed upon them by Soviet inspectors, it being assumed by the United States that the USSR would be entirely businesslike in setting the evaluation. After further delays the news was received that Soviet vessels would call for the nuts and remove them. An agreed value was later placed on the USSR lend-lease account.

Soviet resourcefulness in finding persons who had authority to act within the American administrative apparatus was also cause for some difficulties in conducting the program. As has been indicated, the Congress split lend-lease appropriations three ways soon after the beginning of the war, so that the War and Navy Departments and the Office of Lend-Lease Administration each had separate appropriations from which to procure. Obviously the Army would not procure a frigate, nor the Navy a tank, nor the Lend-Lease Administration a rifle, but there were many borderline items, which the Army or Navy were buying, such as tugs, or which the Army and the Lend-Lease Administration were buying, such as machine tools. The Soviet supply program was prepared annually in consultation with all departments of government and then coordinated with President Roosevelt's policy through Mr. Hopkins as chairman of a coordinating committee.

This resulted in a supply program called a Protocol, four of which were negotiated during the war and all of which have since been published. All possible supplies were covered in some manner, but as no one could foresee a year in advance precisely what types of machine tools would require replacement because of German bombing, or what types of steel would be needed to fill in gaps in Soviet production schedules, many items were expressed in terms of millions of dollars worth of industrial equipment or thousands of tons of steel.

After a program had been agreed upon, the USSR was to file specific requests for items falling within the categories of the supply program. Due to the three agencies with appropriations from Congress, these requests could be filed with any of them which happened to have procurement officers who were engaged in making such purchases. To simplify matters and avoid confusion, the Soviet representatives were advised of the agency which generally was to receive applications for specific requests under each category, but in spite of that fact there were a sufficient number of borderline cases which had not been anticipated. This was particularly so for items filed under a special category for emergencies designed to include anything not previously imagined as being a possible requirement.

Near chaos in a fraction of the program was the result of this situation. It was only a fraction of the program, for most of the program was sufficiently clear to permit no calls upon two or three agencies, but this fraction was the "noisy" fraction—the one that required the telephone calls and caused tempers to rise. It would be learned that an item rejected by one agency because of a belief that it was not sufficiently urgent to the prosecution of the war would be requested of another agency and sometimes granted. This situation gave rise to the expression current in Washington during the war that "The Russians are all over town!" To meet the difficulty, it became necessary to hold meetings at which members of the Navy, Army and civilian staffs could exchange notes as to what was being done so as to avoid differing decisions in different agencies.

The Soviet resourcefulness in finding men with administrative authority, no matter how small that authority, had some amusing aspects. Soviet officials made careful studies of routing procedures within the United States Government. They sought out the person to whom a request would be sent for an opinion as to availability of supply, or relation to the war effort. Some of these people had modest jobs, but they could make a decision which could be effective in denying the Soviet request. Working on the assumption that a man, whether he be American or Middle Eastern, is more likely to decide in one's favor if he has a full stomach, the Soviet Purchasing Commission engaged in an extensive series of informal luncheons and dinners. Small groups of American officials would be invited by Soviet officials of a similar rank to lunch or dine pleasantly and amply at the Purchasing Commission. The hierarchy was usually so carefully observed that an American with relatively little sense of his hierarchical position could tell about where the Soviet officials thought he stood by the persons from the Soviet side who appeared at the affair.

One has to admit that Americans like a good dinner, and they attach some prestige value to a dinner at a foreign embassy, even if only at its commercial wing. The Soviet officials lacked the social prestige value of the British, but still it was pleasant to mention casually among friends that one had been dining with General so-and-so yesterday. Added to that, the Soviet officials were the most cordial of hosts and, quite apart from prestige value, a luncheon or dinner with them was delightful.

No one who was working constantly with Soviet officials failed to appreciate that these dinners or luncheons coincided with requests for specific items which Soviet officials would believe hard to obtain for one reason or another, usually because they were in short supply. It was never a question of security items, for these were completely out of reach of the working level of people for whom the informal luncheons and dinners were designed. The problem lay not with Americans who were familiar with diplomatic niceties, but with the new men who had never been invited to such affairs before, and who suddenly found themselves the center of attention because Soviet officials thought they had some relation to a decision on a type of item not previously the matter of concern. No one in Washington felt that inexperienced Americans could be denied the right to accept invitations, and no one tried to deny them such a right. It did become common gossip, however, that some die-hard had mellowed after a good dinner, and this was the subject of no little merri-

ment among those who negotiated every day and studied Soviet
negotiating techniques.

Soviet determination to obtain a requested item sometimes
led to friction. The legal adviser to the Soviet Purchasing Commission read all United States Government regulations and was
prepared to argue on the basis of those regulations if action was
not taken in accordance with Soviet requests. No one in the War
Production Board could deny an item on the basis of some limitation order without receiving a polite call and having to discuss
the application of that limitation order to the matter in hand.
Let no one who deals with Soviet agencies think that they do not
know what is happening. Their legal staffs are composed of able
men who read everything and who are prepared to argue forcefully, although sometimes mistakenly, for their point of view.

Negotiation with the Soviet lawyers was most extensive when
there was in process of preparation an agreement terminating
lend-lease shipments. The end of the war came at a time when a
considerable number of items were still in production under
orders to meet the supply program to the USSR. It had been
appreciated for some time before the end of the war that the end
was in sight, although there was no idea as to precisely how long
military operations might continue. In view of this appreciation
there was a tendency evident during the final months of the
war to reject applications for industrial equipment of an un-
doubted military value which would require a long time to produce. Several Soviet requests for large industrial plants for making munitions and steel were thus rejected, but some requests
for individual machine tools for multi-purpose use were accepted for production under the program. Some of these were
made to Soviet specifications, and it was believed that they would
have no use in the United States after the war. The idea was hit
upon at top levels that money could be saved the American tax-
payer at the end of the war if these items in varying stages of
production were not cancelled at the supplier, with resulting
severe cancellation charges to the United States Government, but
were continued in production until completion and then sold
to the USSR under an ordinary commercial credit for a term
of years.

With this concept of a commercial credit for such goods as
were in production at the end of the war, whenever that might

be, negotiations of what became known as a "Lend-Lease take out agreement" were commenced. It was clear from the start that the USSR was prepared to accept the principle, and it was certainly to the USSR's advantage, since Soviet reconstruction requirements were large. Nevertheless, the negotiations before the agreement was finally concluded extended over months. A lawyer from the Commissariat of Foreign Trade in Moscow was sent to handle the affair, and he proved to be as meticulous as the best products of the American law firms. His ideas were often excellent and were readily accepted by the American lawyers. Others seemed to stem from a sense of suspicion such as has been described already. Changes were made to suit him, and when he returned another day after consultation with headquarters, still another change would be requested. Patience beyond belief was required on the part of the American negotiators, but in the end their work was rewarded. A workable agreement was reached.

Discussion with junior Soviet officials revealed on many occasions that they wanted to go home and get into the fighting. Several of them told of letters from home advising them of the death of brothers in the army, or the overrunning of their homes and loss of all touch with aged mothers or fathers. They felt that they wanted to have a direct hand in the fighting with the enemy, but they said that they were told they must stay where they were. Most of the ones who talked in this manner were the men in the lower echelons, the section chiefs in the Soviet Purchasing Commission. It was these men who had hourly contact with their opposite numbers in the American organization engaged in the detailed work without which no program can function. On many occasions they exasperated the Americans by constant pressure for speed, when everything possible was being done. Nothing seemed to please them, and almost no heroic effort to push something ahead of what had come to be accepted as the inevitable delays of a large government operation met with open appreciation in the form of a "thank you."

Some of the Americans who had dealt with Russians before the war took it upon themselves to advise the Soviet officials that Americans were glad to be of assistance, but that they were used to being thanked when they did something out of the ordinary. On one occasion early in the war a Soviet air force general called for the fifth time to ask why his request for much needed ammunition had not yet been acted upon. When, at last, the request was met, the officer who had done the work called him to advise him of the affirmative decision. Instead of any response indicating pleasure, he made no comment whatever over the telephone, but asked immediately about the status of his request for some other type of ammunition, rather antagonizing his American colleague. Later, when it seemed appropriate at one of the luncheons, he was asked why he had not thanked the American for his work. He replied quite simply that if the Soviet army stopped to celebrate every time it recaptured a village, it would miss out in the full utilization of every opportunity to take the next village. He was told that his approach might be the best way to win a war against the enemy, but it was not equally effective in dealing with Americans.

All of this campaign of instruction on how to deal with Americans had an amusing sequel. Soviet officials began to preface every meeting with a lengthy statement of their appreciation of all that was being done for them by the official concerned, almost to the point of that official's embarrassment at such fulsome praise. After this approach had been used for an especially important conference with a high official on one occasion, a loquacious member of the Soviet delegation was asked at an appropriate time on a later occasion why there had been so much "palaver." He replied, perhaps with his tongue in his cheek, that Americans seemed to like it, and if they did, who were the Soviets not to provide compliments to please them!

Only once did an occasion come to my attention of rudeness on the part of a Soviet official. He was a section chief who had a particularly brusque manner and a rough voice. When there had been delays in procurement of an item for which he was responsible, he called on the telephone to protest, and he did so in a tone of voice and manner reminiscent of a superior talking to an inferior officer in the Army. This tone was often seen among officials in the Soviet Purchasing Commission when directions had to be given to their own men, but it had not been used previously in talking to Americans. He was advised that nothing would be done for him when he approached the matter in such a way, and his superior in the commission was telephoned and advised of the trouble. The offender apologized later, and no similar incident was subsequently reported.

II

Negotiating on matters concerned with lend-lease during the war was undoubtedly affected by the Soviet desire to get supplies which the United States owned or controlled. In obtaining those supplies it paid to cater to the wishes and even whims of the Americans concerned. For that reason the experience of those on the working level in the lend-lease operation may throw little light on the problem of negotiating with Soviet officials when it is the United States which wishes something. With that consideration always in mind, the conclusions may be stated as to the qualities necessary in the man or woman who would prepare himself or herself for negotiating with Soviet officials.

It is elementary that the American must have a controlled temper, perhaps to be displayed at the appropriate time, but subject to control so that it never appears at the wrong time or blinds the negotiator who lets it run free. It takes a mind untouched by temper or other dulling forces to deal with the usual competent Soviet official who approaches the table. Secondly, the American would probably benefit from the ability to be patient. He who rushes can be lost. This does not mean that there is no reason to put pressure on the Soviet side for a decision when it is needed, but this must be a controlled pressure exercised on the part of a man who utilizes it with care rather than the unreasoning pressure of the exasperated. A full understanding of Russian history and Soviet administrative practices will help in meeting situations which seem to drag on forever. Delays are not always indicative of unwillingness to negotiate, for they may be only the result of inability to get a superior's attention, or a lack of appreciation that time is of the essence.

Some appreciation of Marxist political theory will help the negotiator who wishes to take advantage of every opportunity to press his case. Imputation of false motives can sometimes be avoided by one who knows what motives might be imputed from actions which might seem innocent enough to the American. Straight answers given without an effort to evade the real reason can make for pleasanter relationships with the Soviet negotiator, even though he seems to be evasive at times. Many Americans have felt that by returning the same coin as one receives one is surer to bring a Soviet negotiator to adopt the attitude desired. The sad truth seems to be that in a mudslinging contest with a Soviet official the latter proves to be better equipped than the American. He can exceed anything the American could imagine. It seems to be better never to begin the contest on such a level but to meet any appearance of uncouthness with efforts to clear the air of it, rather than outdo it unless one expects eventually to take to arms. Negotiating under such conditions is not easy and requires the utmost in diplomatic skills with which few are adequately endowed.

Finally, the official who is unable to stand by his decision once it is made on reasonable grounds is lost if he changes it for reasons other than the presentation of new evidence. The mind which is ever ready to change will be subjected to endless argument and constant attack by the Soviet colleague who is quick to sense the opportunity. Pressure from Soviet negotiators will be redoubled and may result in complete exhaustion on the part of the American so that he comes to the point at which he feels that he never wants to see a Russian again and is thoroughly miserable in the performance of his job. For his own peace of mind, if for no other reason, he will do well to act carefully and advisedly and then stand by his decision until circumstances have changed.

CHAPTER THREE

NEGOTIATING ON WAR CRIMES
PROSECUTIONS

Sidney S. Alderman was born in North Carolina and educated at Trinity College, now Duke University. After graduation from law school in 1916 he entered the Army and was Captain, 321st Infantry, during World War I. He engaged in the general practice of law in Greensboro, North Carolina from 1919 to 1930. From 1930 to 1947 he was General Solicitor, Southern Railway Company in Washington, D.C. From 1947 to 1950 he was General Counsel, Southern Railway System Lines and on May 23, 1950, he was appointed Vice President and General Counsel. During 1945 and 1946 he was Special Assistant to the Attorney General of the United States and Assistant to Mr. Justice Robert H. Jackson, United States Representative and Chief of Counsel in the Nuremberg Trial of Major European Axis War Criminals.

Negotiating on War Crimes

Prosecutions, 1945

BY SIDNEY S. ALDERMAN

This symposium is devoted to various negotiations with the Soviet Union and might seem intended to omit any coverage of negotiations with our other allies. However, most of the negotiations, and particularly those of London leading to the war crimes prosecutions, have been negotiations by the Big Four Powers, the United States, the United Kingdom, France and the Soviet Union, each one of the four conducting negotiations with the other three simultaneously. It is as difficult to dissect out of the mass of the negotiations those representing distinctly American-Russian discussions as it is to dissect two eggs out of a four-egg omelet. Indeed it is apter to say a six-egg omelet, since each of the four nations negotiated with each of the other three; so, eliminating duplications, six sets of international discussions comprised the negotiations. And, to add to the complication, all of the discussions were in three languages, by means of interpreters. For-·tunately, we found that the United Kingdom and United States

representatives came sufficiently close to speaking the same language that we needed no interpreters between us.

It seems a work of supererogation, if not of impossibility, to
attempt a coverage, or even the barest summary, of these particular negotiations in one chapter of this symposium. Mr. Justice
Jackson has done a complete job on the negotiations leading to
the Agreement and Charter of August 8, 1945, and it took a book
of 441 pages to do it.[1] This book contains every basic document,
from the Memorandum to President Roosevelt from Secretary
of War Stimson, Secretary of State Stettinius and Attorney General Francis Biddle, of January 22, 1945, on the Trial and Punishment of Nazi War Criminals, sometimes referred to as the
"Yalta Memorandum" and sometimes as the "Crimean Proposal"
and which furnished the groundwork of later drafts submitted
by the United States for an international agreement, down to the
final Report to President Truman by Mr. Justice Jackson, of
October 7, 1946, after the trial before the International Military
Tribunal was concluded. Thus the book contains in full text
each pertinent Presidential Executive Order, each successive
draft and redraft of the agreement presented by either power to
the others, each set of formal criticisms or comments presented
by any one of them, each aide-mémoire submitted by any one of
them, the full minutes in English of all the plenary conferences,
and a number of the reports to Mr. Justice Jackson made by me
as the American representative on the drafting subcommittee together with my detailed notes on a number of the subcommittee
sessions.

The book is admirably constructed in such chronological order that each draft document can be compared with each next-
preceding draft in the light of the intervening discussions, so that
a careful reading makes it clear how the elaborate discussions
step-by-step clarified divergent views, gradually brought them

[1] The main title of his book is *Report of Robert H. Jackson, United States
Representative to the International Conference on Military Trials—London, 1945*
(Department of State, 1949), and the subtitle is "A documentary record of negotiations of the Representatives of the United States of America, the Provisional Government of the French Republic, the United Kingdom of Great Britain and
Northern Ireland, and the Union of Soviet Socialist Republics, culminating in
the agreement and charter of the International Military Tribunal." This book is
for sale by the Superintendent of Documents, United States Government Printing
Office, Washington 25, D.C., for $1.75, and it is indispensable for any student of
these negotiations. No summary could possibly vie with the incomparable preface
to it written by the Justice, or with his final Report to the President at the end of it.

closer and closer together, compromised sometimes sharp differences, refined and refined again the language, until the final Agreement and Charter was accepted by all four negotiators and signed on August 8, 1945.

An entirely distinct chapter of the negotiations, though overlapping in time with those resulting in the Agreement and Charter of August 8, 1945, consists of those concerned with the drafting of the indictment, including the selection of the defendants to be charged with war crimes. The indictment could not be put in final draft, even in accordance with the views of any one of the four powers, until the four had agreed on the list of defendants. The agreement on this list involved a tremendous amount of study and serious difficulties of negotiations. The most difficult stage then came in the negotiations which compromised sharply conflicting views (generally reflecting differing national procedural concepts as to criminal trials) as to what form the indictment should take. These distinct negotiations continued until October 4, 1945, in London, when the four delegations (I was there acting as the deputy of Mr. Justice Jackson, who had moved to Nuremberg) agreed on the final form of the indictment. We read the proofs the next morning and that afternoon I flew to Berlin with the printed document, where it was signed by the four Chief Prosecutors on October 6 and was filed at the first meeting of the Tribunal on October 18.

Mr. Justice Jackson's book does not purport to cover the details of the negotiations leading to the final form of the indictment. Most of the preliminary work was done by drafting subcommittees on which the chiefs of delegations did not sit. The final work was done and agreement was reached in London, where I served as the Justice's deputy and where work was done under such furious pressure that nobody had time to make detailed minutes of our all-day and part-night sessions. My only source for details, aside from recollections five and a half years old, is a full diary that I kept. But the Agreement and Charter obviously would have come to naught if the four powers had not come to agreement on the list of defendants and on the form of the indictment, without which no trial could have been held; so these final negotiations were of no minor importance.

I

There is one outstanding, yet quite simple, reason why these London negotiations were successful, whereas so many recent negotiations with the Soviet Union have been complete failures. It is a reason inherent in human nature rather than in any peculiar characteristics of the Russian nature or temperament. It is the very plain fact that there was no difference or conflict among the four powers as to the ultimate aim of these negotiations. There were differences in concepts as to judicial process, as to procedure, as to what constitutes a fair trial, as to where the trial should be held, even as to substantive international law and definitions of war crimes. But there was no difference as to the one ultimate aim, the creation of an international military tribunal and the indictment, trial, conviction and punishment of the major European Axis war criminals.

Such unanimity as to ultimate aim is the greatest catalytic agent for the fusion of conflicting elements of method. This situation is in no wise comparable to other negotiations with the Soviet Union where ultimate national aims have been in conflict, such aims as fixing of boundaries (Poland, for example), fixing of reparations, making treaties with conquered countries, limitation of armaments, international inspection of atomic weapons, settling of lend-lease, the relations between west and east Germany, or the Berlin blockade and the airlift.

A second important reason for the success of these negotiations is that they were all conducted in secret, confidential sessions. The press was never present. No press releases were ever given as to the details of the discussions, although, as inevitably happens, there were some leaks to or speculations by the press as to supposed differences among the four negotiators. Nevertheless, the Agreement and Charter was an "open covenant" secretly, not openly, arrived at. As a result there was no temptation to make the debates and discussions a sounding-board for home consumption in the four nations or for propaganda by any one nation directed to public opinion in the others or elsewhere.

For these reasons we never had any acrimonious debates. There were no attacks or even insinuations by any one delegation against the motives, views or contentions of the others. The four chief negotiators were four very distinguished lawyers or lawyer-judges. The discussions at all times were kept on a high plane. The Russians were second to none in politeness and tact. They were characteristically stubborn on any matter on which they took a definite position or on which apparently, they were under instructions from Moscow. But they were never rude. They could sit tight on a matter for days and weeks, remaining totally impervious to the arguments of others, without ever giving any offense or departing in the slightest from an attitude of perfect politeness. They would agree to a matter one day and repudiate the agreement the next, evidently having communicated with Moscow in the meantime, without any appearance of embarrassment at the inconsistency and with the blandest suavity of manner. These acts or tactics often harassed, sometimes vexed, the other conferees, but neither the words nor the manners of the Russians ever did. There was a complete absence of any such diatribes and invectives as Vyshinsky, Gromyko and Malik have accustomed us to in recent years.

Individually the Russians were charming, courteous and friendly. Our individual conversations with them were hampered by the constant necessity of an interpreter, but that necessity in no wise prevented, only slowed down, social communication. Sometimes such slowing down of conversation is a good thing. It gives each participant the chance to weigh carefully what the other has said and what his reply will be. It helps to avoid the hasty *faux pas*. They entertained elaborately and well, usually at the Savoy. At one of their parties at the Savoy, I said to Professor Trainin that only good, sound capitalists could afford to live and entertain at such an expensive hotel. He enjoyed the jibe hugely. In the course of our conversation he asked me what I did in "civil" life. I told him that I represented "special interests." He laughed again and said slyly, "Ah, you know, we have some of those in Russia too." They were not only gracious hosts but also genial guests. We formed very close personal attachments for each of them. Not one of us has heard a word, even by indirection, from any of them since they returned behind the "Iron Curtain." Several of us have tried to communicate but never a word of acknowledgment or response. We think we know why.

What has just been written sounds like the cart before the

horse, the conclusions before the premises. However, these are hardly conclusions. They are observations pertinent to all the negotiations, from first to last.

II

The so-called "Yalta Memorandum" or "Crimean Proposal" by the Secretaries of State and War and the Attorney General, of January 22, 1945,[2] was furnished to guide President Roosevelt when he attended the Yalta Conference.[3]

That memorandum set forth the essence of the "American Plan" for which we fought throughout the subsequent negotiations and which substantially was finally adopted by the other three powers and carried out in the trial. It rejected the idea of executing notorious Nazi war criminals out of hand, without trial or hearing, and recommended the judicial process and a fair trial. It recommended the negotiation of an executive agreement of the Big Four that would provide for the establishment of an international tribunal of a military character. It proposed the use of the theory of conspiracy to reach not only individual outrages but also the common plan of the German leaders to conduct a systematic and planned reign of terror within Germany, in the satellite Axis countries, and in the occupied countries of Europe." The memorandum said that this planned course of conduct went back to 1933 when Hitler was appointed Chancellor of the Reich. It continued, "It has been marked by mass murders, imprisonments, expulsions and deportations of populations; the starvation, torture and inhuman treatment of civilians; the wholesale looting of public and private property on a scale unparalleled in history; and, after initiation of 'total war,' its prosecution with utter and ruthless disregard for the laws and customs of war."

That memorandum also contained the other essential feature of the "American Plan" which occupied so much of the London negotiations, the proposal for a procedure by which the

[2] *Ibid.*, p. 3.

[3] For earlier planning which it embodied, see Stimson, Henry L. and McGeorge Bundy *On Active Service in Peace and War*, New York, 1948, Vol. 11, p. 584; Bernays, Murray C. "Legal Basis of the Nürnberg Trials," *Survey Graphic*, January 1946, Vol. 35, p. 4; and Jackson, Robert H. "The Nürnberg Case," New York, 1947, p. v.

Tribunal in the main trial would declare certain Nazi groups and organizations (SA, SS, Gestapo, etc.) to be criminal, as the basis for reaching the many members of those organizations in later trials of individuals at which the Tribunal's finding as to the criminal character of the organizations would be conclusive on that question. This was a strange concept to Russian and French lawyers and even to British and some American lawyers and it took extensive negotiations to harmonize views and to gain its acceptance.

The memorandum indicated acceptance "in principle" by an attached note of Mr. Molotov for the Soviet Union and by an aide-mémoire from the British Embassy to our Department of State. Thus on January 22, 1945, there was good hope of acceptance of the "American Plan" by the Soviet Union and by the United Kingdom. France was in a chaotic condition and had not been heard from.

At Yalta no action was taken other than an agreement for later consideration by the governments there represented.

On April 12, 1945, President Roosevelt died and Harry S. Truman became President. At that time Judge Samuel Rosenman, assistant to the President, was in Europe endeavoring to obtain agreement by the United Kingdom to proceed with the trial of war criminals in general conformity with the plan outlined in the "Yalta Memorandum." Under President Truman's direction, Judge Rosenman continued these efforts at San Francisco at the United Nations Conference on International Organization.

On May 2, 1945, President Truman issued Executive Order 9547 appointing Justice Robert H. Jackson as "Representative of the United States and as its Chief of Counsel in preparing and prosecuting charges of atrocities and war crimes against such of the leaders of the European Axis powers and their principal agents and accessories as the United States may agree with any of the United Nations to bring to trial before an international military tribunal." [4] This order did not specifically charge Justice Jackson with any functions in connection with negotiating the proposed executive agreement. For some time there was

---

[4] For full text, see Jackson, cited above, p. 21. The next morning, May 3, 1945, Mr. Justice Jackson asked me to join him on his mission and he immediately began to organize a small staff.

doubt as to who would handle the negotiations for the United States.

Representatives of State, War and Justice Departments, in conference with Mr. Justice Jackson and his staff, reduced the proposal to a draft "protocol" for an executive agreement of the Big Four which Judge Rosenman, with representatives of the three departments, took to San Francisco. It was informally discussed, certain revisions were made and, as revised, it was delivered to Foreign Ministers Eden of the United Kingdom, Molotov of the Union of Soviet Socialist Republics, and Bidault of the Provisional Government of France. This was the first submission of a proposed agreement by the United States and was the basis on which the Foreign Ministers accepted, in principle, the "American Plan" for trial.[5]

No action was taken at San Francisco other than informal discussions and agreements by the four governments on the following general principles: first, trial of the major war criminals rather than political disposition of their cases; second, return of criminals whose crimes had fixed geographical location to the countries where their crimes were committed; third, an international military tribunal to hear the cases of the major war criminals; and fourth, a committee of four representatives or chiefs of counsel to prepare and manage the prosecution, one to represent each of the four governments. It was further agreed that after the San Francisco Conference, and probably in Washington, meetings of the representatives would be held to formulate definitive agreements.

On May 22, Mr. Justice Jackson, at the direction of President Truman, left for Europe to organize the gathering of evidence, through American military and other channels, to confer as to progress towards an agreement for international trials, and to discuss trial preparations with American military authorities and with the French, British and Soviet officials who would be concerned with such trials.

Discussion with French Foreign Minister Bidault, en route to Paris, resulted in assurances that the Provisional Government agreed in principle with the "American Plan" and would promptly name a representative to engage in negotiation of the

[5] For full text, see *ibid.*, p. 23.

agreement and of a definitive plan and to conduct the prosecution.

In London, Lord Chancellor John Viscount Simon stated that the United Kingdom Government had become convinced of the desirability of proceeding along the general lines outlined in the American proposal.

At a meeting with Attorney General Sir David Patrick Maxwell Fyfe, Treasury-Solicitor Sir Thomas James Barnes and Patrick Dean of the Foreign Office, on May 28, a memorandum of British proposals for amending the agreement as proposed by the United States at San Francisco was handed to Mr. Justice Jackson. It proposed only minor changes.[6] On May 29, the British Government announced the appointment of Sir David as their representative for the negotiations and as their chief of counsel for the prosecution.

Mr. Justice Jackson made a call upon Soviet Ambassador Gusev in London, but secured no information as to the Soviet attitude. He returned to the United States without having learned anything as to the Soviet position.

On June 3, 1945, the British Embassy in Washington presented to our State Department an aide-mémoire which formally informed the State Department that His Majesty's Government had accepted in principle the United States draft as a basis for discussion by the representatives appointed by the allied governments to prepare for the prosecution of war criminals. It suggested that the United States Government might care to represent to the Soviet Government and to the French Government the urgent necessity for reaching agreement on the main principle, at least, of the United States draft agreement and invite those two governments to follow the example of the United States Government and of His Majesty's Government by appointing representatives for the prosecution. The aide-mémoire further suggested that the respective representatives meet in London for the negotiation of the agreement and also for the organization of the proposed prosecuting authority, the preparation of charges and the procedure for the trials.[7]

On June 6, 1945, after his return from Europe, Mr. Justice

6 *Ibid.,* p. 39.
7 *Ibid.,* p. 41.

Jackson made a very full report to the President, reviewing all the work that had been accomplished by the United States up to that date and setting out very fully the American theory of the case and plan for the procedure. It was a great state paper. It was released to the press by the White House, with a statement of the President's approval, and was widely published throughout Europe as well as in the United States. This report was accepted by other governments as the official statement of the position of the United States and as such was placed before all the delegations to the London conference.[8]

On June 11, 1945, the British Ambassador in Washington presented to the Secretary of State an aide-mémoire formally inviting the United States to send representatives to London for discussions beginning on or about June 25. Similar invitations were addressed to the Soviet and French Governments. These invitations were accepted, first by the United States and later by the Soviet and French Governments.

In the meantime, Mr. Justice Jackson and his staff studied the draft of the proposal and, without changing it in principle, prepared a further revised draft, which was transmitted on June 14, 1945, to the embassies of the United Kingdom, the Soviet Union and the Provisional Government of France, at Washington, for the information and consideration of their governments before the approaching London conferences.[9]

These occurrences crystallized the understanding that the negotiation of the international agreement as well as the preparation for and prosecution of the trials would be conducted by the representatives and chiefs of counsel appointed by the four governments. Thereafter, Mr. Justice Jackson rather than the State Department conducted, on our behalf, the negotiations for the international agreement.

Obviously, communications between Washington and Moscow were difficult. On June 14, 1945, Nikolai V. Novikov, Minister-Counselor of the Soviet Embassy at Washington, called on Mr. Justice Jackson and delivered an aide-mémoire in the Russian language which agreed with the United States draft of the agreement in its principles, but which suggested seventeen specific amendments. This aide-mémoire referred to the original

8 *Ibid.*, p. 42.
9 For the full text of the June 14, 1945, revised draft, see *ibid.*, p. 55.

draft protocol considered at San Francisco. Evidently the Soviet Government had not yet received or considered the two subsequent drafts. However, the seventeen suggested amendments were largely applicable to the last draft of June 14, 1945.[10]

Mr. Justice Jackson handed me a copy of the Soviet aide-mémoire, telling me that he was willing to accept at least fourteen of the seventeen proposed amendments out of hand. In the subsequent negotiations in London, we had very little difficulty satisfying the Soviet Union as to all of the amendments suggested in this aide-mémoire.

As the first step in the preparation for the trial, our staff drew up a careful planning memorandum to indicate the application of the provisions of the United States proposals to the various practical problems of the trial.[11] That memorandum was distributed to all delegations at the beginning of the London conference as an aid to their understanding of the meaning of our proposals.

III

On June 18, the day of General Eisenhower's triumphal return to Washington, Mr. Justice Jackson and I, with the nucleus of his staff,[12] flew to London, arriving there the next day. We were met there by William Dwight Whitney, of New York and London, the unusual combination of an American lawyer and a British barrister, who had been named by the Justice as a member of his staff. He had a wide acquaintance with British officialdom and a thorough knowledge of London and was of great help in all our relations with the British.

On the afternoon of June 20, Shea, Whitney, Lt. Donovan and I had an informal, preliminary meeting with Sir Thomas Barnes, Treasury-Solicitor and assistant to Sir David Maxwell Fyfe, B. A. Clyde and E. G. Robey, Sir Thomas' assistants, George Cold-

---

10 For full text of the Soviet aide-mémoire as translated into English, see *ibid.*, p. 61.

11 *Ibid.*, p. 64.

12 Col. Murray C. Bernays, AUS, Francis M. Shea, Assistant Attorney General, Lt. Gordon Dean, USNR, our publicity officer, now Chairman of the Atomic Energy Commission, Lt. James Donovan, USNR, General Counsel of the Office of Strategic Services (Maj. Gen. William J. Donovan, Director of OSS, was a member of the staff but did not take this particular trip), Ens. William E. Jackson, USNR, the Justice's son and assistant, Maj. Lawrence Coleman, AUS, and a number of secretaries.

stream, of the Lord Chancellor's office, Patrick Dean and Robert Scott Fox, of the Foreign Office.

We first had a general discussion about our last draft of the "protocol.' The British said they had a few suggested amendments but no substantial objections to it. They announced that M. Donnedieu de Vabres had been confirmed by the French cabinet as France's representative and chief of counsel. He was distinguished international lawyer and author on international law. We were all comforted at this indication that the Provisional Government of France was getting under way.

The British talked about the probable length of the trial and were strongly of the view that it ought not to last more than three weeks, that public interest would flag if it took longer than that. We were confident that no such compression of the trial could be accomplished, though we agreed that we should aim to make it as short as consistent with making out a full case for the prosecution and giving the defendants a full and fair opportunity to defend.

The British are very keen on the "working subcommittee" system and expressed the view that to expedite the work we ought to appoint small subcommittees of the four delegations to deal with particular subjects, such as the draft of the protocol agreement, rules of procedure for the Tribunal, draft of the indictment, etc. We agreed.

They talked about a tentative list of defendants they had drawn up, a very small list of from seven to ten. I told them that we had in mind a very much larger list of something like fifty or sixty. Mr. Dean said that their approach to the case was to begin with a small segment and enlarge it as the work developed. I told him that our approach had been rather from the opposite direction, to build up a very elaborate case and then trim it down by elimination as we approached the trial. This was characteristic of our respective approaches throughout the negotiations. We agreed that each of our delegations might follow its own approach with the hope that we might meet somewhere in the middle ground.

In the course of our discussion I told our British cousins that I represented the southern part of the United States, whereas all other members of our staff were "damn Yankees." Sir Thomas indicated a sympathetic attitude on the part of the British to the southern viewpoint. Then he praised our Planning Memorandum highly and said that he "cottoned to that document." I asked him where in the world he got that expression, saying it was distinctly a southern colloquialism in the United States. He said that it was current English and I suggested that the reason might be that the United Kingdom was the principal market for our cotton and that our expression probably followed the cotton to the United Kingdom. He agreed.[18]

We had some discussion of the languages which would have to be employed at the trial. They thought, and we agreed, that all documents and all testimony would have to be put in English, French and Russian, as well as in German. I asked if it would be necessary to translate also from English into American and *vice versa*. Sir Thomas very politely suggested that they had not thought that necessary and he proceeded to make use of some other American slang to illustrate his point. My diary notes on this first conference end thus: "The meeting was in Church House, so when we adjourned for the meeting tomorrow, I told Sir Thomas that I would see him in church. He was a wee bit slow on the uptake but he finally appreciated it. I like these people."

On June 21 and June 24, at the invitation of the British, informal meetings of the United States and United Kingdom representatives, and of their respective staffs, were held. These meetings were necessarily informal because we did not want the Russian and French representatives, when they had arrived, to think that the United Kingdom and the United States had undertaken any formal action prior to the start of the four-power negotiation.

The informal meeting on June 21 was especially interesting in that Sir David presented as a basis for discussion a list of defendants consisting of Goering, Hess, Ribbentrop, Ley, Rosenberg, Hans Frank, Frick, Keitel, Streicher and Kaltenbrunner. This was the round number of ten, in line with the views the British representatives had previously expressed. The list is especially interesting because everyone named ultimately showed

[18] Like so many off-the-cuff, amateur etymologies this one was wrong. The Oxford English Dictionary shows the expression "cotton to," in the sense indicated, to have been an English expression dating back at least to the sixteenth century. Many supposed southern colloquialisms in the United States are straight Elizabethan English.

up as a defendant in the trial except Ley, who was named as a defendant, but who committed suicide the night after reading the indictment. The United States representatives agreed that the list of ten names should be considered, but said that they would propose additional names later.

There was a general discussion of the best methods of proof in view of the difficulty and novelty of the case and of the many possible sources of evidence to be explored.

Sir David stated that the United Kingdom hoped that the trial would commence about the first of September. He wanted that set as a target date, although recognizing that a target is not always hit. He referred to the pending elections in which he was, as he said, "wooing the electorate," and said that he had no doubt that, in the event a Labour Government was chosen, it would adhere to the plans made by its predecessors in the present conferences. He suggested Munich, in the United States zone of Germany, as an appropriate place for the trial, partly for its psychological value as the birthplace of the Nazi Party. Mr. Justice Jackson suggested that the choice depended chiefly on facilities that could be made available and undertook to investigate the suitability of Munich. All agreed that the trial should be held on the continent, probably in Germany, and that, if in Germany, it should be held in either the British or the American zone of occupation.

The discussion continued on Sunday, June 24. Sir Basil Newton, of the Foreign Office, advised that the British Ambassador in Moscow had reported that Soviet delegates would attend the conference, but that they had requested that the meeting be deferred to June 26. It was agreed that the British Embassy at Moscow should be notified that the British and American delegations acceded to the Soviet request.

Sir Basil further informed the session that the French had decided to send as their representative for the negotiations Judge Robert Falco of the Cour de Cassation, instead of M. Donnedieu de Vabres, and that Professor André Gros, French member of the United Nations War Crimes Commission, would accompany and assist Judge Falco.

There was an informal discussion of the amendments that had been proposed by the United Kingdom to the United States draft and of the seventeen points raised by the aide-mémoire handed to Mr. Justice Jackson by the Counselor of the Soviet Embassy at Washington. Pending arrival of the other delegations, it was agreed that a subcommittee would attempt to reconcile such differences as there were between the British and American viewpoints in a joint new draft of protocol, but that no commitment should be made by either delegation on any point that was to come before the four-power conference.

Francis Shea and I were named as the United States representatives on this subcommittee, and we met with Sir Thomas Barnes and Clyde and Dean and in two days harmonized all of our differences and came to full agreement upon a new draft of the protocol agreement. This demonstrated how easy it was for us to handle negotiations with the British. However, we did not circulate this new draft and it was not the subject of discussion in the four-power conference, being kept by our two delegations in the nature of a working paper.

On June 26, the Russian and French representatives arrived and the first four-power conference was held. The Russian representatives were General I. T. Nikitchenko, Vice-President of the Supreme Court of the Soviet Union, and Professor A. N. Trainin, member of the Soviet Academy of Sciences and the author of a very excellent book on war crimes, an English translation of which had been made available to us. The French representatives were Robert Falco and André Gros.

In addition to the members of the British delegation already named, there were G. D. Roberts, K. C., General Lord Robert Clive Bridgman of the War Office, E. J. Passant, of the Foreign Office, and M. E. Reed, of the Law Officers' Department.

The conference was called to order by the Attorney General, Sir David, who welcomed the representatives of the other powers on behalf of the host, the United Kingdom. He stated the purpose of the conference in general terms, reviewed the proceedings which had led up to it, and suggested that, inasmuch as the United States had proposed a definite form of agreement, the conference call upon Mr. Justice Jackson to explain in detail the United States proposal, which he did.

General Nikitchenko immediately suggested that, instead of embodying the entire subject in one instrument, there should be a separate and short executive agreement with an annexed "statute" to cover the details, such as the definition of crimes and the rules and procedures to govern the conduct of the trial. This was a very practical suggestion, which was reiterated by the Soviet Union in a number of conferences and was finally agreed to by the other three delegations.

Mr. Justice Jackson's published minutes of this and subsequent conference sessions are indispensable to an understanding of the nature and details of the discussions, which took a very wide scope. Nothing more can be done here than to give some idea of the principal problems about which there were differences of view and difficulties.

One of the first difficulties that arose and continued as ground for debate throughout many conference sessions, was the United States proposal for the conviction of groups and organizations and subsequent prosecution of individual members in which the primary finding of the International Military Tribunal as to the criminality of the organizations themselves could not be challenged. In this first session General Nikitchenko expressed a good deal of puzzlement as to this part of the United States proposal. He took the position that under authority of the surrender documents the Control Council for Germany had abolished all of these Nazi groups and organizations. Since they had been abolished, he thought they were no longer juridical bodies and that a non-existent or abolished group or organization could not be put on trial, although he recognized that individual members of such an organization could be tried. There was a great deal of debate about this proposal, but finally the Soviet representatives absorbed the idea that the abolishment and disbanding by the Control Council of these groups and organizations did not make it impossible to try them as legal entities and to enter a judgment of conviction against them. This acquiescence was, as the detailed minutes of the sessions will show, largely induced by the basic Soviet view that it was already universally known that these groups and organizations were criminal, that there really was no need to try them, but that it would not hurt to have the Military Tribunal put the seal of its approval on what was already universal knowledge.

Among the seventeen points presented by the Soviet Ambassador to Mr. Justice Jackson in Washington was a favorite point of theirs which apparently they always present early in any international conference, an insistence on rotation. They had proposed that the position of presiding officer of the Tribunal should be held in rotation. At this first session, General Nikit-chenko referred to this proposal and pointed out that the last draft of the agreement made provisión that the chairman or presiding officer of the Tribunal should be elected. He very politely asked why the Soviet Union suggestion as to rotation had not been adopted. Mr. Justice Jackson pointed out that in the United States we have never had the practice of rotating a presiding officer except in certain courts and commissions where they rotate by the year. He suggested that it would be very con-fusing to have the presiding officer of the Tribunal rotate day by day or week by week and found considerable difficulty in the suggestion of rotation.

Without pursuing the details from session to session, it is fair to say that the Soviet Union continued to insist on the principle of rotation for a long time. The whole problem was finally re-solved by an agreement that one presiding officer should be elected for the first trial and that there would thereafter be ro-tation for the subsequent trials. It was quite clear that the Soviet Union conceived that there should be a series of trials before the International Military Tribunal, perhaps one in the United States zone, one in the French zone, one in the Soviet Union zone, and one in the United Kingdom zone of occupied Germany. Their principle of rotation logically fitted such a concept and they were finally satisfied. The British and the Americans had pretty definitely in their minds the basic concept that there would be only one trial of major war criminals before the In-ternational Military Tribunal and that thereafter subsequent trials would be separately prosecuted by each occupying power, in occupational courts, in its own zone. This undoubtedly in-fluenced British and American agreement to the principle of rotation and, in fact, only one trial was held before the Inter-national Military Tribunal. In view of these different concepts, and particularly in view of the Soviet Union preoccupation with the idea that there would be a series of trials, it is extremely interesting to note that although the British, the French and the Americans prosecuted subsequent war crimes trials before national occupation courts, so far as we can discover the Russians have never prosecuted any subsequent trial or any individual German since the Nuremberg trial before the International Military Tribunal. This undoubtedly reflects their subsequent campaign to cultivate close relations with east Germany.

IV

The major conflict of views arose out of the basic differences between the Anglo-American legal concepts as to criminal trials and the quite different concepts obtaining on the continent and in particular in the Soviet Union, Germany and France. This first conference included a very extensive discussion of these different systems.

In both France and the Soviet Union a criminal trial is initiated before an inquiring magistrate, which the French call *juge d'instruction*. This magistrate examines the defendants and cross-examines them, subjecting them to an extensive interrogation, bringing them face to face with any inconsistent statements they have made and with any documents inconsistent with their statements. After this is done and the *juge d'instruction* has completed his dossier of evidence, interrogations and documents, the whole dossier is turned over to the prosecuting officer, who studies the dossier and sums up the charges to present to the judges. This is essentially the French system as described by Judge Falco, and as best we could tell from General Nikitchenko's statement, it was substantially the Soviet Union system, with one important difference. The difference was that the French very carefully respect the distinction between the court and its judges, on the one hand, and the prosecuting officer, on the other; in other words, the basic distinction between the judicial function and the executive function, whereas the Soviet Union does not draw that distinction so carefully.

Under both systems the *dossier* compiled by the *juge d'instruction* is filed with the court. Then at the trial the judges of the court interrogate the defendant or defendants, largely on their own initiative, the prosecuting officer taking very little part in the interrogation. Likewise, the counsel for the defendant takes little part in the interrogation. The function of counsel, both prosecutor and counsel for defendant, is largely that of summing up or arguing the case after the judges have completed their interrogation of witnesses. I observed this procedure in the Pétain trial at Paris. Both the French and the Soviet Union had great difficulty understanding our procedure of allowing defendants to testify initially in their own defense under examination by their counsel. Both the Soviet Union and France thought that one person could not be at the same time a defendant and a witness.

The Soviet Union had one point upon which they constantly insisted as constituting the essence of what we call due process or a fair trial, the right of the defendants to make an unsworn statement at the end of the trial, a statement which we Americans came to refer to, somewhat lugubriously, as "the last words of the defendants." Since the other delegations readily agreed to accord the defendants this right to utter their "last words," the Soviet Union was easily satisfied as to its concept of a fair trial.[14]

These different concepts likewise were reflected in correspondingly differing concepts as to the nature of an indictment. With the British and the Americans an indictment is a rather brief document merely charging the offense alleged to have been committed and containing no evidentiary matter or documents. The evidentiary matter and documents are introduced only at the trial. Under the Soviet and French systems, however, the indictment consists of the filing with the court of the *dossier* of interrogations, cross-interrogations, and documents which have been compiled in the preliminary proceedings by the *juge d'instruction*. Obviously, there is much to be said for each of the two conflicting systems. Under the continental system, although the defendant has been subjected to preliminary examination and cross-examination, yet he has seen and has the benefit of all the documents alleged to be in conflict with his statements and all of his own statements or the statements of other witnesses alleged to be in conflict with his interrogation. In this first conference and throughout later conferences, General Nikitchenko and Professor Trainin showed a constant recognition that it would be necessary to select between the two differing systems, to try to pick out the best elements of each, so as to create for the International Military Tribunal a system and procedure which would be expeditious and yet which would contain the essential elements of a fair trial.

[14] This Soviet practice is not unknown in the United States. The criminal law of the State of Georgia denies to a defendant in a criminal case the right to give sworn testimony in his own defense but does accord him the right to make an unsworn final statement. See *Taylor v. Georgia* (1942), 315 U.S. 25.

Another major difficulty throughout the negotiations was created by the Soviet insistence, first, that the trial should take place in Berlin, in the Soviet zone, and second, that in any event, the seat of the Tribunal should be in Berlin even if the "first trial" took place in some other zone.

In our preliminary discussions the British and the Americans had foreseen such insistence and we had quite well agreed between us that we would both resist these proposals to the limit, for obvious reasons. The Soviet Union insisted through many sessions that the first trial should take place in Berlin. We always insisted that the destruction in Berlin was such that there was no available building for the conduct of the trial and no adequate billeting arrangements for handling the prosecuting delegations and no adequate prison arrangements for the defendants. Subsequently, Mr. Justice Jackson, with a group of his assistants, on July 7, flew to Frankfurt and conferred with General Lucius D. Clay, who advised that Nuremberg would be the most suitable place for the trial. Thereupon, Mr. Justice Jackson and the members of his staff proceeded to Nuremberg and inspected the Palace of Justice and the jail, obtained dimensions and floor plans, and examined the billeting facilities in that city. He came firmly to the conclusion that Nuremberg presented the only adequate facilities for the trial in occupied Germany, and he continued to insist on Nuremberg as the place for the trial, finally with success.

However, a dramatic illustration of how persistent the Soviet Union was in its contention about the place of trial occurred later in July. Justice Jackson invited the British, Soviet and French delegations to accompany him on a flight to Nuremberg so that we all might spend a day there examining the courthouse, prison and billeting facilities and so as to give the other three delegations the benefit of such inspection. The Soviet Union, as well as the United Kingdom and France, formally accepted the invitation.

On July 20, the day before the proposed trip, the British, American and French delegations were entertained by the Soviet Union at an elaborate luncheon at the Savoy. Our hosts were very polite and hospitable, but during the cocktail session, Clyde and I learned that General Nikitchenko, Professor Trainin, and young Troyanovsky, their very efficient English interpreter (son of former Ambassador Troyanovsky and a graduate of Dart-

mouth) were all saying that they could not go with us to Nuremberg the following day, in spite of the fact that they had formally
accepted the invitation. I told Justice Jackson what I had learned
and he said there was nothing for us to do but wait and see what
happened, that it was up to them to tell us if they were not going
with us. After the usual toasts and compliments, the luncheon
broke up, and as the Justice was telling Nikitchenko goodby, the
latter, through Troyanovsky, and with obvious embarrassment,
told the Justice that no member of the Soviet delegation could
take the trip with us. The Justice offered to change the date to
any other date that might be more agreeable to them, but
Nikitchenko said that changing the date would make no difference. The refusal to go was categorical. We had no doubt that
Nikitchenko had notified Moscow that he had accepted the invitation and that Moscow had vetoed the trip.

Notwithstanding this *contretemps,* the Soviet Union in the
later stages of the negotiations agreed to hold the first trial before the International Military Tribunal in Nuremberg, provided that the permanent seat of the Tribunal should be in Berlin and that the first meetings of the members of the Tribunal
and of the chief prosecutors should be held in Berlin, and this
agreement was incorporated in Article 22 of the Charter as follows:

> "The permanent seat of the Tribunal shall be in Berlin. The
> first meetings of the members of the Tribunal and of the Chief
> Prosecutors shall be held at Berlin in a place to be designated
> by the Control Council for Germany. The first trial shall be
> held at Nuremberg, and any subsequent trials shall be held at
> such places as the Tribunal may decide."

Another problem on which the Soviet Union stuck so hard that
it never gave up was that raised by the American proposal that
the Tribunal be empowered to appoint Special Masters, or commissioners, to make special investigations, take evidence, and
report to the Tribunal, with power in the Tribunal to act on
such reports. This suggestion, of course, was borrowed from our
very familiar equity practice. Its adoption would have greatly
facilitated this trial. We had in mind such special investigations
as those of particular concentration camps or of other distant
points where particular atrocities occurred, such as the Warsaw
ghetto, so vividly described in John Hersey's *The Wall.*

I think our approach to this proposal was bad psychologically, in that we used the term "Special Masters." I think that term, or whatever its Russian translation was, shocked the Soviet Union and that no amount of explanation on our part ever enabled them to recover from their original sense of shock. In our drafting subcommittee meetings I had a great deal of discussion with Professor Trainin about this matter of Special Masters. The British and the French were in accord with our views that such a procedure would expedite the trial. Professor Trainin's arguments about it took strange turns. At first he argued that the Tribunal would have the inherent power to appoint commissioners to take evidence for it, or "Special Masters," as we called them, and insisted that it was unnecessary to spell that power out expressly in the International Agreement and Charter. I pointed out to him that the Tribunal could have no inherent powers not conferred upon it by the Agreement and Charter, that it was a creature of the Agreement and Charter and could have no powers other than those expressly conferred upon it. Faced with the logic of this, he had no answer to it except to revert categorically to his refusal to accept the proposal. It was obvious that he was opposed to the Tribunal's having the very power which he claimed it would have inherently. The Soviet Union never did agree to that particular proposal.

V

I revert briefly to the chronology of the negotiations and reserve for a little later the difficulties we had arising out of the problem of properly defining wars of aggression.

After the first plenary session on June 26, 1945,[15] the United Kingdom on June 28 presented to the other delegations formal amendments which it proposed to the last United States draft protocol.[16] On the same date the French presented elaborate written observations on the American draft [17] and the Soviet Union presented elaborate written comments and proposals on the American draft.[18]

The Soviet Union's comments and proposals contained most

[15] For the full minutes, see Jackson, cited above, p. 71–85.
[16] *Ibid.*, p. 86.
[17] *Ibid.*, p. 89.
[18] *Ibid.*, p. 92.

of the Soviet positions above discussed: that there should be a short Agreement, with the details and procedure set out in an Annex; that the principle of rotation should be followed; that the proposal for trying and convicting organizations be eliminated; the contention that the four prosecutors should constitute a formal international investigating commission, with functions in line with the continental concept of a preliminary investigation by the *juge d'instruction*, etc. The document ended with this characteristically polite statement:

> "The present considerations are preliminary in character. Their purpose is to make more precise the positions of the delegations and to contribute to the systematic and rapid development of the work of the Commission."

By "Commission" they had reference to their concept of the four prosecutors forming such an international commission.

On June 29 another plenary session was held in which each delegation, British, French, and Soviet, explained its memorandum of amendments, objections and suggestions.[19]

General Nikitchenko's explanation of the Soviet memorandum at that session was highly illuminating as to most of the Soviet concepts and positions. It is well worth detailed study. In the outset he made a statement clearly showing the Soviet concept that the trials were largely formalities, saying:

> "The first is with regard to the character of the trial. We are not dealing here with the usual type of case where it is a question of robbery, or murder, or petty offenses. We are dealing here with the chief war criminals who have already been convicted and whose conviction has been already announced by both the Moscow and Crimea declarations by the heads of the governments, and those declarations both declare to carry out immediately just punishment for the offenses which have been committed."

That was a viewpoint which the British, French and Americans had to counter many times throughout the negotiations. Time and again the Soviets were told that heads of governments, executives, under our concept, cannot convict people of crime. They can only direct and arrange for prosecution before judicial tribunals, and only those tribunals can convict. General Nikitchenko was perfectly willing to go through the form of having

19 *Ibid.,* p. 97.

the Tribunal put its stamp of approval on the conviction, but he
adhered to the view that the Nazi leaders were already convicted criminals by declaration of the conquering powers.

In his explanation of his memorandum he was very helpful on
the point that we should examine all of the systems of procedure, the Anglo-American and the continental, that they all
have good points, and that we should pick out the best points of
all for this special situation.

His attitude towards our Anglo-American principle of complete separation between the judiciary and the executive is
clearly shown in the following quotation from his remarks:

> "Third, with regard to the position of the judge—the Soviet
> Delegation considers that there is no necessity in trials of this
> sort to accept the principle that the judge is a completely dis-
> interested party with no previous knowledge of the case. The
> declaration of the Crimea Conference is quite clear that the
> objective is to bring these criminals to a just and speedy trial.
> Therefore, the judge, before he takes his seat in court, already
> knows what has been quoted in the press of all countries, and it
> is well known about the criminal as accused and the general
> outline of the case against him. The case for the prosecution is
> undoubtedly known to the judge before the trial starts and
> there is, therefore, no necessity to create a sort of fiction that the
> judge is a disinterested person who has no legal knowledge of
> what has happened before. If such procedure is adopted that
> the judge is supposed to be impartial, it would only lead to
> unnecessary delays and offer opportunity for the accused to
> bring delays in the action of the trial.
> "Fourth, the Soviet Delegation points out that, at the time
> when the declaration was made by the leaders of the United
> Nations on the question that the chief criminals should be tried,
> it was not certain whether these criminals would actually be
> tried by a court or would be punished by some purely political
> action. That is to say, they might have been dealt with by
> means other than a trial. Since then it has been decided that
> they shall go through a process of trial, but the object of that
> trial is, of course, the punishment of the criminals, and there-
> fore the role of the prosecutor should be merely a role of as-
> sisting the court in the actual cases. That is the role of either
> the investigation committee or Chiefs of Counsel as proposed
> in these drafts. The difference is that the prosecution would
> assist the judge, and there would be no question that the judge
> has the character of an impartial person. Only rules of fair trial
> must, of course, apply because years and centuries will pass and

it will be to posterity to examine these trials and to decide whether the persons who drew up the rules of the court and carried out the trials did execute their task with fairness and with justice but subject to giving the accused an opportunity for defense to that extent. The whole idea is to secure quick and just punishment for the crime."

In support of his contention that the American provision for trial and conviction of groups and organizations be deleted, General Nikitchenko said:

"The Soviet Delegation explains this point by the fact that organizations such as the S.S. or the Gestapo have already been declared criminal by authorities higher than the Tribunal itself, both in the Moscow and the Crimea declarations, and the fact of their criminality has definitely been established. We cannot imagine any position arising in which the Tribunal might possibly bring out a verdict that any one of these organizations was not criminal when it has most definitely been labeled so by the governments."

On June 30, 1945, the American delegation submitted a further revised draft of the Executive Agreement and what we called "Annex," accompanied with a written memorandum by Mr. Justice Jackson.[20] In this revised draft and in the accompanying memorandum, the American delegation made its best efforts to meet the respective memoranda filed by the other delegations on June 28.

On July 2, 1945, the Soviet Union presented another draft of the Agreement, very brief in its terms and eliminating any provision for the trials of groups and organizations.[21] This precipitated an elaborate discussion, particularly by Mr. Justice Jackson and Sir David Maxwell Fyfe, presenting the proposal for trial of groups and organizations as the very heart of our proposals and the only practicable way in which to reach the many members of these organizations through the organizations themselves.

After extensive discussion, General Nikitchenko made the following statement, which was immediately characterized by Mr. Justice Jackson as a very excellent statement of what the Americans were trying to get expressed in the document:

"The Soviet Delegation says that under the Soviet law there would be no question whatever of a man being permitted to

20 *Ibid.,* p. 119–127.
21 *Ibid.,* p. 128.

raise the point again whether the organization itself was criminal or not. Once the court had decided in any case, no subsequent trial could raise the question whether it is criminal or
not. It has definitely been pronounced criminal. What he can
do is to produce at the trial evidence that he did not belong
to the organization, or took only a minor part in its proceedings,
or possibly did not know for what purposes the organization
existed, or perhaps that he was forced to join it, but those
factors would be considered by the court as providing the basis
for his acquittal or reduction in penalty in his individual case."

However, he added that he was speaking only of Soviet law and
that in the field of international law the criminality of these
organizations had already been declared by the respective governments and that question could not, in his opinion, be reopened by the International Military Tribunal.

The discussions were continued in further plenary sessions on
July 3 and 4.[22] Those discussions brought the conferees closer
together in principle and ended with agreement for the creation
of a drafting subcommittee to undertake the detailed redrafting of the Agreement and Annex, as it was then called. The members named to that subcommittee were Professor Trainin, for
the Soviet Union; Sir Thomas Barnes, for the United Kingdom;
Judge Falco, for France; and Mr. Alderman, for the United
States, with Mr. Clyde to act as secretary. To facilitate the work
of the drafting subcommittee, I prepared and had mimeographed
a draft showing the latest Soviet and American proposals in
parallel columns.[23] This document greatly facilitated our work.
Meetings of the subcommittee were held on Thursday, July 5,
and continued on successive days thereafter, with the exception
of Saturday and Sunday, until July 10.

On July 11 I made a final report to Mr. Justice Jackson as
the American member of the drafting subcommittee, attached
to it my detailed notes of the discussions in the drafting subcommittee, and a new draft of Agreement and Charter, as it was
now called, reported by the drafting subcommittee to the four
delegations. The members of the drafting subcommittee were
in agreement on this new draft, with the exception of certain
provisions in square brackets left for final determination in

[22] *Ibid.,* p. 143–163.
[23] *Ibid.,* p. 165–184.

plenary sessions.[24] It was understood, however, that all of the work of the drafting subcommittee was tentative in the sense that it was all subject to approval or disapproval of the plenary sessions.

Following the original suggestion by the Soviet Union that the documents be divided into two parts, a brief executive agreement providing for the setting up of the International Military Tribunal, and an appendix to cover all the details, the various drafts up to this point had called the appendix either "annex" or "statute." In the drafting subcommittee negotiations, Professor Trainin objected to "annex" as the title for the appendix because the appendix was made an integral part of the agreement itself, although a separate and appended document, and because he felt that the word "annex" indicated that it was not an integral part of the agreement. Both he and Judge Falco preferred the word "statute." I objected to "statute" on the ground that it left an implication that the whole agreement was in the nature of a four-power treaty which, under our Constitution, would have to be ratified by our Senate. We were undertaking to negotiate an executive agreement and we did not want to go through the process of Senate ratification. Sir Thomas Barnes was sympathetic with my view. He and I discussed the matter separately and agreed that a good compromise would be to call the appendix the "charter." I suggested that he present this suggestion to the subcommittee, which he did, invoking the precedent of the Atlantic Charter, which was not ratified by our Senate. Professor Trainin and Judge Falco were satisfied with this and thereafter, and in the final executed form, the whole document was called "Agreement and Charter."

VI

We were not able to accomplish an adequate definition of wars of aggression. The heart of the case, as we Americans conceived it, was to convict the defendants of a conspiracy to launch and wage aggressive war. Throughout the negotiations and, indeed, throughout the Nuremberg trial, all delegations were obviously embarrassed on this basic matter of aggressive war by the fact

---

24 *Ibid.,* p. 185–201.

that our ally, the Soviet Union, had invaded Poland at the same time that Hitler invaded that country, the actual initiation of aggressive war. The Soviet theory seemed to be that they did not wage aggressive war in Poland, that they merely came in the back door, peacefully, to protect their own interests and boundaries at the same time that Hitler waged aggressive war through the front door. This basic inconsistency made the Soviet Union very sensitive to any properly generalized definition of the launching and waging of aggressive war.

The provision of our subcommittee draft of the Charter of July 11, 1945, in its definitions of crimes, in Article 6 (a), first defined "violations of the laws, rules or customs of war" substantially as they were defined under the heading "War Crimes" in the final document. As to the definition of aggressive war, our draft contained the following:

"(b) Launching a war of aggression.

" (c) [Invasion or threat of invasion of or] initiation of war against other countries in breach of treaties, agreements or assurances between nations or otherwise in violation of International Law.

"(d) [Entering into a common plan or enterprise aimed at domination over other nations, which plan or enterprise involved or was reasonably calculated to involve or in its execution did involve the use of unlawful means for its accomplishment, including any or all of the acts set out in subparagraphs (a) to (c) above or the use of the combination of such unlawful means with other means.]"

The brackets indicate portions of the definition on which the subcommittee could not agree and which were specifically reserved for the plenary sessions. It is interesting that Professor Trainin thus reserved the particular words "invasion or threat of invasion of or," since it obviously could hardly be argued that the Soviet Union had not invaded Poland, even if it could be argued that the Soviet Union had not launched or waged aggressive war against Poland.

The brackets around subparagraph (d) show that Professor Trainin was still dubious about the American theory of conspiracy. The final definition of our draft was:

"(e) Atrocities and persecutions and deportations on political, racial or religious grounds [in pursuance of a common plan or enterprise referred to in subparagraph (d) hereof, whether or not in violation of the domestic law of the country where perpetrated.]"

The brackets in this paragraph again indicate the Soviet Union reservation as to our American theory of a common plan or conspiracy even as to atrocities.

One of the important accomplishments in these subcommittee negotiations, achieved by Sir Thomas Barnes and me, with the consistent good help of Judge Falco, was that we finally brought Professor Trainin to agreement on the second main proposal of the American delegation, the question of trial of groups and organizations.

The pertinent provisions agreed to in our subcommittee draft were:

> "10. At the trial of any individual member of any group or organization, the Tribunal may declare (in connection with any act of which the individual may be convicted) that the group or organization of which the individual was a member was a criminal organization.
> "11. In cases where a group or organization is declared criminal by the Tribunal, the competent national authorities of any Signatory have the right to bring individuals to trial for membership therein before national, military or occupation courts. In any such case the criminal nature of the group or organization is considered proved and shall not be questioned."

In the final executed document this definition was contained in Article 9 and Article 10 of the Charter, in exactly the same words, with the exception of an added paragraph in Article 9 providing for the giving of notice adequate to reach the members of groups and organizations so as to give them an opportunity to intervene in defense of the charge that the organization was criminal.

After much argument in the subcommittee, we were unable to get Professor Trainin to agree that the first trial should be held in Nuremberg, since he took the position that he had no authority to make such an agreement; in that draft, therefore, the place for holding the first trial was left blank.

On the matter of empowering the Tribunal to appoint Special Masters, Professor Trainin agreed on the language to be inserted in the draft, but in brackets, so as to reserve that question for the plenary sessions, Article 3 (e) of the Charter stating, among the specific powers to be conferred on the Tribunal:

"[(e) To appoint special officers of the Tribunal to take evidence and to make findings (except findings of guilt) and to certify summaries of evidence to the Tribunal, whether before or during the trial];"

It is fair to say that the British, Russian and French delegations and I and several other members of our delegation were very well pleased with the subcommittee draft of July 11, 1945. We all thought that a good many important and reasonable compromises between conflicting views had been achieved. However, as I have said before, it was understood that all of the work of the subcommittee was subject to decisions by the plenary sessions and not merely the matters specifically reserved as indicated by brackets.

VII

While our subcommittee was working, Mr. Justice Jackson took another trip to Germany and had a number of conferences with General Clay and with others of our military officials. They told him a great deal about the various difficulties they had been having with the Soviet Union on a number of problems. He came back to London in a very pessimistic mood, which made him skeptical as to whether any written agreements made by the Soviet Union would be carried out. Coupled with this basic skepticism was his major disappointment with our failure to obtain Professor Trainin's agreement to two matters of outstanding importance: the holding of the first trial in Nuremberg, and a proper definition of aggressive war. This attitude of the American representative is rather reflected in the detailed minutes of the plenary sessions beginning July 13, 1945, and ending with the signing of the Agreement and Charter on August 8, 1945.[25]

It is impossible to review in detail here these subsequent plenary sessions, the minutes of which occupy 208 pages of Mr. Justice Jackson's book. While many detailed questions of procedure were elaborately discussed in these sessions, the three outstanding problems dealt with were: (1) the place of the first trial, (2) an adequate definition of aggressive war, (3) a provision empowering the Tribunal to appoint Special Masters,

[25] *Ibid.*, p. 211–419.

or commissioners, to take evidence and report to the Tribunal, all of which questions had been reserved by Professor Trainin in the subcommittee negotiations.

The minutes of the plenary session of July 13, 1945, and of subsequent sessions show that Mr. Justice Jackson took a strong attitude, going so far as frankly to state that unless the four delegations could promptly arrive at an agreement satisfactory to the basic concepts of the American Plan, the American delegation was prepared to withdraw from the negotiations, proceed to Nuremberg, try the prisoners in American hands, and go home, leaving the other three powers to their own devices. The United Kingdom and France were somewhat dismayed at this peeling off of the customary kid gloves of diplomacy. However, it was language which the Soviet realists understood. They, no less than the United Kingdom and France, did not want to contemplate the withdrawal of the Americans from this international trial and they became much more amenable to reason in the plenary sessions beginning July 13.

To justify the foregoing statement, I quote in this connection from Mr. Justice Jackson's preface the following:

> "The most serious disagreement, and one on which the United States declined to recede from its position even if it meant the failure of the conference, concerned the definition of crimes. The Soviet Delegation proposed and until the last meeting pressed a definition which, in our view, had the effect of declaring certain acts crimes only when committed by the Nazis. The United States contended that the criminal character of such acts could not depend on who committed them and that international crimes could only be defined in broad terms applicable to statesmen of any nation guilty of the proscribed conduct. At the final meeting the Soviet qualifications were dropped and agreement was reached on a generic definition acceptable to all." [26]

The Soviet Union, throughout the negotiations, proposed definitions of wars of aggression limited to aggressions on other nations carried out by what they habitually referred to as "the Hitlerite Fascist criminals." They objected to any more generalized definition which might include aggressions by others. In the light of subsequent history, it is fairly obvious why they adhered to such objections.

[26] *Ibid.*, vii–viii.

On July 19, 1945, the American delegation presented to the others a rather detailed definition of aggression, for consideration with Article 6 of the Charter, which would have denounced as an aggressor any state which was the first to commit any of the following actions: (1) declaration of war upon another state; (2) invasion by its armed forces, with or without a declaration of war, of the territory of another state; (3) attack by its land, naval, or air forces, with or without a declaration of war, on the territory, vessels, or aircraft of another state; (4) naval blockade of the coasts or ports of another state; (5) provision of support to armed bands formed in its territory of another state, or refusal, notwithstanding the request of the invaded state, to take in its own territory all the measures in its power to deprive those bands of all assistance or protection. The definition further stated that no political, military, economic or other consideration should serve as an excuse or justification for such action and only reserved as an excuse the right of legitimate self-defense.

Again, in the light of subsequent history, it is quite obvious why the Soviet Union did not agree to any such detailed definition. That proposal was the subject of debate for weeks in the plenary sessions. While the Soviet Union, as Mr. Justice Jackson states, in the final meeting, dropped its qualification of limiting the definition of aggressive war to acts committed by the Nazis, the definition as contained in the final executed document went into no such detail as the American proposal of July 19, and did not differ materially from the definition contained in our subcommittee draft of July 11. The definition in the final document reads:

> "(a) Crimes Against Peace: Namely, planning, preparation, initiation or waging of a war of aggression, or a war in violation of international treaties, or assurances, or participation in a common plan or conspiracy for the accomplishment of any of the foregoing;"

Under Mr. Justice Jackson's forceful handling of the later plenary sessions, the Soviet Union and the other delegations did, as has already been said, agree that the first trial should be held in Nuremberg, provided that the permanent seat of the Tribunal and the first meeting of the Tribunal and of the Prosecutors should be held in Berlin.

Again, as already stated, the Soviet Union never gave up on its objection to empowering the Tribunal to appoint Special Masters, or commissioners, and that provision was not incorporated in the final document.

After the election in which the Churchill Government was superseded by the Labor Government, the final work of the conference was conducted for the United Kingdom by the new Lord Chancellor, William Viscount Jowett of Stevenage. The new Labor Attorney General, Sir Hartley Shawcross, was named Chief Prosecutor for the United Kingdom. However, with the remarkable sense of continuity which the United Kingdom shows, regardless of changes in the party in power, Lord Chancellor Jowett and the new Prosecutor, Sir Hartley Shawcross, adopted all of the previous work of the United Kingdom delegation, as Sir David Maxwell Fyfe had predicted would occur if a Labor Government should be elected.

Lord Chancellor Jowett signed the final document for the United Kingdom. One of Sir Hartley Shawcross's first acts, after his appointment as United Kingdom Prosecutor, was to name Sir David Maxwell Fyfe as his first deputy, and Sir David continued throughout the trial as the wheel-horse of the United Kingdom team.

After the signing of the Agreement and Charter of August 8, 1945, General Nikitchenko was named by the Soviet Union as its member of the Tribunal, with Lt. Col. A. F. Volchkov as alternate member. The French named M. Donnedieu de Vabres as their member of the Tribunal, with Judge Falco as alternate. The United Kingdom named Lord Justice Lawrence as its member, with Mr. Justice Norman Birkett as alternate. The United States Government named Francis Biddle as its member, with Judge John J. Parker as alternate. Lord Justice Lawrence was elected to preside, and did preside, throughout the trial and there was no rotation.

The Soviet Union named as its Chief Prosecutor General R. A. Rudenko. Chief Prosecutor for France was first M. François de Menthon and later M. Auguste Champetier de Ribes. Sir Hartley Shawcross was Chief Prosecutor for the United Kingdom and Mr. Justice Jackson for the United States.

VIII

Following our preliminary conference with the United Kingdom on June 21, 1945, at which they proposed the appointment of working committees for drafting not only the executive agreement but also the indictment (including the selection of defendants), trial procedures and rules, and other details, and at which they proposed their suggested list of ten Nazi defendants, Mr. Justice Jackson named Mr. Alderman, Col. Bernays and Lt. Donovan as the American members of the committee on the draft of the indictment and the selection of defendants. Sir David Maxwell Fyfe appointed Mr. Roberts, Mr. Robey and Mr. Patrick Dean to that committee as the United Kingdom representatives. We and the United Kingdom representatives did a considerable amount of basic work before the Soviet and French delegations arrived in London on June 26.

The British and American representatives on the committee met on June 23. We first dealt with the question of the list of prospective defendants, discussing the list of ten defendants originally proposed by the United Kingdom. We tried to find out the theory on which their selection had been made, and it seemed to be nothing more definite than that they sought a small and select list of well-known names of principal offenders. Looking at their list of ten Mr. Clyde said that he was immediately struck by the omission of Baldur von Schirach, the head of the German youth movement and of the vicious Nazi indoctrination of the youth. I said that I had missed von Schirach on our various tentative lists and thought he ought to be included. He was finally included as a defendant.

In preparation for this meeting the American members of the committee had had a session the day before, and Col. Bernays and Lt. Donovan had undertaken to compile a list of defendants under the headings of five of the principal Nazi groups and organizations to which they had belonged. This produced a list of forty-six, but there were numerous duplications under different organizations and after eliminating those we had a total list of twenty-six. I thought that twenty-six defendants, with twenty-six defense counsel examining and cross-examining, making objections and arguments, would unduly prolong the trial, and I suggested that before the meeting with the British the next day, Lt. Donovan take the list of twenty-six, make further eliminations, and see if he could not produce a more compact list which still would be fully representative of the principal Nazi groups and organizations. The result was that at the meeting on June 23 with the British we presented a reduced list of sixteen, as follows: Hitler, Goering, Hess, Ley, Rosenberg, Frick, Ribbentrop, Streicher, Hans Frank, Schacht, Keitel, Seyss-Inquart, Kaltenbrunner, Doenitz, Funk, Speer.

It will at once be noted that all of these, with the exception of Hitler and Ley, who were dead, finally showed up in the dock as defendants.

The United Kingdom seemed to be pleased with our list, and I felt rather confident that we could ultimately use it as a working basis, though we all recognized that undoubtedly France and the Soviet Union would have other names to propose and that there might be additional changes or eliminations.

Both the British and we were somewhat doubtful as to the wisdom of including Gross-Admiral Doenitz in the list. The British Admiralty had Doenitz's diary, but they had found nothing in it that would incriminate him, though the study of it had not been completed. The general view of the British Admiralty was that, as compared with land and air warfare, the German Navy came much closer to following the rules of war and of chivalry, although they had in mind one particular case of the shooting up of survivors of a sunken vessel, *The Peleus.* I presented the further consideration that Doenitz was the man who finally authorized the unconditional surrender.

I suggested that we might make use of the headings outlining offenses within Germany and outside Germany, as set out in the American planning memorandum, as a kind of basis for drafting the indictment and also that we study in that connection the somewhat elaborate bill of indictment and bill of particulars in the Washington sedition trial. I said that, although that trial was a fiasco, that was not because the bill of indictment was defective but because the trial judge was not able to keep control of the trial. More particularly, I suggested the view that the indictment should start with a general description of the conspiratorial plan; that there should then follow an intermediate series of allegations alleging what were the elements that constituted the criminal enterprise or conspiracy: that we then descend to the allegations of particular means and acts resorted to in the carrying out of the conspiratorial plan; and that we then name individual defendants in separate counts, alleging their particular connection with the plan and the criminal acts. I may say that the final form of the indictment in its main outlines largely followed this suggestion.

The meeting ended with the understanding that the British and we would each undertake to produce a preliminary draft of the indictment for further consideration.

During previous months the OSS and various expatriated German historians on our staff had done a tremendous amount of basic work compiling the detailed biographies of the principal Nazi leaders and undertaking in detail to connect each of them with the conspiracy or with particular crimes and atrocities. After our tentative consideration of our American list of sixteen, the work of these technicians was concentrated on that list.

After the Soviet and French delegations, of only two members each, reached London, their time was completely taken up with the plenary sessions and the meetings of the drafting sub- committee working on the executive agreement. They had no members to assign to the subcommittee for drafting the indictment and selecting the list of defendants. It was tacitly agreed that the United Kingdom and United States would go ahead with this detailed work and would submit the results from time to time to the Soviet and French delegations.

On July 17 the British delegation submitted to the others an illustrative draft of indictment, including their original list of ten defendants and, for consideration, the additional names of von Schirach and Sauckel. That draft is quite interesting as showing the United Kingdom view as to how simple an indictment could be. It occupied only two and a half printed pages and contained only eight counts. Count 1 charged, in one sentence, the unlawful conspiracy. Count 2 charged, in one sentence, the means adopted to carry it out. Count 3 charged a breach of the Treaty of Versailles by the establishment of the Luftwaffe. Count 4 charged that defendants violated said treaty by reintroducing conscription in Germany and fixing the peacetime strength of the German Army at 550,000. Count 5 charged a breach of that treaty by sending armed forces into the demilitarized Rhineland. Count 6 charged nine additional breaches of treaties in the invasions of Austria, Czechoslovakia and Denmark, in the attacks on the Soviet Union and Yugoslavia, and in the invasions of Belgium, Luxembourg and Holland. An additional charge of a breach of treaty in the invasion of Poland was left in brackets, evidently out of tenderness for the feeling of our Soviet allies who entered Poland with their armies at the same time. Counts 7 and 8 charged breaches of Hague Conventions in the pursuance of the common plan and conspiracy and in the commission of wholesale atrocities, setting out briefly some of the specifications and details. We Americans conceived of a considerably more elaborate indictment than that.

Working technicians on our staff, following weeks of work, produced a mimeographed document about five inches thick. It contained a very detailed draft of an indictment substantially along the lines of my original suggestion and, in an appendix, contained exhaustive biographical notes on each of the proposed defendants as a basis for a bill of particulars to connect them with particular crimes. This was an important compilation of working materials. We submitted copies of it to the other delegations merely as such working materials and not at all as being our suggestion as to a final draft of the indictment.

The Russians seemed much pleased with these materials. They seemed to comport with the Soviet idea of a *dossier* compiled by a *juge d'instruction,* with attached documents. The Russians seemed to consider the biographical materials as documents to be attached to the indictments. The French were amazed at the amount of work that had gone into producing these materials but were puzzled as to how we could condense them into an actual indictment.

From the time of the submission of these materials the Russians seemed to be basically satisfied about the indictment, provided it included sufficient details as to particular atrocities against the Soviet Union, and were mainly interested in the addition to the list of defendants of important Nazis captured by the Soviet Army. For a long time, however, the Soviet delegation did not know what important Nazis were among their prisoners. For instance, for a long time it was generally supposed that Bormann was one of their prisoners, and all delegations thought he ought to be a defendant. The Russians finally were informed that he was not one of their prisoners. He was not found elsewhere. He was included in the final list of defendants but was never found, and was tried and convicted *in absentia*.

On August 12 Clyde told me that General Nikitchenko had been talking with the British about how to divide the case up for presentation among the four Chief Prosecutors. General Nikitchenko had expressed the view that such a division would be a great contribution to simplification of the case, and he tentatively suggested the following division: (1) the Americans to present the general conspiracy theory and the crime of aggressive war; (2) the British to present violations of treaties and crimes on the high seas; (3) the French and the Russians, each for their own territories and subjects, to present the details of atrocities, concentration camps, religious and racial persecutions, etc. This suggestion appealed to all of the other delegations as being highly practicable, and, finally, the indictment itself followed largely General Nikitchenko's outline of the division of the case.

Count One of the indictment, The Common Plan or Conspiracy, presented the conspiratorial plan and the crime of wars of aggression and the means in detail whereby the conspiracy was carried out.

Count Two, Crimes against Peace, alleged the treaty violations involved in the offenses covered by Count One.

Count Three, War Crimes, alleged the particulars of violations of the rules of land and sea warfare in different areas.

Count Four, Crimes against Humanity, alleged the details of many other atrocities carried out in pursuance of the criminal conspiracy and going beyond what would otherwise have been violations of the rules of land and sea warfare in the classical sense.

Appendix A to the indictment set out a bill of particulars against each of the individual defendants, and Appendix B set out a bill of particulars against each of the groups and organizations charged with criminality.[27]

On August 24 Justice Jackson told our staff that the most immediately pressing problem then was putting the indictment in

[27] For the full text of the indictment, see *International Military Tribunal, Trial of the Major War Criminals*—Official Documents—Nuremberg, 14 November 1945 to October 1946, published in Nuremberg, Germany, 1947, vol. I, p. 27–92. It was a document of 65 printed pages as reproduced in this official record.

final form. He had the definite impression from the British that they would furnish nothing more than a bare outline draft, like their illustrative draft of indictment submitted on July 17, merely charging offenses in line with the definition of crimes in the Agreement and Charter. We Americans all recognized that something much more elaborate than that would be necessary, and the Justice appointed a number of special experts on our staff to work with me on putting the indictment in final form. He himself, with a substantial part of his staff, left almost immediately for Nuremberg. He left me in London as his deputy for putting the indictment in final form.

IX

Meanwhile, on August 21, the Russians called a special meeting of the four delegations and insisted on adding a number of names to the list of defendants, including certain prisoners in their hands. The French also had two of their prisoners whom they wished added, von Papen and von Neurath. As a result of this, the four delegations agreed to add to our previous list of sixteen the following additional nine names: Gustav Krupp von Bohlen und Halbach, Erich Raeder, von Schirach, Sauckel, Alfred Jodl, Martin Bormann, Franz von Papen, Constantin von Neurath, Hans Fritzsche.

Hitler was eliminated from the list of sixteen on information that he was dead, and, with this elimination and the additions insisted on by both the Russians and the French, the final list became the following twenty-four: Goering, Hess, Ribbentrop, Ley, Keitel, Kaltenbrunner, Rosenberg, Hans Frank, Frick, Streicher, Funk, Schacht, Gustav Krupp, Doenitz, Raeder, von Schirach, Sauckel, Jodl, Bormann, von Papen, Seyss-Inquart, Speer, von Neurath, Fritzsche.

Of these twenty-four, Ley was not tried, having committed suicide, and Gustav Krupp was not tried, since the court, upon the unanimous report of an international commission of physicians, found that he was suffering from senile dementia and was neither mentally nor physically able to stand trial. Bormann, who was never found but was tried *in absentia,* of course did not appear in court. The result was that only twenty-one of the twenty-four actually appeared and were tried in person.

On September 13 I personally delivered to each of the other delegations two mimeographed copies of our five-inch-thick working materials for the indictment and tried to make them all understand that the imposing document was to be considered as working material rather than as a suggested actual draft of the indictment. When I went to the Soviet Embassy I was sent to another building and there had to wait about twenty minutes for M. Ivanov, who was absolutely alone, with no secretary, no translator, and no help of any kind. I tried to make him understand the nature of our materials and suggested that he would have a terrific job undertaking to translate them into Russian.

The United Kingdom was much pleased with these materials. On September 15 we worked on the materials with the British. Sir David Maxwell Fyfe presented a rough draft of Counts One and Two, based largely on our materials, with some condensation and editing. Meanwhile, Mr. Roberts was working on his draft of Count Three, War Crimes, and Count Four, Crimes against Humanity, and he was largely disregarding the American materials and putting these two counts in the form of a very skeleton outline indictment.

At a further meeting on September 17 the French produced, in writing, a very elaborate critique of our materials, which they evidently had considered as a suggested final draft of the indictment. The French thought that we had tied everything too much to the aggressive quality of the war. They thought that the war crimes, in the classical sense, were the essential thing, and yet, with somewhat strange logic, they sought for what they called the "link of unity" in the case, not in war or a war of aggression or in war crimes but in the nazification of Germany. Still, they expressed the greatest interest in war crimes as such.

The Soviet Union, in turn, expressed prime interest in the crimes against humanity and seemed to argue that the whole case could be tried around those offenses.

I made quite an argument at that session. I began by telling the French that I was, perhaps, not as much impressed by their famous *"esprit critique"* as others might be, because I have been continuously exposed to the French critical spirit for twenty-six years.[28] I argued that the only possible link of unity in the case was the war itself, which was an aggressive war; that with-

[28] My wife is French.

out the war there could have been no war crimes; that, while crimes against humanity might have taken place without a war, they would not have risen to the rank of international crimes; and that they only became of international concern because they were related to the preparation of and the carrying out of the war.

At this session the new Soviet Chief Prosecutor, General Rudenko, appeared for the first time for the Russians, with Lt. Col. Petrovsky, M. Ivanov, and a lady Russian-English interpreter. She had a fair knowledge of English but obviously had little understanding of legal terms, either in Russian or in English, and it was extremely difficult for General Rudenko to understand us, the British and the French, and for any of the other delegations to understand him.

At this meeting General Rudenko produced and deposited before the four delegations a tremendous file of certified and authenticated Russian evidence, following the constant Soviet concept of the prosecutors as forming a commission, with which evidence to be attached to the indictment should be filed. He had, however, only brought one set of the evidence in Russian, except for photostats of certain captured German documents in German. He blandly overlooked the fact that each Chief Prosecutor and his staff would need at least one set of these materials. We, in turn, would have had an almost impossible problem to translate them into English and French. He further dismayed us by announcing that he would have another section of evidentiary material of equal volume.

On September 18 there was a further meeting of the four delegations, which went much better than the previous meeting. There was general agreement in principle as to how the redraft of the indictment should be attempted. The only major dispute was whether the work should continue in London or in Nuremberg. Under instructions from Mr. Justice Jackson, I insisted that the work continue in Nuremberg. The other delegations voted three to one against me.

Sir David announced that he was going to Nuremberg the next day to spend the rest of the week, and M. de Menthon said he was going there for a day or two that week.

The French requested a further meeting of Chief Prosecutors for Wednesday of the following week and invited us to Paris, although stating their willingness to meet in London. General Rudenko said he intended to stay in London two more weeks at least. It was very obvious that the British intended to stay in London as long as possible. The meeting was tentatively set for the following week in London, subject to whatever effort Mr. Justice Jackson and I might make in Nuremberg to convince Sir David and M. de Menthon that the meeting should be in Nuremberg. The meeting on September 18 broke up with the general impression that all four delegations had substantially agreed on the last draft of Counts One and Two of the indictment worked out by the Americans and the British.

On September 19 I flew to Nuremberg and on September 21 attended a conference between Mr. Justice Jackson, Sir David Maxwell Fyfe and M. de Menthon, which was very helpful on our various problems, but unfortunately the Soviet Union was not represented. Sir David and M. de Menthon were very anxious for the Justice to attend a meeting of the Chiefs in London the following week to settle the final form of the indictment. He would not commit himself but indicated that either he would go or that he would send me.

Following that conference a formal press conference was held, at which Justice Jackson presided but in which both Sir David and M. de Menthon participated. It was a new experience for them, neither of them ever having held a press conference. They were not familiar with this American custom. The press conference lasted an hour and a quarter. The reporters were excellent cross-examiners and asked most of the tough questions. They pressed Justice Jackson on when the trial would open. He limited himself to saying, "Not before November 1."

The really crucial question was reached when Justice Jackson made a reference to the making of aggressive war as an international crime and one of the reporters said that there were reports in the press that the French delegation did not agree with the view that the making of aggressive war was a crime and asked the Justice whether that was so. He had to take the gamble and pass the question to M. de Menthon, but the French Chief "rang the bell." He talked about the Briand-Kellogg Pact and said that the French delegation was in complete agreement that the making of aggressive war was a violation of international law and a crime. That statement was a great relief to all of us in view of the efforts of the French delegation at London to confine the matter to war crimes, in the classical sense.

On the evening of September 23 Mr. Justice Jackson sent me a copy of a redraft of Count One of the indictment which he had written himself and in which he had undertaken to incorporate some new ideas which had occurred to him since he left London. He said that his redraft was merely a suggestion, but he asked me to take it and work it over with others of our staff and get it in shape. The Justice had given a copy of his draft to Sir David before his departure for London that day, and I anticipated "fireworks" in London because the other delegations thought we had pretty well agreed on Count One in the last London conference.

On September 24 Col. Telford Taylor, later Brigadier General and Chief Prosecutor for the subsequent American Nuremberg Trials under Control Council Law No. 10, called me from London in much agitation, saying that the British were very much disturbed that a whole new draft of Count One had been produced in Nuremberg. We had a number of staff conferences about the Justice's new draft of Count One, and finally Benjamin Kaplan, now Professor of Law in Harvard Law School, and Sidney Kaplan, now practicing law in Minneapolis, and I worked out a complete new redraft of Counts One and Two, together with a detailed outline of headings for the entire indictment. In this draft I, for the first time, spelled out in detail a formulation of just what we alleged the conspiracy or common plan to be. We had all been talking for months about a common plan and conspiracy, but nobody had ever formulated and put down on paper just what that conspiracy was. The Kaplans and I completed our redraft and submitted it to Mr. Justice Jackson on September 26, and he approved it.

The United Kingdom was so disturbed about the new Nuremberg draft that it sent a special delegation to Nuremberg on September 27. On that day and the next the Kaplans and I, after all-day conferences with the British team, were able to come to complete agreement with them on our redraft of Counts One and Two, save for certain reservations in brackets which they had to submit to the Attorney General. Meanwhile, Col. Taylor was working with the British, French and Soviet delegations in London on drafts of Counts Three and Four. Mr. Justice Jackson instructed me to return to London to undertake, with the help of the British, to sell the French and Russians on the last Nuremberg redraft of Counts One and Two. Meanwhile, much to the surprise of all of us, the French delegation had itself made a new and complete redraft of the indictment, which came to Mr. Justice Jackson in Nuremberg and which he handed to me on September 30. I flew back to London on October 1.

The next morning Col. Taylor told me that the French had said that unless Mr. Justice Jackson came to the meeting in London M. de Menthon would not come. The situation looked bad.

I received a peremptory call from the French delegation saying that they must have precise and definite information as to whether Mr. Justice Jackson was coming because they had to communicate with M. de Menthon in Paris. I went around to see M. Dubost, M. de Menthon's deputy, who spoke no English. I used my best French, and a little flattery, and told him that I was in London with full authority to agree finally. I suggested to him that Mr. Justice Jackson had been in London for two months constantly attending meetings, during which time there was no authorized French representative. He looked embarrassed, assured me that they were not raising a formal point of prestige, but that they merely considered it futile for M. de Menthon to come to London if no one was authorized to act finally for the Americans. Upon my assurance that I was authorized to act finally, I secured a definite promise from him that M. de Menthon would come without demanding the presence of Mr. Justice Jackson.

I then performed another diplomatic mission with the Russians and delivered to General Rudenko extra copies of our latest draft. I was fortunate in having with me Dr. John Hazard,[29] of our staff, who had a thorough speaking knowledge of Russian, interpreted well, and kept the Russians in the best of good humor. General Rudenko was highly complimentary of our latest drafts of Counts One and Two. That afternoon we had a four-power meeting: M. Dubost, for France; Sir David Maxwell Fyfe, for the United Kingdom; General Rudenko for the Soviet Union,

[29] For Dr. Hazard's impressions of Negotiating with the Russians, in a slightly different context, see Chapter Two.

and I, and we made great strides towards final agreement on the latest redrafts of all four counts.

That night, after I had obtained the promise that M. de Menthon would come to London, on the representation that I had full authority to act finally for the American delegation, I received instructions from Mr. Justice Jackson by telephone that I must not agree to any indictment which did not include the German General Staff or some recognizable category of the High Command as a defendant organization alleged to be criminal. Thus my plenipotentiary authority was severely restricted. Up to that time none of the drafts had included a charge of criminality against the German General Staff and High Command, for the very good reason that we could not find anywhere in the German Tables of Organization any such entity as the General Staff or the High Command. The next morning, October 3, I told the Attorney General, Sir Hartley Shawcross, about my instructions regarding the High Command question, and he told me that he would have to oppose that proposal bitterly.

M. de Menthon arrived from Paris about noon on October 3, and we went into plenary session. I presented my instructions as to the necessity of including the German General Staff and High Command and made for about an hour the best argument I could make in support of the new proposal. Sir Hartley Shawcross made a very vigorous argument in opposition, so vigorous that a number of members of his staff later apologized to me. I told them that he had been no more vigorous than I would have been in his position. Much to my surprise, France and the Soviet Union voted in full support of my position, and Sir Hartley Shawcross took his three-to-one defeat very gracefully.

With the help of a very skillful British intelligence officer, Wing Commander Peter Calvocaressi, who had previously been loaned to our staff, we had ready to present his draft of a formula to define the German Staff and High Command group. He presented this formula to the plenary session, and it was adopted and incorporated in the indictment. It is worthy of noting at this point that the International Military Tribunal ultimately refused to convict the group so defined.

Mr. Justice Jackson, in the same telephone conversation, had insisted that I insist on the addition of two or three additional defendants from among German industrialists. In the afternoon plenary session on October 3 I was forced to bring up this new additional proposal. Sir Hartley Shawcross gave me advance notice that he would oppose this with all the power at his command, and he certainly kept his promise. He made another argument against me so vigorous as to embarrass his associates. I made the best argument I could in support of the proposal, but this time France and the Soviet Union voted with the United Kingdom, and I had to accept the three-to-one vote against me. The other three delegations opposed the additional names largely because they thought their incorporation in the list of defendants would substantially delay the beginning of the trial.

On October 4, the four delegations spent the whole day and much of the night polishing up the draft of Counts One and Two and incorporating the French and Soviet insertions in Counts Three and Four of the particular atrocities in each of their sectors.

The rush of these last sessions was such that it was all the French and the Russians could do to keep current translations into their languages of the body of the indictment itself and of the appendices, with verbal changes from session to session. If General Rudenko had expected that the mass of Russian documents he had deposited with the Chief Prosecutors would be attached to and filed with the indictment, he very conveniently forgot the matter. The mere matter of translation into English, French and German would have made it physically impossible. The French had deposited no such documents. Both they and the Soviet Union conveniently forgot, in the last mad rush, their previous insistence that evidentiary documents should be filed with the indictment.

On October 5 we had proofs of the indictment and of the appendices. We read the proofs and got copies of the final printed documents about noon. I flew to Berlin that afternoon with the printed documents.

Mr. Justice Jackson, Sir Hartley Shawcross, M. de Menthon and General Rudenko arrived in Berlin on Saturday, October 6, and, to my great satisfaction, the Justice approved my handling in London. The four Chiefs signed the indictment that day.

Two very thorny questions arose from the last insertions of allegations by the Soviet Union of crimes in eastern territories.

In Count Three—War Crimes (A) 2 in the heading, the Soviet Union inserted the following definition of the Union of Soviet Socialist Republics:

> "In the U.S.S.R., *i.e.,* in the Bielorussian, Ukranian, Estonian, Latvian, Lithuanian, Karelo-Finnish, and Moldavian Soviet Socialist Republics . . . ,"

thereafter listing specific atrocities. I had discussed this definition with Patrick Dean of the British Foreign Office in our last sessions in London and had communicated with Mr. Justice Jackson in Nuremberg about it. Neither the United Kingdom nor the United States had ever recognized the Soviets' acquisition of Estonia, Latvia and Lithuania, and we feared that the signing of the indictment containing that definition of the Union of Soviet Socialist Republics by the British and American Chiefs of Counsel might be construed by the Soviet Union as an admission by the United Kingdom and by the United States that the Soviet Union had lawfully incorporated those three countries into their union.

We took the matter up with General Rudenko. He was very suave about the matter and indicated that our signature of the indictment would not be construed as evidence of a diplomatic recognition by the United Kingdom and by the United States of the incorporation of Estonia, Latvia and Lithuania into the Soviet Union, although he declared that they had lawfully been absorbed.

I had an opportunity to confer about the matter with Averell Harriman, our Ambassador to Moscow, and with James Dunn, of the State Department, both of whom happened to be in London. They both felt that the signing of the indictment containing the definition in question could not be construed to constitute a diplomatic recognition by the United States of the absorption of Estonia, Latvia and Lithuania into the Soviet Union, and they thought by all means that no controversy over this question ought to be precipitated which would delay the filing of the indictment and the starting of the trial. I communicated their views to Mr. Justice Jackson, in Nuremberg, together with my recommendation to the same effect.

Nevertheless, Mr. Justice Jackson was worried about the matter and when he signed the indictment on October 6, he took the precaution of addressing to M. François de Menthon, Sir Hartley Shawcross and General R. A. Rudenko a letter of reservation by the United States Prosecutor in regard to the wording of the indictment. In it he stated that the language making reference to Estonia, Latvia, Lithuania and certain other territories as being within the area of the U.S.S.R. was accepted to avoid the delay which would be occasioned by insistence on an alteration in the text. He further insisted that the indictment was signed by him subject to the reservation and understanding: that he had no authority either to admit or to challenge on behalf of the United States of America Soviet claims to sovereignty over such territory. He asserted that nothing, therefore, in the indictment was to be construed as a recognition by the United States of such sovereignty or as indicating any attitude, either on the part of the United States or on his part, toward any claim to recognition of such sovereignty.[30]

General Rudenko accepted the filing of this letter of reservation in good part and made no objection to it.

The other controversial insertion by the Soviet Union in the indictment, under the same count, inserted by them at the last London conference, was a specific allegation against the Germans, as follows:

> "In September, 1941, 925 Polish officers who were prisoners of war were killed in the Katyn Forest near Smolensk."

I had extended conferences with Patrick Dean about that allegation after it was inserted in the London draft. There was grave doubt as to who had murdered the Polish officers in the Katyn Forest. The Soviet Union claimed that the Germans had murdered them and the Germans claimed that the Russians had murdered them. The Germans further claimed that when the bodies were exhumed their state of disintegration proved that the murders had dated from a time when the Russian armies were in the possession of Katyn Forest. There had been extensive debates about the merits of this controversy in the public press. We were embarrassed about including that allegation in the indictment, but finally concluded that it was up to the Soviet Union and that if it thought it could sustain the allegation by

[30] International Military Tribunal, Trial of the Major War Criminals—Official Documents—Nuremberg, 1947, vol. I, p. 95.

proof, it had the right to make the charge in the indictment.

After the signature of the indictment by the four Chief Prosecutors on October 6, twelve days were spent in Berlin reconciling discrepancies between the German translation of the indictment and the English, Russian and French versions. Suddenly, about October 18, General Rudenko insisted on changing the above quoted allegation so as to make it read:

> "In September, 1941, 11,000 [instead of 925] Polish officers who were prisoners of war were killed in the Katyn Forest near Smolensk."

At the time of this change in the allegation I was in Washington on a mission for Mr. Justice Jackson, and Francis M. Shea was representing him in Berlin. The change in the allegation was highly embarrassing to the British, French and American Prosecutors. The change had to be teletyped to me in Washington so that I could incorporate it in the English version of the indictment which I was correcting for the American press.

When the change was made it called the attention of the American press sharply to the whole question of the merits of the allegation as to the murders of Polish officers in the Katyn Forest and resurrected the whole controversy. That controversy caused embarrassing difficulties in the trial itself. However, the altered allegation remained in the indictment.[31]

On October 18, the Tribunal held its opening formal session in Berlin and on that date Sir Hartley Shawcross, General Rudenko, the French Deputy Chief Prosecutor, M. Dubost, and Mr. Justice Jackson's representative, Francis M. Shea, formally filed the indictment with the Tribunal.[32] The London negotiations were completed.

X

My conclusions are very simple. You can successfully negotiate with the Soviet Union if your ultimate ends and theirs are the same. There will always be difficulties as to language and as to concepts. There will always be differences as to procedures. But on a mission like ours, where the ultimate aims are not in con-

[31] *Ibid.,* p. 59.
[32] *Ibid.,* p. 24.

flict, all these difficulties are readily overcome. They are skillful negotiators and can be extremely cooperative.

Whether we can successfully negotiate with them on matters as to which ultimate aims are in conflict will have to be tested by other negotiations where that condition exists. I can imagine few things more difficult. They have a genius for obstruction when they desire to use it.

NEGOTIATING AT BRETTON WOODS

Raymond F. Mikesell has been Professor of Economics at the University of Virginia since 1946. Born in Ohio, he received his undergraduate and graduate training at Ohio State University, was Assistant Professor at the University of Washington from 1937 to 1941 and since then has served as a member of the staff or as an economic consultant to a number of Departments of the United States Government. He was representative of the Treasury Department in Cairo, Egypt in 1943–44 and the United States delegate to the Middle East Financial Conference in Cairo in April, 1944. He was a member of the technical staff of the Bretton Woods Monetary and Financial Conference, has been a consultant to the Treasury Department and the Department of State, was a member of the United States Currency Mission to Saudi Arabia in 1948, and was a consultant on the White House staff to the Special Assistant to the President (Gordon Gray) during the summer of 1951 During the spring and summer of 1951 he was a member of the staff of the President's Materials Policy Commission and Chief of the Foreign Resources Division. He has been a member of the editorial board of the Middle East Journal since 1947 and is the author of United States Economic Policy and International Relations (1951), and co-author (with Hollis B. Chenery) of Arabian Oil (1949).

Negotiating at Bretton

Woods, 1944

BY RAYMOND F. MIKESELL *

The American planners of the postwar world confidently believed that a way could be found whereby nations with capitalistic, socialistic and "mixed" economies could live together in harmony and carry on mutually beneficial commercial and financial transactions with one another. Although the Monetary Fund and Bank were designed in large measure to deal with the problems of free-enterprise economies in the light of prewar experience, it was expected from the beginning that the USSR and other socialist countries would become members. The inclusion of the USSR as an important member of all of our postwar international institutions was considered first of all to be of the greatest political significance and a condition of their successful operation. In addition, however, Russian membership in the Fund and Bank was believed by the United States to have considerable economic significance for the realization

* The author is indebted to Mr. John Bowles for his valuable research in connection with the preparation of this article.

of its foreign economic policy, although American officials were somewhat vague as to just what significance Russian membership in the Fund was likely to have.

Although the USSR did not join the Fund and Bank it participated to perhaps a greater degree than has generally been realized in the preparation of the charters of these institutions and a number of the provisions of these documents were determined or influenced by the Russian negotiators. In considerable measure, however, the fundamental decisions with respect to the Articles of Agreement of the Fund and Bank were arrived at before the Bretton Woods Conference, and in particular the basic negotiations with the Russian representatives regarding points of difference between the American and Russian positions were carried on in Washington prior to the conference.[1] Hence it will be necessary to survey these pre-Bretton Woods discussions in order to understand why the American representatives supported certain provisions favored by the Russians at Bretton Woods and rejected others.

The basic outlines of the American proposals for the Fund and Bank were developed in 1942 and a copy of the draft of the Fund plan was given to the Russians early in 1943, as well as to several other governments. Although there were exploratory discussions with Soviet representatives in 1943 and in June 1943 Soviet representatives participated in a three day informal conference of nineteen countries in the United States Treasury Department, the important informal negotiations with the Russian representatives did not begin until February 1944, when there were held a series of conferences between a Soviet delegation headed by N. F. Chechulin, Assistant Chairman of the State Bank of the USSR and an American technical group headed by Dr. Harry D. White of the United States Treasury. The American group included representatives from the Departments of State, Commerce, the Federal Reserve Board, the Export-Import Bank and the Foreign Economic Administration. The purpose of these meetings was to consider a draft of the "Joint Statement of Experts on the Establishment of the International Monetary Fund of the United and Associated Nations," [2] which had been

---

[1] This was also true with respect to the negotiations with the British.

[2] The final draft of the *Joint Statement* was later published in April 1944. See *Proceedings and Documents of United Nations Monetary and Financial Conference*, Vol. II, Department of State, 1948, Washington, D.C., p. 1629–1636.

prepared as a result of joint discussions between American and British technicians. The conference with the Russians also considered the American draft proposal for an International Bank for Reconstruction and Development.[3] The objective of the American representatives was to determine whether or not the Russians would agree to the two proposals as a basis for an international conference and also to determine what position the USSR would take on the various provisions of the proposals.

It should be said that the Russian representatives had done their homework well and were well aware of the provisions which affected their own interests. They were, however, not interested in the solution of the fundamental problems with which the Fund was designed to deal, namely, stable exchange rates, the elimination of exchange restrictions and the creation of a multilateral payments system. Rather their interest in the proposals was largely confined to four general categories: 1) what it would cost them to join; 2) how much could they get out of it in the way of credits; 3) how would the obligations of Fund membership interfere with their internal and external economic practices; and 4) the voice of the USSR in the management of the two institutions.

In April 1944 during the course of the bilateral discussions with the Soviet representatives, which continued intermittently from early in February through April 1944, the head of the Soviet delegation, Mr. Chechulin, announced that the Soviet Government would participate in a United Nations Monetary and Financial Conference planned for July of that year at Bretton Woods, New Hampshire. It was also agreed that the *Joint Statement* (which was published on April 31, 1944) was to serve as a basis for negotiation on the establishment of the Monetary Fund. It should be said that in general the Russians, while proposing a number of additions to and modifications of the language of the *Joint Statement*, did not seek to change the fundamental principles of the *Joint Statement* which had been agreed to as a frame of reference for the Bretton Woods negotiations.

In June 1944 a preliminary conference was held in Atlantic City to draft the agenda for the Bretton Woods meeting. The USSR was represented at this conference but its representa-

---

[3] The American proposal for an International Bank was published in November 1943; see *Proceedings and Documents,* Vol. II, p. 1616–1628.

tives did not take an especially active part in the discussions except to make known their position on a number of issues.[4] The chairman of the USSR delegation at the Bretton Woods Conference was M. S. Stepanov, Deputy People's Commissar of Foreign Trade. Five other members were included in the delegation,[5] assisted by three advisors and fourteen other technicians and clerical assistants. The Soviet delegates participated actively in all phases of the conference except that their chairman, unlike many of the other heads of delegations, was not addicted to making flowery speeches. When the occasion required it, Mr. Stepanov would make a few remarks in Russian in which he invariably pointed to the stand which the Russians were making against Hitler's hordes in their homeland. Beyond this the Russian members confined their remarks in meetings strictly to the business at hand. At social gatherings the Russians were friendly although naturally cautious and reticent on subjects relating to their political and economic system. They went to the cocktail parties, formed a volley-ball team and played (very seriously) against the teams of other countries and occasionally came down to the night club in the basement of the Bretton Woods Hotel. On the latter occasions we joined with them in singing the Red Army songs and stimulated by considerable quantities of vodka, they joined in singing familiar American songs.

I

Before taking up the details of the negotiations, several characteristics of the Soviet negotiating methods as displayed at the Bretton Woods Conference are worth noting. First of all the Russians refrained from extensive debate and counter-argumentation. They stated their proposal or objection to someone else's proposal, presented a few simple reasons, and then countered every contrary argument by a simple restatement of their original position. It was evident that they counted not on logic and persuasion for winning their point but upon sheer doggedness and the fact

[4] No minutes were kept of the proceedings of the Atlantic City Conference.
[5] The other USSR delegates were: N. A. Maletin, Deputy People's Commissar of Finance; N. F. Chechulin, Assistant Chairman of the State Bank; I. D. Zlobin, Chief, Monetary Division of the People's Commissariat of Finance; A. A. Arutinunian, Expert-Consultant of the People's Commissariat for Foreign Affairs; A. N. Morozov, Member of the Collegium; Chief, Monetary Division of the People's Commissariat for Foreign Trade.

that they knew that the United States delegation would make every effort to satisfy them because of the political importance of Soviet membership. By not compromising they believed they could wring greater concessions towards their position. This inflexibility of position was of course due in part to the rigid instructions under which the Soviet delegates had to operate. Any deviation required cabling Moscow and frequently the conference was delayed in settling issues for several days while the Soviets were awaiting new instructions. An example of Russian inflexibility carried to a ridiculous degree, was the insistence of the Soviet delegate upon the inclusion of both "restoration" and "reconstruction" in Article III, Section 1 (b),[6] of the Articles of Agreement for the International Bank. All of the other members of the committee argued that the use of both terms was redundant but the Soviet delegate kept repeating his point until the other members gave in out of sheer exhaustion.

In one notable instance the delay in obtaining cabled instructions from Moscow made a considerable difference in the United States subscription to, and aggregate capital of, the International Bank. The USSR had insisted that its subscription to the Bank, which was in no way related to its ability to borrow from that institution, should be $300 million smaller than its agreed quota in the Fund ($1,200 million) which determined its normal drawing right as well as its contributions to the Fund. Since, however, membership in the Bank was to a number of countries an important condition for their membership in the Fund, it was feared that a substantial reduction in the capital of the Bank would have resulted in a failure of certain countries to join the two institutions. The Soviet delegation was finally prevailed upon to cable Moscow for permission to accept a quota of $1,200 million in the Bank, but the cable failed to arrive. Meanwhile in order to save the conference the American delegation agreed to raise its subscription to the Bank by $300 million to $3,175 million. However, the evening before the conference closed the chairman of the Soviet delegation made the dramatic announcement that the cable had arrived and that the Soviet subscription

---

[6] This was proposed by the Soviet delegation. It provides that the Bank in determining the conditions and terms of loans made to members whose home territories have suffered from enemy occupation, "shall pay special regard to lightening the financial burden and expediting the completion of such restoration and reconstruction".

to the Bank would be $1,200 million. This incident explains why the aggregate capital of the International Bank is $300 million larger than that of the Fund, since the United States did not withdraw its last minute offer to increase its own subscription to the Bank.

Another characteristic of the Soviet negotiations at Bretton Woods was the almost exclusive concern of its delegates with those matters which directly affected the Soviet Union and an almost complete lack of interest in the broad purposes which the Fund and Bank were designed to accomplish. This was perhaps a reflection of the fact that the USSR regarded the problems which the Fund was designed to solve as being peculiar to those of capitalistic economies. The American delegation on the other hand sincerely believed that certain of the rules for an orderly world trading system required the cooperation of the Soviet Union and that all countries would benefit by the establishment of such a system. For example, the establishment of a world-wide system of multilateral payments and the avoidance of bilateral payments arrangements certainly required the submission of the Soviet Union to the Fund's rules. But this would have required a willingness on the part of the Soviet Union to adopt a policy of conducting its trade in accordance with purely commercial principles, *i.e.*, buying in the cheapest market and selling its exports on world markets at prices related to internal costs. There is little evidence that the USSR accepted the basic economic philosophy of the Monetary Fund. On the other hand the Soviet representatives did not attack these principles at the conference nor did they engage in any of the propaganda tactics which have characterized Soviet participation in international conferences in recent years.

It will not be possible in the course of this chapter to take up all of the points raised by the Russians at the Bretton Woods and pre-Bretton Woods conferences, or to go into all of the technical complications regarding the points which will be discussed. The matters chosen for discussion are therefore to be regarded as illustrative and no attempt will be made to present a comprehensive analysis of the USSR's participation in the Bretton Woods Conference.

II

The draft of the *Joint Statement* on the Fund which had been submitted to the USSR in January 1944 provided that each member must contribute in gold an amount equal to 25 percent of its quota or 10 percent of its net official holdings of gold and dollars, whichever is the smaller. The *Joint Statement* also provided that when members were in debt to the Fund they must use one-half of any increase in their gold and dollar holdings to repay the Fund. The Soviet representatives proposed the following substitute provisions: 1) that all members contribute an amount of gold equal to 15 percent of their quota except that the gold contribution of members whose territories had been wholly or substantially occupied by the enemy be reduced by 50 percent; and 2) that the provision for repaying the Fund with half of any increase in gold and dollar holdings should not apply to newly mined gold.

The reasons for the Russians' attitude were obvious. They had large gold holdings, variously estimated from $3 to $6 billion and hence they would not benefit from any provision which cut down the gold contribution for countries with low monetary reserves. They wanted the amount of the gold contribution to depend in large measure upon whether or not a country had been occupied by the enemy. Finally, since they are large gold producers (the amount of current production is not known but probably runs to several hundred million dollars annually), they did not want to be required to use any part of it to repay the Fund.[7]

In the course of the negotiations the American technicians pointed out that the gold contributions put forward in the American draft of the Fund's Articles published in July 1943 had been cut from 50 percent to 25 percent of the quotas and that to cut it to 15 percent would have involved too great an impairment of the Fund's resources. Moreover many countries had very low monetary reserves and to apply a flat percentage of the quota to all countries was impossible.[8] Nevertheless an effort was made to

[7] The Soviet delegation also objected to the provisions of the *Joint Statement*, later embodied in the Articles of Agreement, that members whose monetary reserves were less than half of their quota might pay the Fund's charges partly in local currency instead of in gold.

[8] It should be pointed out that the July 10, 1943 draft did provide that countries

satisfy the USSR by proposing that its quota should be increased from the $900 million originally suggested to $1,200 million. The Russians refused to compromise this issue and continued to press for a reduction in the gold contributions of members occupied by the enemy, the elimination of newly mined gold from the calculations of the increase in monetary reserves to be applied to repaying the Fund and for the elimination of special treatment for members with low monetary reserves in making the initial subscription to the Fund and in the payment of charges on borrowed funds. At the Bretton Woods Conference a provision for reducing the gold subscription of enemy-occupied countries was introduced and argued for by the Soviet delegation but it was opposed by the United States and a majority of the delegates of the other countries on the grounds that the reconstruction needs of the enemy-occupied countries were to be taken care of by the International Bank and that it would be highly undesirable to weaken the Fund by making a special concession to the occupied countries on their gold subscriptions. The Russians also proposed that members whose territories have been occupied by the enemy should not be required to count the increase in stocks of newly mined gold in calculating the increase in their monetary reserves for the purpose of determining the amount of compulsory repayment of credits borrowed from the Fund. This proposal was likewise rejected.

A final Russian proposal on gold contribution to be noted was one which provided that the Fund would hold in each of the four countries having the largest quota an amount of its gold equal to that country's gold subscriptions. In practice this would have given the Soviet Union a veto over the use of its subscription to the Fund.

The attempts of the Soviets to reduce their gold contribution and the calculation of their obligation to repay credits from the Fund were closely related to their general interest in obtaining the maximum net benefits from the Fund. In addition the Soviets bargained for a higher quota than that originally calculated by the American technicians prior to the conference, and more favorable treatment in the granting of credits and loans by the Fund and Bank for countries whose home territories had

whose home territory had been occupied by the enemy would be required to make only 75 percent of their normal gold contributions.

been devastated by the enemy. The quota for the USSR which was finally agreed upon bore little relation to its importance in world trade and was set almost entirely in recognition of its political and potential economic importance. The proposal of the Soviets that the Fund make large credits available to enemy-occupied countries immediately after its inauguration was rejected by the American technicians in the bilateral discussion prior to Bretton Woods on the grounds that the Fund's resources were not designed for rehabilitation and reconstruction. The Soviets dropped this proposal but continued to press for special treatment for enemy-occupied areas by the Bank. Article III, Section 1(b) of the Bank's charter was included in an attempt to meet the Soviet position.[9] However, the conference rejected the Soviet proposal to include the phrase "and shall establish favorable interest and commission rates for such loans".

III

Probably the greatest source of Soviet concern in the negotiations on the Fund and Bank had to do with the extent to which membership might involve interference with Soviet practices or the revelation of information. Any international organization which is designed to determine and enforce rules for international conduct must involve some voluntary giving up of sovereignty or the rights of its members to act entirely in their own interest. The USSR has never accepted this principle with respect to its own affairs. One important example of this desire to avoid any interference with Soviet economic practices had to do with the obligation of the Fund regarding the maintenance of exchange rates. In the course of the bilateral discussions with the Soviet representatives in the spring of 1944, the Soviet delegates argued that since the ruble was not used in international trade, the USSR should not be subject to the Fund's rules on the maintenance of exchange rate parities. The Soviets further pointed out that there was no relationship between their internal price and cost structure and their official exchange rate of

[9] Article III, Section 1 (b) is as follows: For the purpose of facilitating the restoration and reconstruction of the economy of members whose metropolitan territories have suffered great devastation from enemy occupation or hostilities, the Bank, in determining the conditions and terms of loans made to such members, shall pay special regard to lightening the financial burden and expediting the completion of such restoration and reconstruction.

5.3 rubles to the dollar. Therefore except for tourist travel and remittances the exchange rate had virtually no international significance.

Persuaded by this argument the American technicians agreed to support the provision in the Fund's Articles (Article IV, Section 5e) which states: "A member may change the par value of its currency without concurrence of the Fund if the change does not affect the international transactions of members of the Fund." What this provision did in effect, however, was to sanction a system of international trading in which the prices of exports bore no necessary relation to domestic costs, and the internal prices of imports bore no relation to foreign export prices. Such a system makes tariff negotiations and exchange rates meaningless. It also violates the principles of maximum advantage in international trade and makes for an uneconomical use of resources in the Soviet Union as well as abroad and opens the door to the use of state trading organizations for accomplishing non-commercial objectives. The fact that the USSR has a socialist economy and all of its trade is conducted by the state does not prevent it from fitting into an orderly trading system with rules of fair practice. What prevents it from getting into such a system is its unwillingness to do business on a purely commercial basis and to bring its domestic accounting system into line with its system of foreign trade accounting.

The USSR also insisted that the Fund's obligations regarding the use of exchange restrictions had no relevance for it because the state is the only trader and the ruble was not an international currency. This is not true, however, since the USSR does participate in clearing arrangements which involve an offsetting of bilateral trade balances, and certain of these arrangements could probably be construed as discriminatory currency arrangements. It should be pointed out, however, that the Fund Agreement does not deal with trade practices as such and that it was anticipated at the Bretton Woods Conference that the establishment of the Fund would be followed by an international agreement and organization which would deal with restrictive and discriminatory trading practices.[10]

[10] The Bretton Woods Conference adopted a resolution recommending the calling of a conference to deal with matters relating to the conduct of international trade, international commodity agreements and international measures for the

Another source of Soviet concern on matters related to its internal affairs was with the requirement that members must furnish information needed by the Fund in its operations. The American draft of July 10, 1943 (Article VII, Section 7) provided that members were obligated "to furnish the Fund with all information it needs for its operations and to furnish such reports as the Fund may require in the forms and at the times requested by the Fund". The Russian representatives objected to this provision and in the course of the bilateral discussions with the United States officials in Washington suggested that the provision be changed to read: "The member country will furnish the Fund information and reports in the form agreed upon between the Fund and the member country." This was unacceptable to the American group on the grounds that the Fund must have clear authority to obtain all of the information which it needs for its operations. This controversy was carried over into the Bretton Woods Conference where the Russian delegation proposed to limit the obligatory information to the gold holdings of each member's treasury and central bank, and that further information would be obtained by agreement between the Fund and the country concerned. (Since to the Russians the Fund's only significance was a source of credits there was little need for further information.) The United States delegation opposed the Russian proposal and suggested the provision which was finally adopted in modified form. This provision included a list of information which members are required "as a minimum" to supply the Fund upon request.[11]

maintenance of high levels of employment. This resolution foreshadowed the International Conference on Trade and Employment at Havana, Cuba which prepared the Charter for an International Trade Organization in March 1948. The USSR did not participate in this conference.

11 Article VIII, Section 5 (a) is as follows: The Fund may require members to furnish it with such information as it deems necessary for its operations, including, as the minimum necessary for the effective discharge of the Fund's duties, national data on the following matters:

(i) Official holdings at home and abroad, of (1) gold, (2) foreign exchange.
(ii) Holdings at home and abroad by banking and financial agencies, other than official agencies, of (1) gold, (2) foreign exchange.
(iii) Production of gold.
(iv) Gold exports and imports according to countries of destination and origin.
(v) Total exports and imports of merchandise, in terms of local currency values, according to countries of destination and origin.
(vi) International balance of payments, including (1) trade in goods and services, (2) gold transactions, (3) known capital transactions, and (4) other items.
(vii) International investment position, *i.e.*, investments within the territories of

This information requirement has frequently been cited as a reason why the USSR refused to join the Fund. It is worth noting, however, that this matter was not mentioned in the list of reservations which the Soviet delegation made regarding the Articles of Agreement at the close of the conference.[12] Moreover in the light of the Soviet Government's well-known ability to manipulate its statistics it is difficult to believe that its decision not to join the Fund and Bank was largely determined by this issue.

The Soviet delegates raised a similar issue in the Articles of Agreement of the Bank. The United States draft of November 1943 of the International Bank proposal [13] and the final version at Bretton Woods requires that before a loan is made a competent committee of the Bank must make a careful study of the merits of the project and that the Bank must also make arrangements to assure that the proceeds of the loan are actually used for the purpose for which the loan was approved. During the preliminary discussions on the Bank proposal with the American officials in Washington prior to the conference the Soviet representatives argued that such investigation was unnecessary in the case of state trading countries. Obviously the Russians were fearful that the Bank would require the sending of a mission to the Soviet Union which could obtain detailed information on the project. Also the Soviets were opposed to the idea of any strings on the use to which they might put funds borrowed from the Bank. The author can find no record, however, of the Russians proposing any substitute provision on this point at Bretton Woods or of objecting to the provision as now written.

the member owned abroad and investments abroad owned by persons in its territories so far as it is possible to furnish this information.
(viii) National income.
  (ix) Price indices, *i.e.*, indices of commodity prices in wholesale and retail markets and of export and import prices.
   (x) Buying and selling rates for foreign currencies.
  (xi) Exchange controls, *i.e.*, a comprehensive statement of exchange controls in effect at the time of assuming membership in the Fund and details of subsequent changes as they occur.
 (xii) Where official clearing arrangements exist, details of amounts awaiting clearance in respect of commercial and financial transactions, and of the length of time during which such arrears have been outstanding.

[12] See *Proceedings and Documents*, Vol. I, p. 1090–1091, for a list of the Soviet reservations to the Articles of Agreement of the Fund.

[13] *Proceedings and Documents*, Vol. II, p. 1616–1628. See also Article III, Sections 4 and 5 of the Articles of Agreement of the Bank.

While the Soviet delegation was defeated on a number of issues, it recognized the rule of the majority of the drafting delegates with good grace and the conference ended on a note of friendliness and good will. This is indicated in the following excerpt from an address by Mr. Stepanov at the closing session: (translation)

> "We, the representatives of 44 democratic nations, have elaborated this Act in a friendly atmosphere. The questions which we deliberated upon at Bretton Woods were very difficult and complex, they gave rise to the prolonged discussions inevitable in a meeting of this nature. Nor could it be otherwise at a Conference of the representatives of democratic countries who freely express their opinions.
> "However, of great weight and value is the fact that although on separate questions some of us maintained our own points of view, the Conference has nevertheless successfully worked out draft agreements for the establishment of the Fund and Bank which are now submitted for the consideration of the governments of the countries represented here.
> "As regards the amount of the USSR subscriptions to the capital of the Bank, as you have already heard from Mr. Morgenthau, the USSR, willing to meet the wishes of some other delegations at the Conference and in particular the wishes of Mr. Morgenthau, has decided to determine the amount of the USSR subscription to the capital of the Bank at 1,200 million dollars . . .
> "I second the motion of Lord Keynes, the Chairman of the U. K. Delegation, and appeal to the Conference to accept the Final Act and to submit it to the respective Governments for consideration." [14]

Like a number of other delegations the USSR asked to have recorded in the minutes of the conference certain reservations regarding the Articles of Agreement as drafted. These reservations included some of the Russian proposals which had been defeated such as the reduction in initial gold payments to the Fund by members whose territories had suffered substantial damage during the war.[15] None of these reservations with respect to the Articles of the Fund or of the Bank appeared to be sufficiently important to account for the USSR's failure to join the Bretton Woods institutions. In fact the Russian delegates gave

[14] *Proceedings and Documents*, Vol. I, p. 1111–1112.
[15] *Ibid.*, p. 1090–1091.

the impression at the close of the conference that they were fairly
well satisfied with the results.

IV

Acceptance of the Bretton Woods Agreements was open to
countries represented at the Bretton Woods Conference until
December 31, 1945, and on December 29, 1945 the representatives of 38 countries signed the Articles of Agreement in Washington, D.C.[16] Up until the last minute it was hoped that the
Soviet Union would join. In response to an inquiry by the United
States Government the USSR replied that its officials had not
yet had sufficient time to study the proposals! The USSR was
invited to send an observer to the inaugural meeting of the
Board of Governors of the Fund and Bank held at Savannah,
Georgia in March 1946. It sent a low-ranking observer, Professor F. P. Bystrov, who was an advisor to the Soviet Purchasing Commission in the United States and had been a member
of the Soviet technical staff at the Bretton Woods Conference.
Bystrov was accompanied by D. L. Dolotov, a Russian economist
with the Purchasing Commission and three clerical assistants.
In contrast with their friendly behavior at Bretton Woods, the
Soviet representatives at Savannah kept strictly to themselves
and so far as the writer could observe attended no social functions. They gave no hint of the Soviet Union's attitude toward
joining the Fund and Bank but were apparently interested in
having the door left open as long as possible for Russian participation on the same basis as other members represented at the
Bretton Woods Conference. The Czechoslovakian delegate proposed that countries represented at Bretton Woods should be
admitted on the same basis as the original members until December 31, 1946. Although this was an extension of six months beyond the time limit suggested by the United States delegation,
the Czech resolution was adopted.[17] The period of extension
elapsed without further word from the Soviet Government.

The explanation of the Soviet Union's failure to join the
Fund and the Bank must lie in the realm of speculation. I think

[16] Colombia became a member of the Fund only, but subsequently joined the
Bank.
[17] See *Selected Documents,* Board of Governors Inaugural Meeting (International
Monetary Fund, Washington, D.C., April 1946), p. 27-28.

it is to be found in the whole complex of political developments subsequent to the Bretton Woods Conference rather than in an unwillingness of the USSR to accept the obligations imposed upon it by membership in these financial institutions. As was pointed out above, the Soviet technicians were convinced from the very beginning that the rules of the Fund applied only to capitalist countries and not to state-trading nations. Moreover the USSR has not been adverse to breaking international agreements. The growing political rift between the USSR and the United States and its western European allies has made economic cooperation impossible. At the time the Export-Import Act of 1945 was passed (July 31, 1945) it was expected that the United States would make a loan of a billion dollars to the USSR but within a few months the political atmosphere was such that negotiations on the loan could not get under way. Had the USSR joined the Fund and the Bank the political obstacles to any United States concurrence on the extension of credits to the USSR would have probably been prohibitive. The Soviet Government must have realized that it was shutting itself off from the United States credits directly or indirectly, when it embarked upon its program of violating treaties and of political, economic and military aggression.

Even if the political atmosphere of the past five years had been more favorable to economic cooperation, it is difficult to see how Russian membership in the Bretton Woods institutions could have contributed to their success without a substantial change in the whole economic and political philosophy of the Soviet Union. As has been indicated above, this conclusion is not based on the fact that the USSR has a socialist economic system and maintains a state monopoly of all foreign trading. The Monetary Fund or something like it, would be a useful institution in a world of socialist, state-trading nations. The difficulty lies in the fact that the USSR is not willing to organize its trade on a purely commercial basis and conduct its buying and selling in world markets in a non-discriminatory manner and in accordance with the principles of maximum advantage from international specialization and trade. Russian trading practices violate these principles in several ways. First, there is no relationship between its internal system of costs and prices and external prices. From a purely economic standpoint the Soviet Union would gain if there were such a relationship. Secondly, it prefers barter arrangements to buying and selling in free world markets. The Soviet Union is able to gain from such tactics both by reason of its political power over many of the countries with which it deals and also it is able to improve its terms of trade by exploiting its position as a discriminating monopolist or monopsonist. Any orderly system of trade among nations must rule out the use of such discriminatory tactics. Finally, the USSR uses its trade as a means of gaining political objectives. Economic cooperation for the development of a multilateral trade and payments system is of course impossible to achieve with a country whose foreign trade is an instrument of power politics.

One final word regarding the motives of the American officials at the Bretton Woods and pre-Bretton Woods conferences in negotiating with the Russians. Although every effort was made to meet the points of view of the Soviet representatives without endangering the objectives of the Fund and Bank, just as a similar or even greater effort was made to meet the points of view of the United Kingdom and other countries represented, there was absolutely no evidence that any member of the American delegation deliberately compromised the interests of the United States or "sold out" to the Russians. Secretary Morgenthau, Dr. Harry D. White and other American delegates argued vigorously for the American position as determined by a committee representing various branches of the United States Government and the congressional leaders present at the conference. The negotiations with the Russians at Bretton Woods were carried out within the framework of the United States's general political policy toward our Russian ally in the war, which had been determined by President Roosevelt and his Cabinet and was supported by a majority of the members of Congress.

CHAPTER FIVE

NEGOTIATING TO ESTABLISH THE FAR EASTERN COMMISSION

George H. Blakeslee is Political Advisor to the Chairman of the Far Eastern Commission. For many years Professor of History and International Relations at Clark University, Dr. Blakeslee was also, from 1933 to 1943, Professor of Diplomacy and International Politics at Fletcher School of Law and Diplomacy, a Lecturer at the Naval War College from 1922 to 1942 and at the Army War College from 1923 to 1929 and again in 1932. He was Special Assistant to the American Legation in Peiping and Counselor to the American member of the Lytton Commission in 1932. During 1942 and 1943 he was a consultant for the Department of State, served as an officer of the Department from 1943 to 1945 and since that date has been a Special Assistant to the Director of the Office of Far Eastern Affairs.

Negotiating to Establish the

Far Eastern Commission, 1945

BY GEORGE H. BLAKESLEE

The surrender of Japan led to the problem of determining the kind of administration which should be set up for the occupied country. This problem led in turn to a conflict of view and of policy between the United States and the Soviet Union. The United States was willing, and intended, to consult the other Allied states in regard to the policies to be adopted during the occupation, but wished to have the controlling voice in the determination of these policies, and wished the implementation of these policies and the control of Japan to remain solely with General MacArthur who, as Supreme Commander for the Allied Powers, had already been authorized by the Allied Powers to take such steps as he deemed proper to effectuate the terms of surrender. The Soviet Union, while willing to recognize the leadership of the United States in the occupation of Japan, claimed the right of responsible participation in the control of Japan and in both formulating and implementing the policies for the occupation. During four months the United States and the Soviet Union carried on negotiations in regard to the administration to be established for occupied Japan. Both Governments made substantial concessions. They finally reached an agreement, acceptable also to the United Kingdom and China, the two other major Powers, which was expressed in the Terms of Reference of the Far Eastern Commission and of the Allied Council for Japan. This chapter will outline the steps in the negotiations.

I

In the early months of 1945, as the defeat of Japan became increasingly certain, the United States Government began more earnestly to consider measures for the post-surrender control of Japan. It decided to invite the states which were helping to win the war to participate in the discussions of the policies to be adopted for Japan while the United States would retain for itself a dominant position and the deciding voice. In accordance with this general plan the United States Government drafted terms of reference for a Far Eastern Advisory Commission, which, after some revision, were submitted on August 21 to the Governments of the United Kingdom, China and the Soviet Union. The United States in its communications to these three Governments stated that it would propose that the governments to be invited to be members of the Far Eastern Advisory Commission in addition to the four major Allies be the Governments of France, the Philippine Islands, Australia, Canada, New Zealand and the Netherlands.

The outstanding features of the proposed Terms of Reference were:

(1) the functions of the Far Eastern Advisory Commission would be limited to making recommendations to the participating Governments:

> *a.* "On the formulation of policies, principles and standards by which the fulfillment by Japan of its obligations under the instrument of surrender may be determined:
> *b.* On the steps necessary and on the machinery required to ensure the strict compliance by Japan with the provisions of the instrument of surrender."

(2) its headquarters were to be in Washington and

(3) it would cease to function at the request of any one of the four Allied Powers.

The Terms of Reference were silent as to methods of voting within the Far Eastern Advisory Commission and as to the procedure which would be followed after the participating Governments had received the recommendations of the Commission. The view of the United States Government, however, was clear: it wished to consult with its Allies but it intended to retain the controlling authority.

This policy of the United States Government was publicly expressed in the "United States Initial Post-Surrender Policy for Japan," which was prepared jointly by the Departments of State, War and Navy, and approved by the President on September 6, 1945. The pertinent paragraph stated:

> "Although every effort will be made, by consultation and by constitution of appropriate advisory bodies to establish policies for the conduct of the occupation and the control of Japan which will satisfy the principal Allied Powers, in the event of any differences of opinion among them, the policies of the United States will govern."

The proposal of the United States Government, submitted on August 21, that a Far Eastern Advisory Commission should be formed, was shortly accepted by the Governments of China and the Soviet Union, neither of which raised objection to the draft Terms of Reference. The United Kingdom Government, which wished a control council to be set up, also agreed by October 1 to the establishment of the Advisory Commission, but objected to the draft Terms of Reference and submitted an alternative draft.

The Soviet Government, however, after some weeks changed its mind in regard to the desirability of the proposed Advisory Commission whose only function would be to make recommendations on policy. Generalissimo Stalin said that his representative in Tokyo, Lieutenant General Derevyanko, was neither informed nor consulted. The Soviet Union, Stalin declared, was being treated as a satellite state and not as an ally, and this did not become the dignity of his nation.

The dissatisfaction of the Soviet Government became apparent at the London meeting of Foreign Ministers in September. Mr. Molotov urged that the question of Japan be placed on the Agenda, but the Secretary of State, Mr. Byrnes, declined to discuss the subject during the London meeting since he had had no opportunity to consider the matter in advance with his advisors in Washington. On September 24th, however, Mr. Molotov read to the other Foreign Ministers a statement of the views of the Soviet Government in regard to the administration of Japan. The statement said that the responsibility for the occupation of Japan rested on the four Allied Powers and could not be assumed solely by the United States. The Soviet Government, therefore, submitted the following proposals:

(1) An Allied Control Council for Japan should be set up at once in Tokyo composed of representatives of the four Allied Powers, under the chairmanship of the representative of the United States;

(2) The task of the Control Council should be "to define and formulate the policy of the Allies towards Japan in political, military, economic, financial and other matters";

(3) The measures to carry into effect the policies formulated by the Control Council should be taken by the Chairman of the Council "through the executive agencies of the Control Council," on which representatives of the four Powers might be included.

By these proposals the Soviet Government claimed an equal share with the United States, the United Kingdom and China in determining the policy of the Allies toward Japan in all matters, and a part in carrying out these policies. The Soviet position was explained further by Mr. Molotov a few days later in a letter to the Secretary of State. Mr. Molotov said that so long as the Japanese military forces had not been disarmed there had been justification for concentrating all functions for the control of Japan in the hands of the Allied Commander-in-chief, but that now there should be an Allied organ through which "the four Powers who played the decisive role in the defeat of Japan would put into effect in relation to Japan an agreed policy and assume joint responsibility." It would be wise, he added, to have in addition an Allied Advisory Commission, as envisaged in the United States proposal, which would also be under the presidency of the representative of the United States, and would include more countries than the four major Allied Powers. The Soviet Government, however, could not agree to the formation of a Far Eastern Advisory Commission until the four Powers had created a Control Council.

The Secretary of State, however, in view of the fact that the four major Allied Powers had officially approved the plan for the proposed Far Eastern Advisory Commission, announced that the Commission would meet shortly and would be asked to consider whether a Control Council for Japan should be established and, if so, what should be its powers.

The conflicting positions of the United States and of the Soviet Union were thus fairly clear. The United States wished to have the controlling voice in the occupation of Japan, and to have General MacArthur exercise full authority under the United States, in carrying out occupation policy. The United States, however, proposed that its Allies should participate in recommending policies to be adopted. On the other hand, the Soviet Union wished to share with the United States the responsibility both of formulating and executing occupation policies, and therefore urged the creation of a Control Council for Japan in which joint responsibility would rest with the four major Allied Powers, including the Soviet Union.

In exchanges of view between the United States and the Soviet Governments which took place during the greater part of October, the Soviet Government modified its demand that the four major Allied Powers should exercise "joint responsibility" for the occupation of Japan through an Allied Control Council. Generalissimo Stalin said that the Control Commission in Japan should be similar to the Control Commission in Rumania, and that General MacArthur, as Chairman, would have the final voice in most matters as the Soviet Commander had in Rumania as Chairman of the Rumanian Control Commission.

The United States made even greater concessions. To meet the views of the Soviet Government it suggested that there should be an Allied Military Council in Japan—which it really did not want—and that the Far Eastern Advisory Commission, with its powers only to make recommendations, should be replaced by a Far Eastern Commission with authority not to recommend but to determine the policies for the occupation of Japan.

On October 27th the United States Government submitted

to the Governments of the Soviet Union, the United Kingdom and China Terms of Reference for a Far Eastern Commission and for an Allied Military Council. The Terms of Reference for a Far Eastern Commission contained the following main provisions: The Far Eastern Commission, to be composed of representatives of states on the Far Eastern Advisory Commission plus India, should have the function to formulate "policies, principles and standards" required to give full effect to the instrument of surrender; "the Commission shall respect existing control machinery in Japan including the chain of command from the United States Government to the Supreme Commander and the Supreme Commander's command of occupation forces"; "the United States Government shall prepare directives based on the policy decisions of the Commission and shall transmit them to the Supreme Commander through the appropriate United States Government Agency"; "The United States Government may issue interim directives to the Supreme Commander pending action by the Commission whenever urgent matters arise not covered by policies already formulated by the Commission"; "the Commission may take action by less than unanimous vote provided that action shall have the concurrence of at least a majority of all the representatives including the representatives of three of the four major Allied powers"; and the Far Eastern Commission shall have its headquarters in Washington, although it may meet at other places including Tokyo.

The Terms of Reference proposed by the United States for an Allied Military Council provided that the Council, to be composed of representatives of the United States, the British Commonwealth, the Soviet Union and China, should have its seat in Tokyo, under the chairmanship of the Supreme Commander for the Allied Powers, and should have the function of "consulting with and advising the Supreme Commander in regard to the implementation of the terms of surrender and occupation of Japan and of directives supplementary thereto." The Supreme Commander should issue all orders and be the sole executive authority for the Allied Powers in Japan. "His decision upon all matters shall be controlling."

The Soviet Government was not satisfied with these proposals of the United States although the United States Government believed that its suggested Terms of Reference for the Far Eastern

Commission and the Allied Military Council went far to meet the Soviet demands. In consequence further negotiations between the United States and the Soviet Governments were carried on through the last of October and all of November. The United States Ambassador in Moscow, acting under frequent and detailed instructions from Washington, had long discussions with both Molotov and Stalin.

The Soviet Government wished a substantial share of the responsibility in formulating policies for the occupation, in supervising the execution of these policies and in the general control of Japan. It therefore proposed that the Terms of Reference of the Far Eastern Commission should specify that the four major Powers, together with a majority of all members of the Commission, must approve any policy decision to be adopted by the Commission and that the United States should not have the right of issuing an interim directive. According to these Soviet amendments the Soviet Government would have to give its approval before any policy decision could be adopted by the Far Eastern Commission or any directive be sent to the Supreme Commander for the Allied Powers. The proposal that the four major Powers must approve all policy decisions passed by the Commission would give to each of these Powers, including the Soviet Union, the right to veto any action proposed to be taken by the Far Eastern Commission. The Soviet Government also objected to India's being included in the Far Eastern Commission, although it was a member of the Far Eastern Advisory Commission. The British Government had asked that India be a member of the Advisory Commission, and the Governments of the United States and China had consented and the Soviet Union for some time had raised no objection. The United States Government, therefore, invited India to be a member of the Far Eastern Advisory Commission and India accepted the invitation.

In regard to the Allied Military Council, proposed by the United States, the Soviet Government wished the name to be "Allied Control Council" or "Allied Control Commission." In addition to its other duties, it should have "control over the execution of the terms of surrender of Japan"; that is, the Council should have "control" of the administration of Japan, a function which the United States insisted belonged solely to the Supreme Commander. Further, in accordance with the Soviet proposal, the Supreme Commander "will consult and advise with the Council upon orders involving questions of principle in advance of their issuance. If there is disagreement on the part of one of the members of the Council with the Supreme Commander (or his deputy) on questions of principle . . . the decision of the Supreme Commander on these questions shall be withheld from execution until agreement on these questions has been reached between Governments or in the Far Eastern Commission." Of less importance, the Soviet Government wished a provision to be included in the Terms of Reference for the Allied Council authorizing each member to be accompanied by an appropriate staff consisting of military and civilian members.

In supporting and explaining their position the Soviet nego‐tiators said that the Soviet representatives on the Far Eastern Commission and the Allied Control Council should not be, as Molotov expressed it, "only decorative" or, as Stalin phrased it, a mere "piece of furniture." The Soviet Government should share in the responsibility for the occupation of Japan. Gen‐eralissimo Stalin recognized that the United States had a greater measure of responsibility in Japanese affairs than the other Al‐lies, but he said that he had not agreed that the United States alone should have this responsibility since he considered that those Allied Powers whose forces took an active part in the defeat of Japan should share this responsibility. The Soviet negotiators pointed out that in the beginning of the occupation, during the period when the Japanese troops were being dis‐armed, August–September 1945, the Supreme Commander nat‐urally operated without the supervision of any Allied control organ. After the disarmament of the Japanese troops, however, the Supreme Commander should not continue to exercise all the rights and privileges which he enjoyed during the earlier period; it was necessary that an Allied control organ should be created to solve new questions of a political, economic, cultural, administrative and financial character. This Allied control organ should be similar to the Control Commissions established in Rumania and Hungary. Stalin recognized that the Supreme Com‐mander, as the permanent Chairman of the control organ, should in the majority of issues have the decisive voice; but in those few cases which involved matters of principle, such as questions of a change in the regime of control of Japan and changes in the composition of the Japanese Government, unanimous agreement should be required among the members of the Control Council, as was the case in matters of principle in the Control Commissions in Rumania and Hungary. In the Far Eastern Commission, the Soviet Government stated, the principle of the unanimity of the principal Powers should also be preserved. That principle had been successfully applied during the war, and was continued as the basis for the voting procedure in the Security Council of the United Nations.

In the exchanges of view the Soviets gave the impression that they were suspicious that United States policies might lead to the development of a Japan which would be antagonistic and a threat to the Soviet Union. They pointed out that Japan for two generations had been a constant menace to Russian security in the Far East and that they wished now to be free from this threat.

The United States Government was opposed to these Soviet changes in the United States draft since the Soviet proposals appeared to constitute a fundamental attack upon the basic principle of the primary responsibility of the United States in Japan. The Department of State pointed out that the United States Government and the United States forces had occupied Japan on behalf of the United Nations and that they had the responsibility for carrying out the terms of surrender and for the occupation of Japan and that neither the United States Government nor General MacArthur could be divested of nor share the responsibility for making and enforcing final decisions. However, the Department of State contended, the Soviet Government by its suggested changes was proposing that the United States Government could send to the Supreme Commander no directives not in accordance with decisions of the Far Eastern Commission which had been adopted by the unanimous agreement of the four principal Allies, including the Soviet Union. The power of the United States Government to issue interim directives would be taken away. It thus appeared that the United States Government, which had the responsibility for carrying out the surrender terms in Japan and the responsibility of enforcing these terms by its own military establishment, would be utterly unable to fulfill this responsibility.

The Soviet proposals, also, seemed to the United States Government to constitute a complete departure from the earlier statement of Generalissimo Stalin that he was willing to take as a model for a control council in Japan the Control Commissions for Rumania and Hungary on which the Soviet General, Chairman of the Commission, had the "last word." General MacArthur, Stalin had said, would also have the "last word" in making decisions for Japan. The recent Soviet proposals, however, appeared to the United States to disregard the precedent of the Control Commissions for Rumania and Hungary, and to aim at imposing on the Allied Council in Japan the same rule of unanimity which had caused such difficulty in the Allied Control Council in Germany.

In the view of the United States the Allies should participate in the Far Eastern Commission in making basic policy decisions and in the Allied Military Council should have an opportunity to advise and consult with the Supreme Commander for the Allied Powers upon the manner of carrying out these policies, but the right to speak the "last word" in the Council should belong to General MacArthur. It seemed to the United States that the procedures which it had proposed in its draft terms of reference for a Far Eastern Commission and an Allied Military Council in Japan would give considerably more privileges to the Soviet representatives than the Soviets gave to the United States representatives on the Control Commissions in Rumania and Hungary. Under these circumstances, the State Department said, except for the Soviet proposal that each member of the Commission and of the Council might be accompanied by an appropriate staff—a provision which would be acceptable—the United States could not consent to any substantive changes in the draft Terms of Reference for the Allied Military Council, or to any impairment of the right of the United States to issue interim directives pending action by the Far Eastern Commission. The United States Ambassador, however, explained to Mr. Molotov that if the Soviet Government should accept the fundamental principle of primary United States responsibility, the question of voting procedure would be open for negotiation. This proposal must have appealed strongly to the Soviets since they were especially anxious to obtain the right of "veto" in the Far Eastern Commission, a right which would accrue to the Soviet Representative as a result of the adoption of a voting procedure which would require for any action by the Commission the unanimous approval of the four major Allied Powers.

Mr. Molotov, in replying to these statements, summarized the Soviet position and in conclusion said that the United States Government might rest assured that the Soviet Government did not intend to diminish the preeminent rights of the United States in Japanese affairs. The Soviet proposals had simple and elementary objectives:

(1) To see to it that the participation of the Soviet Union in the control over Japan would not be merely "decorative," and

(2) To secure conditions of cooperation in the control over Japan through which the Soviet Union as well as the United States might bear responsibility.

After receiving Mr. Molotov's explanation, the United States Government in a further effort to meet the Soviet wishes offered additional concessions and the United States Ambassador gave a further detailed clarification of the position of the United States.

In regard to the Allied Military Council, the Ambassador said, the United States was willing to accept the name "Allied Council for Japan,"—but not "Allied Control Council"—in order to avoid any impression that the Council would occupy itself only with military affairs and not with the implementation of directives involving matters of political, economic and cultural character. There would be no objection by the United States to adding to the draft of the Terms of Reference for the Allied Council for Japan a statement that each representative would be entitled to have an appropriate staff the size of which would be fixed in agreement with the Chairman of the Council. Provisions could be made in the Terms of Reference for periodic meetings of the Council at stated intervals, perhaps every two weeks. Further, the following paragraph might be added to the Terms of Reference:

> "Action to modify the agreed regime of Allied Control for Japan or to approve revisions or modifications of the Japanese Constitution will be taken only in accordance with decisions of the Far Eastern Commission."

The United States Ambassador explained to Molotov that in the view of the United States Government the Far Eastern Commission was the proper body for the formulation and determination of basic policies towards Japan and that the proposed Allied Council for Japan under the chairmanship of General MacArthur would have no power to determine on its own initiative fundamental questions such as the change in the regime of control or changes in the Japanese constitutional structure. So far as changes in the personnel of a Japanese Government were concerned, to take this power from the Supreme Commander by requiring the unanimous agreement of the four Powers would deprive him of the essential and fundamental authority to enforce his orders.

The United States Ambassador said further that the terms of reference proposed by the United States for the Allied Council for Japan provided for a full measure of consultation by the Allied Council with regard to the administration of Japan, and for the observation of the manner in which the administration was being carried out. If there should be disagreement between the Chairman and one or more members of the Council, as to whether an action of the Supreme Commander was consistent with policy decisions of the Far Eastern Commission or with directives of the United States any Government could raise the issue involved either in the Far Eastern Commission or by direct approach to the United States Government. If it should be clear that the action of the Supreme Commander had been at variance with the reasonable interpretation of the policy directives on which such action was based, measures could then be taken to modify the action in dispute. In view of the primary responsibility of the United States for the control and administration of Japan, the United States Government could not accept an arrangement by which in the event of disagreement in the Council the Supreme Commander would be unable to take essential action pending an agreement between the interested governments. Any indication that the authority of the Supreme Commander was not final in relation to the Japanese authorities and in the execution of policies in Japan could only serve to weaken his authority and control over the Japanese Government and thus imperil the efficient administration of Allied policy in Japan.

In regard to the precedent established by the Allied Control Commissions in Rumania, Hungary and Bulgaria the Ambassador pointed out to Molotov that the Soviet Government had never consented to any interpretation of the functions of these Control Commissions which would tie the hands of the Soviet Chairman in the event of disagreement with the American and British members or require him to withhold action pending agreement between the Governments represented on the Commission. To be sure, at the Berlin (Potsdam) Conference, July 17th to August 2, 1945 the Heads of Government of the United States, the Soviet Union and the United Kingdom accepted as a basis for the Control Commissions in Rumania, Bulgaria and Hungary the following Soviet proposal for the terms of procedure for the Allied Control Commission in Hungary:

> "Directives of the Allied Control Commission on questions of principle will be issued to the Hungarian authorities by the President of the Allied Control Commission after agreement on these directives with the English and American representatives."

The United States Government, however, contended that the Russian word for agreement, "Soglasovanie," had been consistently interpreted by the Soviet authorities to mean "consultation and discussion" and not agreement; and that no case was known where the Soviet Government had interpreted this provision of the Potsdam Conference to mean that the Chairman of the Control Commission could act only after agreement on the part of the other members. It was therefore obvious that if the Allied Council for Japan were to follow the precedent of the Allied Control Commissions in Rumania, Hungary and Bulgaria, General MacArthur, as Chairman of the Allied Council for Japan, would be under obligation only to consult his colleagues on the Council but not to wait for their agreement. In any case, it might be pointed out that the Soviet contention that unanimity in the Allied Commissions was required by the provision of the Potsdam Conference, applied only to "questions of principle" and not to ordinary decisions.

In regard to the Far Eastern Commission the Ambassador said that the United States Government would be prepared to include in the terms of reference of the Commission a clause to the effect that any directives dealing with fundamental changes in the Japanese constitutional structure, or in the regime of occupation would only be issued following prior consultation and agreement in the Commission. If the right of the United States to issue interim directives should be retained, the United States Government would not object to a voting procedure in the Commission which would embody the principle of unanimity among the four principal Allies. These interim directives would be subject to review by the Commission and would be issued by the United States only in cases where the situation in Japan would not permit delay.

In both the Allied Council and the Far Eastern Commission the United States Government stated that it wished to afford the maximum opportunity for consultation and the working out of agreed Allied policies. The United States, however, could not accept arrangements under which any action could be indefinitely delayed because of disagreement or differences between the Allied nations involved. The essential safeguards upon which the United States must insist were intended merely to insure that the entire administration of Japan, for which the United States admittedly bore the primary responsibility, did not break down pending the adjustment of differences which might arise between the interested governments.

The Soviet Government in replying to this statement of the views of the United States made the following comments. The Soviet Government assumed that there was no basis for objection to accepting the procedure which would require unanimous agreement among the four Allied Powers in reaching decisions in those important cases which concerned questions of principle, such as questions of changing the regime of control over Japan and changes in the composition of the Japanese Government. In all other questions which might come before the Allied Council for Japan the Commander-in-Chief of the American occupation troops in Japan, since he had "sufficiently broad opportunities" and had military force for taking prompt measures, would have the decisive voice. There was thus no ground for apprehension that the acceptance of the principle of agreement among the four Allies in regard to questions of principle would weaken the authority of the Commander-in-Chief. Therefore the Soviet Government believed that major questions of control over Japan should not be decided solely by the Commander-in-Chief but by the unanimous agreement of the four Allies. As to the Far Eastern Commission the Soviet Government assumed that the voting procedure in the Commission should also express the principle of unanimity of the four Allied Powers not only in questions concerning basic changes in the constitutional structure or in the regime of control of Japan but also in such a question as a change in the Japanese Government as a whole, including the Prime Minister. This principle of unanimity should also apply to the procedure of issuing interim directives on questions other than those relating to matters of principle.

Substantial progress had thus been made in the negotiations during October and November 1945, in clarifying and in some measure in reconciling the divergent views of the United States and Soviet Governments. Mr. Molotov said that in the opinion of the Soviet Government the negotiations of these two months had been both useful and fruitful and that the views of the United States and the Soviet Union had been brought closer together. The United States had made major concessions to the Soviets by agreeing to (a) an Allied Council in Tokyo, (b) a Far Eastern Commission to replace the Far Eastern Advisory Commission and (c) a voting procedure in the Commission which would give the Soviet Representative a "veto." The Soviet Government, in turn, had modified the demands which it had presented at the opening of the negotiations. There were, however, important differences remaining when on December 16th the Foreign Secretaries of the United States, the United Kingdom, and the Soviet Union met in Conference at Moscow.

II

At the opening session of the Moscow Conference Secretary Byrnes presented to the Soviet and British Foreign Ministers revised drafts of the terms of reference for the Far Eastern Commission and the Allied Council. These drafts were based on the United States drafts submitted on October 27, and contained the further concessions to which the United States Government had agreed during the negotiations following October 27th. These later proposed concessions were in part as follows:

(a) In regard to the Allied Council, the name "Allied Military Council" was changed to "Allied Council"; the Council should meet not less often than once every two weeks; each representative on the Council would be entitled to have an appropriate staff the size of which would be fixed in agreement with the

Chairman of the Council; and "Action to modify the agreed regime of Allied control for Japan or to approve revisions or modifications of the Japanese Constitution will be taken only in accordance with decisions of the Far Eastern Commission";

(b) In regard to the Far Eastern Commission, the draft of December 16 provided that the concurrence of all four major Powers would be necessary to make valid any action by the Commission; interim directives issued by the United States Government would be subject to review by the Commission at the request of any member; and "Any directives dealing with fundamental changes in Japanese constitutional structure, or in the regime of occupation, will only be issued following prior consultation and agreement in the Far Eastern Commission."

The Soviet Government was not satisfied with these additional concessions. The Soviets wanted a larger share than the United States offered both in the formulation of policy for the occupation of Japan and in the "control" of Japan during the occupation. They wished to restrict so far as possible the unilateral authority of the United States and of General MacArthur. With this objective in view, Mr. Molotov on December 18th submitted a number of amendments to the United States drafts of the 16th. The most important of these were, in regard to the Allied Council: the name should be "Allied Control Council" or "Allied Control Commission," and it should function "for the purpose of control over the execution of the terms of surrender of Japan" as well as for "the purpose of consulting and advising the Supreme Commander"; the size of the staff of each member of the Allied Council should not be subject to an "agreement with the Chairman of the Council"; and the provisions in the United States draft limiting the final authority of the Supreme Commander in basic matters of principle should be clarified in these words:

> "On questions concerning the implementation of decrees of the Far Eastern Commission the decisions of the Supreme Commander shall be final with the exception of questions of principle, such as questions concerning a change in the regime of control over Japan, changes in the constitutional structure, of a change in the Japanese Government as a whole. In the event that a member of the Council disagrees with the Supreme Commander (or his deputy) regarding the implementation of the aforementioned decrees involving questions of principle, the

decisions of the Supreme Commander on these questions will not be put into effect prior to agreement (soglasovanie) on these questions in the Far Eastern Commission.

"In cases of necessity the Supreme Commander may take decisions concerning the change of individual ministers of the Japanese Government after appropriate preliminary consultation with representatives of the other Allied Powers on the Allied Control Council."

As to the Far Eastern Commission the important Soviet amendments to the United States draft of the Terms of Reference were: The United States Government should have no authority to issue interim directives; India should be omitted from the list of Governments represented on the Far Eastern Commission; the words "The Commission in its activities will proceed from the fact that there has been formed an Allied Control Council" should be inserted in the United States draft before the words: "The Commission shall respect existing control machinery in Japan including the chain of command from the United States Government to the Supreme Commander and the Supreme Commander's command of occupation forces"; and "a change in the Japanese Government as a whole" should be added to the list of subjects regarding which no directive should be issued without consultation and "the attainment of agreement in the Far Eastern Commission."

On the following day Secretary Byrnes submitted an additional revision of the United States drafts to meet still further the views of the Soviet Government. In regard to the Allied Council the United States draft of December 19th adopted the Soviet amendment which deleted the provision that the size of the staff of each member should be fixed in consultation with the Chairman of the Commission and incorporated with some rearrangement the Soviet draft, given in a preceding paragraph, which provided that the decision of the Supreme Commander in regard to the implementation of policy decisions should be final except as to "questions of principle." Secretary Byrnes declined, however, to agree either to the Soviet proposal that the title of the Allied Council should be "Allied Control Council" or that the Council should be organized in part "for the purpose of control over the execution of the terms of surrender of Japan." As to the terms of reference of the Far Eastern Commission Secretary Byrnes accepted in substance the Soviet redrafting of two paragraphs. He did not accept the omission of India from the Far Eastern Commission or the deletion of the right of the United States to issue interim directives.

During the two days of discussions following the submission of the revised United States drafts on December 19th, Mr. Molotov on behalf of the Soviet Government accepted the United States position on all the remaining issues. He raised no further objection to the right of the United States to issue interim directives. He agreed that India should be a member of the Far Eastern Commission, in deference, he said, to Mr. Bevin's strong wishes. He dropped the suggestion that the Allied Council should be named the "Allied Control Council." He first presented and then withdrew a new proposal. In the draft Terms of Reference for the Allied Council paragraph 4 stated that the Supreme Commander "will consult and advise with the Council in advance of the issuance of orders on matters of substance, the exigencies of the situation permitting." Mr. Molotov expressed the wish, in order that this provision should be mandatory on the Supreme Commander in all circumstances, to drop the phrase "the exigencies of the situation permitting." When Secretary Byrnes explained that he could not acquiesce in this request, Mr. Molotov dropped it.

Viewing in perspective these negotiations of some four months between the United States and the Soviet Union an appreciation of the extent of the concessions made by each may best be gained by contrasting in summary the original plans of each with their final agreement.

The United States in the beginning planned to control the occupation of Japan, both in the formulation of policy and in its execution by General MacArthur. It was willing to consult with other countries in regard to policy but was opposed to any other country interfering with the authority of the United States. After the negotiations were concluded the United States had transferred its right to formulate policy—with the exception of interim directives—to the Far Eastern Commission, in which the Soviet Union had a veto; and consented to the establishment of an Allied Council in Tokyo composed of the four major Powers with the function of consulting with and advising the Supreme Commander.

The Soviet Government at first aimed to obtain a substantial share in the control and administration of occupied Japan. It asked for a Control Council in Tokyo, of which it would be a member, which would have the authority to formulate policy and to supervise its execution. By concessions during the negotiations it gave up the substance of its original objective. Although the Soviet Union obtained the veto in the Far Eastern Commission, the predominance of the United States in the occupation of Japan remained. While the United States could not by itself pass a policy decision in the Commission, it could by its veto prevent the approval of any policy decision which it opposed, and on its own authority it could send to the Supreme Commander interim directives on urgent matters. In Japan the authority of the Supreme Commander as sole executive of the occupation remained in nearly all matters unrestricted by the action of any country other than the United States.

The official views of the United States and Soviet Governments in regard to the issues which had arisen over the Far Eastern Commission and the Allied Council were expressed in an exchange of letters between President Truman and Generalissimo Stalin. In a letter to Generalissimo Stalin carried to him by Secretary Byrnes President Truman said:

> Secretary Byrnes and I have sought to go as far as we have felt able to meet your views with reference to the Allied Council for Japan and to the Far Eastern Commission, and I sincerely hope that your Government will accept the proposals which we have made.

As to the attitude of the people of the United States he stated:

> I repeat my assurances to you that it is my earnest wish, and I am sure that it is the wish of the people of the United States, that the people of the Soviet Union and the people of the United States should work together to restore and maintain peace. I am sure that the common interest of our two countries in keeping the peace far out-weighs any possible differences between us.

Generalissimo Stalin in reply in a letter to the President dated December 23rd, wrote in part:

> I agree with you that the peoples of the Soviet Union and the United States must strive to work together in the cause of the restoration and maintenance of peace and that we must proceed from the fact that the common interests of both our countries are higher than individual differences between them.

E. F. Penrose was educated at the University of Cambridge and Stanford University. He spent five years in research and teaching at the Nagoya College of Commerce, Japan; five years in research at the Food Research Institute, Stanford University; five years on the Economics faculty of the University of California, Berkeley; three years as Economic Advisor to the International Labor Office, Geneva; five years in the Foreign Service as Economic Advisor to Ambassador Winant in London during the war and one year at Lake Success as Advisor on Economic and Social Affairs to the United States representative on the Economic and Social Council. Since 1947 he has been B. Havell Griswold Jr. Professor of Geography and International Relations at the Johns Hopkins University. He is the author of Food Supply and Raw Materials in Japan; Population Theories and Their Application, with Special Reference to Japan; *and part author* Economic Aspects of Medical Services, with Special Reference to California; Industrialization of Japan and Manchuria, 1930–1940; *and a forthcoming publication,* Economic Errors of the Peace.

CHAPTER SIX

Negotiating on Refugees and

Displaced Persons, 1946

BY E. F. PENROSE

There are few subjects on which more prolonged and exhaustive negotiations have been carried on between the Soviet Union and the western world than on the subject of refugees and displaced persons. For the most part these negotiations were carried on in international committees and the controversies to which they gave rise were controversies which involved other eastern as well as western countries. Most of the negotiations took place in 1946, when central and eastern Europe, although subject to political pressure from the Soviet Union, were less dominated by her than they came to be in later years, and still occasionally exercised independent judgment in international affairs, at least on matters of detail. It was a time, too, when the western world had not given up hope of reaching an accommodation with the Soviet Union, at least on some aspects of international relations, and was anxious to leave the way open to compromise wherever practicable and to avoid the appearance of a political combination against the Russian representatives at international gatherings. The negotiators showed immense patience, and every possible opening through which there seemed to be any chance, however remote, of reaching general agreement was explored, not once only but time after time during the year, until the fabric of the discussion was worn threadbare and new speeches could no longer get beyond the repetition of old arguments and the reiteration of old charges.

There is thus a mass of material relating to negotiations over displaced persons. The earlier discussions which took place between SHAEF and Russian military authorities regarding Russians in the ranks of the German armies who were taken prisoner on the western front were in a sense related to the subject of displaced persons, though it is not necessary to go into them in this discussion.[1] Then, when foreign laborers in Germany were released, the military authorities in the western zones and in Italy and Austria had to make provision for repatriation of some and care of other displaced persons among whom a number of Russians were to be found who, it was claimed by the Russian authorities, were Soviet citizens, although some of them declared their unwillingness to return to the Soviet Union. UNRRA later took over the maintenance and operation of most of the assembly centers and questions relating to displaced persons came up at the annual or semi-annual meetings of the UNRRA Council and at the monthly meetings of the Committee of the Council of Europe which sat in London.

But the most systematic and extensive negotiations on refugees and displaced persons in which the Soviet Union took part were initiated within the new United Nations organization which began its work early in 1946. They started with discussions in plenary sessions and in the Third Committee of the United Nations Assembly, between January 10 and February 14. The Assembly adopted an important resolution on general principles and appointed a Special Committee on Refugees and Displaced Persons which met in London between April 8 and June 1, 1946, and drew up an extensive report including a suggested draft constitution of an International Refugee Organization. The report was referred to the Economic and Social Council at its Second Session held in New York in June and July 1946.

---

[1] For details of these negotiations, see the chapter by Major General John R. Deane, p. 3.

The suggested constitution was discussed in great detail and a number of amendments were adopted. The Council, which only represented eighteen countries, decided to circulate the amended draft to all the United Nations, to review at its next session the comments which it received from them and to submit the amended draft to the Assembly in the autumn. At its next meeting, held in Lake Success in September, the draft constitution was debated once more both in a subcommittee and in the full council meetings and an amended draft was put before the Assembly in October. This was referred to the Third Committee of the Assembly and absorbed most of the Committee's time from October 24 to December 12. The entire ground was covered again in exhaustive—and exhausting—detail. Finally, after debate in two plenary sessions of the Assembly the draft constitution of a new specialized agency, to be known as the International Refugee Organization, was adopted by a vote of 30 to 5 with 18 abstentions.

I

Notwithstanding the large numbers—amounting perhaps to about seven and a half million—of displaced persons who were in Germany when the Allied armies entered, within a short time only about one million remained in the western zones of Germany and Austria. Of these the Poles formed much the largest single group—roughly two-thirds. They were composed mainly of Roman Catholic and Jewish Poles, the former in a substantial majority. The second largest group, rather less than one-third the size of the Polish group, was made up of Baltic peoples. Next there were Jewish displaced persons not attributed to any one nationality. In Italy there were probably over 100,000 displaced persons: the precise number was unknown since the majority were not in camps. Among them were included a number of the Yugoslav adherents of King Peter who had fought in the army of the United Kingdom and a number of Chetniks who had belonged to the Mihailovich forces.

Thus the controversies which arose over displaced persons were not the outcome of simple and straightforward differences between the Soviet Union and the west. Other countries were involved in them and even if the Soviet Union had kept out of them the negotiations would not have been easy and frictionless. A devastating war, and an enemy occupation which had spread over all Europe east of the Pyrenees, except for Sweden and Switzerland, had left deep social as well as material scars: accusations of collaboration with the enemy and demands for retribution had aroused bitter controversies after liberation. The important part played by the Soviet Union in the negotiations over displaced persons should be viewed against this wider background.

The chief issues concerning refugees and displaced persons seem fairly clear and straightforward at first sight, and an uninitiated observer might wonder why so many millions of words were uttered in the prolonged debate on them. How were refugees and displaced persons to be defined? Were they to be permitted to choose freely between the alternatives of going back to their countries of origin and remaining outside them? If so, what, if any, international aid should be given to those who chose to remain outside? These three questions go to the heart of the entire controversy throughout 1946. Simple as they appear on the surface, they raised far-reaching issues that touched fundamental questions of human liberty on which divergent views were held among the nations whose representatives met in London and New York to decide the fate of a million of these homeless people. Even when broad, general principles were accepted by all, there was much dispute over their application. Dangerous pitfalls were often hidden under apparently innocuous phrases and negotiators could not afford to relax for a moment in their search for the true meaning and the ramifications of each of the numerous amendments and compromises that were proposed between the time when the first draft proposals were drawn up and the time when the final vote on the charter of the new International Refugee Organization was taken.

The first important landmark in the negotiations on refugees and displaced persons in the new United Nations machinery is to be found in the resolution passed by the Assembly on January 29, 1946.[2] It was important not only because of the principles embodied in it but also because the representatives of the Soviet Union, notwithstanding the rejection of some amendments

[2] United Nations General Assembly, Document A/64, July 1, 1946, p. 12.

which they had proposed, voted with the other countries in favor of it. The resolution referred the question as one of urgency to the Economic and Social Council, recommending that the Council appoint a special committee to examine it promptly and thoroughly and laying down principles to guide its work. First, the problem was to be considered as "international in scope and nature". Second, refugees or displaced persons who had ". . . finally and definitely, in complete freedom, and after receiving full knowledge of the facts, including adequate information from the governments of their countries of origin, expressed valid objections to returning to their countries of origin," and who were not "war criminals, quislings and traitors", were not to be "compelled to return to their country (*sic*) of origin," but were to "become the concern of whatever international body" might be established to deal with them. Third, "the main task concerning displaced persons" was "to encourage and assist in every way possible their early return to their countries of origin."

In the Third Committee of the Assembly, where this text was drafted, the Soviet Union had introduced a resolution of its own which at some points resembled that adopted but differed from it, first, in requiring "the consent of the Government of the country whose citizens they are" as a condition of international assistance for the resettlement of genuine refugees who did not wish to return to their countries; second, in prescribing that the staff of the refugee camps should consist mainly of citizens of the countries of origin of the refugees; [3] third, in demanding the immediate return of quislings, traitors and war criminals; and fourth, in prohibiting propaganda in the camps against the "interests" of any member of the United Nations. The objections of the western countries to the first two points are obvious; as to the third, the western occupying powers held that the task of apprehending in Germany and Austria and in appropriate cases of handing back alleged war criminals, traitors and quislings to their countries of origin was one for the military authorities, acting in accordance with instructions from the governments of their countries, and it was not for those concerned with displaced persons to undertake, or to intervene in the performance of, this

[3] United Nations General Assembly, 3d Committee, *Official Records* (1st session, 1st part), p. 54–55.

police function: rather their proper concern was merely to interpose no obstacle to the discharge of this function by the properly constituted authorities. On the fourth point, concerning alleged propaganda in the camps, the spokesmen for western countries maintained that a general prohibition could not be enforced without infringing on legitimate freedom of speech.

During an earlier visit to many of the camps in the United States and British zones of Germany I had been impressed with the complexity of this problem. Many groups of displaced persons held, and expressed, strong views on the existing governments of their countries of origin. The camp authorities could ban organized meetings and demonstration against these governments and against repatriation but, unless a Gestapo were to be organized, they could not, even if they had wished to do so, prevent informal conversations on such matters among the displaced persons in their quarters.

These proposed amendments were defeated in committee, but the last three of them were introduced against at the plenary session during the discussion on the committee's report, this time by the eloquent and vivacious Mr. Vyshinsky. Again, however, they were defeated, although France, Norway and Denmark joined the group which voted for the amendment prohibiting propaganda in the camps.[4]

Although its amendments were not accepted, the Soviet Union voted for the Assembly resolution [5] and more generally it may be said that the Russian representatives were much more conciliatory on displaced persons at the meetings of the Assembly in January and February than they were later at those from October to December. Their position in committee was in substance more conciliatory than that of Yugoslavia, which at the outset argued that repatriation and delivery of war criminals would dispose completely of the problem of refugees and displaced persons and that, therefore, there was no need to create international organizations to deal with it. Even the original Russian draft resolution presented to the Third Committee acknowledged that the problem was international in scope and

[4] United Nations General Assembly, *Official Records* (1st session, 1st part), p. 412–439.
[5] *Ibid.*

recommended the establishment of a specialized international agency to deal with it. At the same time the western delegates treated the Russian delegates with respect and went as far as they could to produce a resolution acceptable to all. The clause in the final draft of the Committee's resolution which stated that repatriation was "the main task" concerning displaced persons was inserted in an attempt to meet the viewpoint of the countries of origin of the refugees. Some of us were doubtful of the relevance of the statement to the facts of the situation. In interviews with many widely distributed displaced persons in Germany late in 1945, I had found little indication of willingness among them to return to their countries of origin and had concluded that all the Baltic and large numbers of the Polish displaced persons would have to be resettled. However, at the time the future of the Polish Government was obscure and there was still a fair prospect that many of the Poles would return, as indeed a considerable number did in 1946.

It is important, I think, to keep in mind the close relation between the attitude of the representatives of the Soviet Union in negotiations on social and economic questions and the attitudes of the Kremlin towards the "top level" political questions of the moment. An unfavorable turn in the relations between the Soviet Union and the western world on the leading international political questions of the day is quickly reflected on a variety of "technical" committees concerned with other questions. This contrasts sharply with the conduct of international relations among the western powers.[6]

II

The action of the Assembly was followed by the establishment at the meeting of the Economic and Social Council of a Special Committee on Refugees and Displaced Persons. The Committee met in London between April 8 and June 1. Its report, together with the comments of the rapporteur, ranged over the whole field in far greater detail than had been possible during the meeting of the Assembly.[7]

[6] However, it must be acknowledged that some congressmen in Washington at times call for the use of similar tactics by the United States even in dealings with its Allies.

[7] United Nations Economic and Social Council, *Official Records* (1st year, 2d session), Special Supplement No. 1.

First, an attempt was made to define in detail both "refugees" and displaced persons. The term refugees was taken to cover recognized prewar refugees; victims of the Spanish falangist regime; victims of nazi, fascist or quisling regimes; victims of racial, religious or political persecution; and in addition any refugee "who is outside his country of nationality or former habitual residence, and who, as a result of events subsequent to the outbreak of the Second World War, is unable or unwilling to avail himself of the protection of the government of his country of nationality or former nationality." [8] The term "displaced person" was to cover one who had been "deported from or . . . obliged to leave his country of nationality or former habitual residence, such as persons who were compelled to undertake forced labor or who were deported for racial, religious or political reasons."

The exceedingly broad and general terms in which the last two categories were drawn might be used to cover the Baltic peoples in Germany whose position was a source of embarrassment to all the Great Powers and who did not all fit easily into the other categories. During my investigations in Germany I heard conflicting views among the British and American personnel in military government and in UNRRA on the Baltic refugees: some believed that large numbers of them aided the Germans willingly, came to Germany voluntarily, and regarded the Soviet Union as their chief if not their sole enemy. From questioning many of them individually I derived a strong impression that they intensely disliked both the Soviet Union and Germany. It seemed to me that if they had been as pro-German as some of the occupying officials believed them to be they would have been willing to resettle in Germany: in fact, however, they expressed a stronger desire than any other group of refugees and displaced persons did to be resettled overseas. Nonetheless, it appeared that some of them fled, not before the earlier German advance but before the final victorious Russian advance, and that these preferred to work for the Germans rather than to remain under Russian occupation.

The western occupying powers were in a peculiar position with respect to the Baltic refugees. They had not recognized *de jure* the *de facto* absorption or reabsorption of the Baltic coun-

[8] *Ibid.*, p. 66.

tries into the Soviet Union. The United States had held that the settlement of territorial questions should be carried out after the war. The Soviet Union had formally accepted this view but in practice had regarded its act of annexation as a closed issue.[9] In these circumstances it was inconceivable that the western occupying powers would bring any pressure to bear on the Baltic peoples to return to their native lands. Here was a clear-cut case for resettlement and the case was facilitated by the high standards of literacy, skill and industry which made this group outstanding among refugees and displaced persons.

The discussions of this, as of a number of other points, were carried on throughout the whole negotiations in an indirect and veiled manner. The status of the former Baltic nations was never raised officially. The delegates talked in more or less abstract terms, though they were well aware of what lay behind the abstractions and their definitions were designed to cover thoroughly concrete cases.

Having defined refugees and displaced persons the Committee attempted to give greater precision to the phrase "valid objections" to repatriation which the Assembly resolution had used. The terms "persecution or fear based on reasonable grounds of persecution" were adopted mainly to cover Jewish refugees. Family reasons and illness or infirmity were readily accepted. But sharp differences occurred again over "objections of a political nature" and unanimity could not be obtained. More than six months before the Committee met, a Russian representative in London had explained the position to me privately as follows: "We are aware that some displaced persons who are not criminals or traitors will not wish to return to their countries because they do not like their governments. We do not ask that they shall be forced to return: if they can settle in other countries they will be free to do so. But we cannot agree that they should receive international assistance to resettle or that they should be the concern of an international organization. How could you expect us to contribute towards the support and resettlement of those who are politically opposed to us and wish to work for other countries." This argument had much force and no agreement was reached then or has been reached since on the matter. In private

9 From a "technical" point of view they held that each of these former independent republics had elected to become a Soviet Socialist Republic within the USSR.

conversations with Russian representatives I maintained that it was to the advantage of the countries of origin, and might even be worth their contributing a small sum, that refugees who did not want to return should be assisted to resettle in other continents: in this way their sense of grievance against the governments of their countries of origin would be minimized, and they would have less time and inclination to conduct agitation against those governments than they would if nothing were done for them and they floated about Germany and Austria under precarious conditions of livelihood.[10] But whether or not individual Russians were impressed by this reasoning the Kremlin certainly was not! Statesmanship with any appearance of magnanimity is foreign to the present state of political development in the Soviet Union.[11]

In defining refugees the exact period of time during which the forced or voluntary migration took place was important. The Soviet Union, with some support from eastern European countries, wished to set a deadline at the termination of hostilities with Germany and Japan. But there were some persons in Germany and Austria who had left their countries after that time, either in fear of violence or out of dislike of a newly established government or a change of regime. A considerable area of prewar Poland had been transferred to the Soviet Union. In conversing with Polish displaced persons in the assembly centers in 1945 I found that most Poles from these territories, regardless of the date when they had left their homes, were not ready even to consider repatriation. Most of them were simple peasant folk to whom "Poland" meant their former homes and the immediate neighboring areas. When these were lost to them and came under Russian rule they seemed to have no more interest in Poland. In their view the rest of Poland would go the same way or at least would come under complete Russian domination in five or ten years. Even if it did not they had no interest in trying to re-

[10] In Munich, in 1945, I had come across a group of refugees who were averse to resettlement overseas because they believed that the government of their country of origin would soon be overthrown and they wished to take part in the agitation and the upheavals which they believed would effect the change.

[11] This is not necessarily peculiar to those Russians who profess to be communists. But in the earlier stages of the Russian Revolution there were a number of instances in which magnanimous policies were advocated. Stalin, with his pessimistic outlook on human nature, put an end to the last traces of such an attitude.

establish themselves in new areas of Poland and among Polish people unknown to them.

But in late 1945 and early 1946 a considerable number of Polish Jews were leaving Poland, traveling across the Soviet zone in Germany and entering Berlin. From there they moved to the displaced persons centers in the United States zone. Some of these had previously been in Germany and had returned after the war to Poland for a time. In the jargon of the day they came to be known as "infiltrees." [12] For the purposes of the present discussion, the significant point regarding the movement is that it was permitted by the Soviet Union, whose occupation forces could have stopped it or forced it to take a more circuitous route. In my investigations in December 1945 I visited the Soviet sector in Berlin to question the "infiltrees," a group of whom were lodged in an old building and fed by the local German authorities. It was late at night and I noticed during my conversations that they were preparing to leave. It turned out that the Russian authorities had given notice that on the next day they would be moved to a suitable camp in the Russian zone outside Berlin. This decision had followed a discussion of the problem in the Commandatura, when the Russian representative had stated that the movement was illegal and that the proper steps would be taken to carry out the regulations. However, before the night ended the refugees had scattered and when the Russian trucks arrived for them in the morning they were all in the French and American zones. From the point of view of occupation law the whole movement was as illegal in the United States as in the Russian zone. In the United States zone at that time the law was not enforced against Jewish refugees and some of the camps were becoming overcrowded with the new influx of postwar refugees fleeing from real or supposed persecution in Poland. [13]

[12] This movement caught the public eye momentarily through a press interview given by General Sir Frederick Morgan, head of the UNRRA operations on displaced persons in Germany, and through the heated reactions to it in a part of the New York press which accused the General of anti-semitism. Never was there a greater gulf between the facts as seen by those on the spot and the representation of them at a distance! I had spent a day with the General a week before the incident occurred and found him full of deep humanitarian concern for the Jewish "infiltrees" and anxious to help them. This was recognized fully by the head of the American Jewish Distribution Committee in Germany, and subsequently by Mr. (now Senator) Lehman and the late Rabbi Wise.

[13] I could not find "infiltrees" who had suffered violence in Poland but many

In Vienna I found a smaller movement of the same character from Hungary.

It was this movement which led the United States representatives to seek a draft permitting "infiltrees" to be considered as genuine refugees and displaced persons which is partly responsible for the wording of certain clauses in the definitions, notably the following:

> ". . . the term refugee also applies to a person of Jewish origin who was a victim of Nazi persecution in Germany or Austria, and who was detained in, or who was obliged to flee from, and was subsequently returned to, one of those countries as a result of enemy action, or of war circumstances, and who has not yet been firmly established therein." [14]

This clause was opposed by the Soviet representatives, notwithstanding their generally cautious attitude on Jewish questions.[15] They were not alone in questioning it: there were others who doubted the wisdom of singling out a specific group of people for special mention and special treatment and would have preferred to cover all groups in abstract terms. However it is probable that the Russian objections were based, not on any issue relating to the Jewish people, but on the precedent that would be created by including what were, in effect, postwar refugees among those for whom international responsibility was acknowledged.

But a much sharper difference arose out of the renewal of the controversy over alleged traitors and war criminals in the displaced persons camps. The western countries were willing to exclude those who took part in organizations advocating "the overthrow by armed force of the government of their country of origin" or of any other member of the United Nations, and those who led movements hostile to the governments of their countries of origin or against repatriation. But the Russians wished to go further and ban those who engaged in "hostile activities"

of them appeared to have been threatened. The motive may have been the fear of claims by Polish Jews returning to Poland for the restoration of property which had fallen into the hands of non-Jewish Poles. To this extent anti-semitism was a cloak for economic motives.

[14] Special Supplement, cited above, p. 66–67.

[15] Much earlier, in London, Russian representatives had informed me privately that they were willing to give special consideration to Jewish refugees, recognizing the extreme persecution to which Jews had been subjected. They were also careful to avoid involvement in any controversy over Zionism.

against the governments of those countries of origin—a phase which might be interpreted broadly to include all who belonged or had belonged to any organizations opposed to the governments of their countries of origin.[16]

Another aspect of camp administration on which sharp controversy arose was the method of transmitting to the refugees information concerning conditions in the countries of origin. The Russians proposed that "as a general rule" such information should be "communicated directly to the refugees by the representatives of those countries." But the majority view which prevailed was that the new international body should be the channel of communication. There was a widespread fear in the west that if the representatives of the countries of origin were given access to the camps they would pursue other aims beyond the transmission of information. Experience in the camps in 1945 on this question had been unfavorable. I visited a camp where a Polish representative made a stupid speech the gist of which was that the refugees had better return to Poland at once if they wished to avoid punishment. In some camps I found that riots had broken out when attempts were made to hold meetings to be addressed by representatives of the Polish Government. These illustrations show the great difficulties in practice of procedures which on the surface appeared to many outsiders to be reasonable. Even France and China voted with the Soviet Union on this question.

But on a closely related matter the Soviet representatives gained the day in a close vote, obtaining the insertion of a clause which would oblige the Executive Committee of the proposed new international body to "establish commissions, including representatives of the countries concerned, to visit camps, hostels, or assembly points . . ." and to ". . . give instructions to the Director General in consequence of the results of such investigations." This was clearly a dangerous provision which might have enabled individual refugees to be identified by representatives of their countries of origin and to be intimidated indirectly if not directly.[17]

[16] The doctrine of "guilt by association" is an integral part of Russian justice but at that time it had not made the great inroads into American practice which it has made since.

[17] As the United States representative on the Committee of the Council of Europe for UNRRA I had strenuously fought against similar proposals, which, un-

A related controversy which was also to be continued throughout the year, arose over the proposed registration of refugees and displaced persons. The Soviet Union, Poland and Yugoslavia argued not only that the names should be handed over to them but also that they should be allowed to appoint official agents to take part in the work. The British and American view, however, was that this work should be carried out by the secretariat of the international organization which would treat personal information as confidential. In view of the familiar methods in authoritarian regimes of bringing pressure to bear on nationals abroad through relatives at home, the capital importance of what seemed at first sight to be a purely administrative matter is obvious.

However, throughout the negotiations, it was difficult to defeat once and for all a specific proposal that seemed to endanger the rights of the refugees. No sooner had one proposal been disposed of than another was put forward on a different part of the agenda which, if it did not reopen all the dangers of the first, threatened partially to undermine the decision already reached.

The Soviet Union gained much ground in the drafting of the clauses relating to the structure of the proposed new international organization. The draft provided for a powerful Executive Committee of nine national representatives who were to "issue directions on policy to the Director General and exercise control over his activities" and was to be "so organized as to be able to function continuously during the first year . . ."[18] These clauses were designed to restrict the Director General's powers and to exalt those of a small committee of national representatives. They were in accord with the practices of the Russians who circumscribed their commissars and set a watch on them to ensure that they would have no opportunity to depart from the true faith. If the Russians had gained their own way completely they would have reduced the Director General's position to that of a secretary charged with carrying out the orders of a standing committee in permanent session. This would have opened the way for continual interference by national representatives in the day-to-day business of the organization.

fortunately, seemed reasonable at first sight to some western representatives. These proposals were defeated though the voting was close.

[18] Article VI.

III

The report and recommendations of the Special Committee were presented to the Economic and Social Council at its second session, which began on May 25. They were referred at once to the Committee of the Whole, against the wishes of the Soviet representatives who argued that there should first be a general discussion at a session of the Council. This was the usual course followed by Russian delegations: the full Council sessions attracted more public attention than the meetings of committees of the Council and from the time when Mr. Byrnes had insisted on more open sessions and more publicity at international meetings, the Russians, after initial hesitations, had seized the opportunity to obtain wider publicity for their point of view.

A week went by without any Council meeting: the whole time of the members was occupied with the meetings of the Committee of the Whole on refugees and displaced persons. The Russians reintroduced the amendments which they had failed to carry in the Special Committee. On the United States side we aimed at reducing the functions and powers of the Executive Committee of the proposed international refugee body. The outcome was more satisfactory to the western countries than to the Soviet Union and other countries of origin. The Russian amendments concerning propaganda in the camps, circulation of names of refugees to governments, and provision of information on conditions in the countries of origin, were rejected, and a series of amendments submitted by Mr. George L. Warren, designated by Ambassador Winant to represent the United States on the Committee of the Whole, reduced the powers of the Executive Committee, particularly by eliminating the clause requiring the Committee to visit refugee camps and to order the Director General to carry out any instructions based on the findings.[19]

During this session and subsequent sessions we strove to explain in detail in private conversations with some of the delegates the precise significance of each amendment that was proposed.

[19] Compare Article VI in the draft adopted on June 21 (United Nations Economic and Social Council, *Journal of the Economic and Social Council* [1st year], No. 29, p. 471–472) with that adopted by the Special Committee (Special Supplement, cited above, p. 76).

Some of the countries represented had no direct interest in refugees and displaced persons and their delegates were not familiar with the questions that arose. On some issues it was not practicable or advisable for our representatives to speak with complete frankness in committee, still less in open sessions of the Council. For instance it would have been unwise at that time to have said bluntly and openly in recorded meetings that we feared the consequences to relatives of refugees if the names compiled during the registration were turned over to the Soviet Union. But it was important to explain such matters in personal conversations with delegates who had had no previous experience of refugee questions.

The Committee of the Whole reported to the full Council session on June 21. It had revised and amended the draft constitution of an International Refugee Organization which the Special Committee had prepared in London. The Council adopted the draft but not until the Russian representatives had insisted on moving a series of amendments. As the British representative remarked:

> "Not one of the amendments put forward was new. All, except one, had been debated at least three times and all of them had been discussed in the Committee of the Whole." [20]

. The Council, which represented only about one-third of the United Nations, rejected the amendments and circulated the draft constitution to all member countries of the United Nations with a request for comments and suggestions which were to be discussed at the next meeting in September.

The chances of creating an international refugee organization in 1946 were seriously jeopardized by the insistence of the Soviet Union on reviving the same or similar amendments and repeating the same or similar arguments on every occasion permitted by the rules of procedure. All organs of the United Nations had to deal with large agenda on which refugees constituted only one item. Other business was delayed by the great lengths to which the debates on refugees were carried. Sooner or later a limit had to be set on these delays and in the summer of 1946 we were concerned over the difficulties of getting a completed and agreed draft constitution to the Assembly in time for it to act in 1946.

[20] United Nations Economic and Social Council, *Official Records* (1st year, 2d session), p. 125.

The next session of the Economic and Social Council opened on September 11. The Assembly was to open on October 23. There was no time to be lost, since the Council had to deal with a packed agenda.

But the Russians and Yugoslavs were determined to reopen every item once more on the Council in September and October. At this session, too, a Yugoslav chairman presided who, though a man of high integrity and attainments, would probably have been subjected to great pressure if he had attempted to curtail debate sharply. There was a serious danger, if not of an outright "filibuster," at least of a prolongation of debate which would have reduced the chances of placing a completed document before the Assembly in time to be acted on during its resumed session due to begin in October. It had become clear, too, by this time that the Soviet Union would reopen every issue at each successive meeting until the Organization was established and much time would be required in the Assembly before the final stages were reached.

Faced with this difficulty a change of approach became necessary if the IRO was to be established in time to be useful. The Soviet Union still advocated the establishment of the Organization and its delaying tactics seemed to be designed not to sabotage it but to try to shape it more in accord with its own desires. In these circumstances I suggested to Ambassador Winant, to Mr. George L. Warren and to the British representatives, Mr. Hector McNeil and Sir George Rendel, that we should discuss the points of difference privately with the Soviet representatives. This suggestion was accepted and we examined the issues in detail in prolonged meetings lasting two nights.[21]

The outcome was a temporary compromise on certain points on the explicit understanding that none of the parties would be in the slightest degree bound by it when the matter came before the Assembly. On the Anglo-American side the compromises affected the functions of the Executive Committee and the position of "unaccompanied children." The clause referred to above, which directed the Executive Committee to visit the camps in

[21] A press report spoke of "meetings starting at midnight in Kremlin fashion." Doubtless such journalistic gloss makes for livelier reading but the dull fact remains that midnight was the earliest hour at which the whole group was free from its other working engagements! Refugees made up only one of many subjects on which we were working simultaneously.

person and issue orders to the Director General in accord with
the findings, was reintroduced in a modified permissive form, the
word "shall" being changed to the word "may."

The issue concerning "unaccompanied children" or war orphans was difficult to judge. A number of unaccompanied children whose nationality was that of one of the countries of origin
were left in the countries of refuge. Some of them were orphans;
the whereabouts of the parents of others were unknown. Some
were taken care of by the friends of their dead parents in the
camps, others had been adopted into families, including in some
cases German families. The countries of origin demanded the
repatriation of all such children. There can be little doubt that
the United States, if placed in an analogous position, would have
made the same demand. However there were cases where, for
example, Polish orphans were cared for by relatives or close
friends of their families who refused repatriation and wished to
take the children with them when they were resettled in a new
land. Should these orphans be returned to a Poland in which
they might have no surviving relatives? There was no easy solution by any general formula, and the clause referring to the subject had been changed at each meeting. Even within the western
delegations there were differences of opinion on the question.

The first draft,[22] made in London, included as refugees "war
orphans or unaccompanied children who are outside their
countries of origin, when compelling reasons prevent their repatriation." This was obviously faulty since it would, strictly
interpreted, shut off from the services of the organization those
who were to be repatriated. At the ECOSOC meeting in June,
therefore, the words "pending their repatriation or" [23] were
inserted after the comma in the sentence. The countries of origin, however, continued vigorously to demand that orphans of
their nationality should be repatriated and were particularly
incensed at the idea that any of them should be adopted into
German families as it was claimed that some Polish children had
been. The temporary compromise draft at the second meeting
of ECOSOC declared that such children should be given "all
possible priority assistance, including, in the case of those whose

[22] Special Supplement, cited above, p. 67.
[23] *Journal of the Economic and Social Council,* cited above, p. 478.

nationality can be determined, assistance in repatriation, to which there should be no obstacles." [24]

Though there were misgivings within some of the western delegations this temporary compromise enabled the draft report and recommendations of the Economic and Social Council to be rapidly completed and transmitted to the Assembly in time for early consideration.

IV

The course of the negotiations now entered its last and longest lap. Formidable obstacles remained before the foundations of an International Refugee Organization could be completed. So far the main part of the work had been done in committees not exceeding eighteen members: now the results were to be examined in detail by a committee of fifty-two members which included representatives of many countries without any direct interest in or experience with refugees and displaced persons but whose votes counted equally with those of the countries of origin and the countries which exercised ultimate jurisdiction in the areas of refuge. The outlook was uncertain. The Assembly referred the subject to its Third Committee and at an early stage we found that no less than seventy-five amendments to the Charter as it came from the Economic and Social Council had been sent in.

The United States had been particularly fortunate in its chief representatives in the negotiations. On the Special Committee Mr. George L. Warren, State Department Advisor on Displaced Persons, and in the Economic and Social Council Ambassador John G. Winant and Mr. Warren, had been the representatives. In the final stage in the Assembly Mrs. Franklin D. Roosevelt was the United States representative on the Third Committee with Mr. Warren as her chief advisor and alternate on refugee questions. The wide international experience and prestige of Ambassador Winant and Mrs. Roosevelt combined with Mr. Warren's unrivaled grasp of every detail of the subject ensured that the United States position would be worthily repre-

[24] United Nations Economic and Social Council, Document E/245/Rev. 1, May 3, 1947, p. 43.

sented. When the Assembly's session opened the Ambassador designated me to assist Mrs. Roosevelt and Mr. Warren in every way possible.

From the flood of amendments it was clear that the Soviet Union and Yugoslavia, and to a lesser extent Poland, intended to raise again almost all the issues which had been fought over since the beginning of the year. Russian persistence was indeed an outstanding characteristic of most international negotiations in 1946: on no issue did it penetrate further into details than on refugees and displaced persons. The delegations surged to and fro again and again over the same ground: when pushed back at one point the Russians sometimes made progress at another, at least in the earlier stages, but whether or not they made progress anywhere they came back to the charge again and again, using the same tactics, repeating the same war cries, attacking the same strongholds with undiminished vigor.

It is unnecessary to enter in detail into the whole course of the discussions in the Assembly: much of it was a repetition of earlier debates, this time before an audience three times as large.[25] We suspected that at times the Russian representatives took the notes of their old speeches off the shelves, dusted them, and with slight variations of expression repeated them in substance.

Mr. Vyshinsky attended the second meeting to give the keynote speech for the Soviet Union. It was a lively performance. He gesticulated; he thumped the table as he spoke of "fascist elements" in the camps who "sought to use the genuine refugees as pawns in their aggressive imperialistic designs." He seemed to go even further than he had gone in January in opposing resettlement and calling for early repatriation. He gave long accounts of alleged incidents in Germany, Austria and Italy in which the British and American military authorities permitted traitors and quislings and "all sorts of dissident elements" to carry on activities in the refugee camps against the Soviet Union. He did not demand forced repatriation of refugees but he contended that the IRO should not assist those who did not wish to return to their native countries.[26] The account of his speech in

[25] For the student interested in all aspects of refugee questions this part of the negotiations may be one of the most significant parts of all because of the wider geographical participation in them. For a detailed account, see United Nations General Assembly, 3d Committee, *Official Records* (1st session, 2d part).

[26] The Soviet position was more precisely stated later by Mr. Gousev on an

the *Official Records* was compressed considerably and left out a number of additional points on which he expressed views that were not strictly in accord with the position of the Soviet delegations. He was at times carried away by his oratorical fervor and improvised hurriedly when he either lost sight of his notes or had gone beyond them. The speech contained stale accusations against the British and American military authorities which had been made much earlier, and had been investigated thoroughly and proved to be unfounded in some cases and based on magnification of small incidents in others. Detailed replies had been sent to Moscow months earlier. What Mr. Vyshinsky did was to pull out old papers prepared months before and rehash discredited charges with oratorical flourishes and with his eyes on the spectators as well as the delegates.[27] Notwithstanding the vituperative elements in his speech he almost appeared to be in a good humor and when I went out into the corridor during the translation of the speech I saw him surrounded by his advisors, the whole group convulsed with laughter, and apparently pleased with the show that he had put on in the committee room.

The subsequent proceedings were dull by comparison. Day after day the committee ploughed through the scores of amendments which reopened every issue that had been voted on in earlier meetings since the beginning of the year. The old arguments were trotted out again and however boring they might be the United States and western European delegations could never afford to relax or be content with perfunctory replies. For there were new listeners at the table and their votes would determine the outcome. As yet it could not be foreseen which way some of them would turn.

Under more normal conditions many details might have been turned over to subcommittees. The Soviet representatives did

amendment which he moved. He "did not mean to propose a form of compulsory repatriation but simply insisted that refugees who refused such repatriation should not be the concern of the organization." *Ibid.* p. 172.

[27] At a later meeting Mrs. Roosevelt pointed out that "recent reexamination of these charges had still failed to substantiate them. A similar list of accusations had been presented to the United States European theatre commander by the commander-in-chief of the USSR occupation force in Germany in June, 1946. In October the latter had been advised that a thorough examination had identified only one of the organizations mentioned, the Ukrainian Aid Committee, which had been dissolved in September, 1945. None of the organizations listed had any official status or recognition whatsoever and none of the persons listed was known in the U.S. zone of Germany." *Ibid.,* p. 263.

indeed propose the appointment of a subcommittee. But we had learned from long experience that subcommittees are useless, except occasionally for drafting, in international organizations in which the Soviet Union takes part. The defeat of a Russian proposal in a subcommittee never settled anything: the same proposal was introduced into the main committee and the same or similar speeches were made again. Hence we and the British worked for the defeat of the attempt to set up a subcommittee. It was cumbrous and exhausting to work through 75 amendments in a committee of 52 members but there was no alternative. There are no short cuts in negotiating with the Soviet Union.

General speeches took up much time at the outset. Here was a familiar dilemma. How much time should be given to refuting the wholesale charges made by the Russians against the United Kingdom and the United States? Such charges might have been safely ignored if they had been heard before by representatives of all the countries in the Assembly. But since only one-third of the countries had been represented at previous meetings it would have been unsafe to have ignored them entirely. Nevertheless the replies were restrained and confined mainly to statements of fact. Mrs. Roosevelt was the embodiment of a spirit of integrity and was an ideal representative for meeting insinuations of bad faith. The United Kingdom representative, Mr. Beswick, reflected the United Kingdom's loyalty to allies when, in reply to Mr. Vyshinsky's attack on General Anders' army, he pointed out first that they did not come in the scope of IRO and second that ". . . they had been among the first to fight fascism and the United Kingdom was proud to be able to repay its debt to them." [28] The significance of the last sentence was not lost on the Russian representatives.

From the time of Mr. Vyshinsky's speech it was clear that the Soviet delegation to the Assembly would pay no attention to the temporary compromise reached on the Economic and Social Council and would strive to reintroduce almost every amendment which it had proposed and failed to carry at previous meetings. There was no breach of faith whatever in this: it had been clearly understood on all sides at the meeting of the Economic and Social Council that no party to the temporary compromise would be bound by it at the meeting of the Assembly.

[28] *Ibid.*, p. 97.

Nevertheless the United States and British delegations did not consider it necessary to undo on their side all the concessions made in the summer. The mandatory term "shall" had been removed from the clause concerning direct investigations in the camps by the Executive Committee or its commissions, and the permissive clause which remained would not be likely to be misused unless the countries of origin obtained a majority on the Executive Committee. Even if the permissive clause were taken out there would be nothing to prevent the Committee from undertaking such investigations. The only safeguard was to maintain a majority of votes in the organization on the side of the countries holding the views of the United-States and the United Kingdom on this matter, and that could not be legislated for!

An exception was made, however, on the clause relating to "unaccompanied children." The representatives of the Low Countries had been uneasy over this perplexing issue and we agreed to support them in any amendment which would provide a better safeguard for the interests of the children concerned. It was desired particularly to prevent compulsory repatriation of orphans already adopted happily into families, and to make it possible to postpone repatriation to avoid interruption of education. A drafting committee made up of representatives of France, the Netherlands, Belgium, Norway and Poland brought in a revised amendment which set an age limit of sixteen years for "unaccompanied children" and specified that they should "be given all possible priority assistance, including, normally, assistance in repatriation in the case of those whose nationality can be determined." [29] This amendment was vigorously opposed by the Soviet Union and Yugoslavia, Mr. Gousev particularly attacking the idea of an age limit. But the Poles, who had the largest number of unaccompanied children in the camps, and who understood the difficulties of the question where Jewish children were concerned, voted with the majority.

It is unnecessary to summarize the discussions on issues already treated in detail in the analysis of previous meetings. But it should not be overlooked that the difficulties of defeating some of the Russian proposals were greater at this meeting than in

[29] United Nations General Assembly, *Official Records: Resolutions* (1st session, 2d part), p. 112.

winked into making concessions to the Soviet Union in the naive belief that the Russians might in that way be induced to join. Thus Mr. James B. Reston said:

> "Sometimes concessions made by the West to meet the objections of the Soviet negotiators merely result in the weakening of the international institutions, without winning the support of the Soviet Union. The protracted negotiations over the constitution of the International Refugee Organization were a case in point. The Russians took an active interest in these negotiations. The other powers weakened the constitution of that organization considerably in order to meet Soviet objections, but in the end the Soviet Union did not join. There is now in operation, consequently an organization that not only does not have the membership of the Soviet Union but is much weaker than it would have been but for Moscow's amendments." [30]

Confident assertions are often made by journalists and politicians about Russian motives and intentions, but it is always difficult and usually impossible to test their validity. For over two and a half years I talked frequently with Russian officials about refugees and many other topics. I have argued with Russian representatives, and listened to hundreds of speeches by them in committees. But I cannot claim to do more than frame hypotheses about the motives and intentions of those who guide the destinies of the Soviet Union.

In international affairs there is a danger in excessively subtle as well as in excessively simplified interpretations of the motives and intentions of others. Throughout 1946 the Russian representatives consistently spoke in favor of the establishment of an international organization to deal with refugees and displaced persons. But they opposed with increasing vigor the idea of using the international organization to assist in the resettlement of refugees who for political reasons refused to be repatriated. They also showed reluctance to enter into any arrangements that would require them to make a financial contribution towards the organization. My hypothesis is simply that the Russians meant what they said, that they sincerely desired that a temporary international body should be set up, with the object of registering refugees and displaced persons, arranging for their repatriation and helping to maintain them during the inevitable delay

[30] Reston, James B. "Negotiating with the Russians." *Harper's Magazine*, August 1947, p. 102.

between registration and repatriation, and, finally, that they would have joined the organization if it had been confined to the performance of these tasks alone. But their efforts so to restrict its scope were frustrated and they decided later that the constitution of the organization which was adopted on December 14 was so little to their liking that they preferred to remain outside it and induced or put pressure on the other countries of origin to follow the same course, hoping, and for a time expecting, that it would be impossible to obtain ratification from a sufficient number of countries to bring it into existence.[81]

Some support may be found for this hypothesis in the attitude of the Soviet representatives towards the General Assembly's resolution of January 29, 1946, for which they themselves voted. They seemed to deprecate references to the resolution in the later discussions. Most of the resolution was consistent with Russian policy. Even the principle that refugees who did not desire repatriation should not be compelled to go back was never challenged by them; in fact they explicitly affirmed it several times. I suspect the embarrassing section of the resolution to them was the single statement in the middle of paragraph c(ii) that, "The future of such refugees or displaced persons [*i.e.* those who objected to repatriation] shall become the concern of whatever international body may be recognized or established. . . ." It is possible that for this reason they regretted having voted for the Assembly resolution.

It is only on this point, if at all, that the consistency of the Russian position on refugees can be questioned. As we have seen the Soviet delegates strove unsuccessfully to amend the Assembly resolution, then formally accepted it but subsequently tried again to undermine one of its provisions. Whether defensible or not their attitude is hardly surprising. They and the other countries of origin were in effect being asked to join and to pay contributions to an organization one of whose functions would be to assist in the resettlement of refugees who disliked the governments of the Soviet Union and of other countries of origin. Is it certain that the United States Congress would agree

81 Some Americans feared a similar outcome. After one of the meetings Senator Vandenberg remarked skeptically to me and to one of my colleagues: "Do you people think you will ever get fifteen countries to sign that?" Later, in Washington he himself played a distinguished part in helping to secure United States ratification.

the meetings of the smaller Economic and Social Council and the results on many issues were by no means a foregone conclusion. Even the Latin American countries were divided on some issues and the Arab countries were highly suspicious of the United States because of its policy—if it could be said to have had one—on Palestine. At the outset I found it extraordinarily difficult in private conversations to convince Arab representatives that the IRO would have nothing to do with the question of admitting Jews to Palestine. It was only by the most strenuous efforts over six weeks that we and the British and western European countries were able to win the necessary votes to stave off the scores of hostile amendments moved by the Soviet Union and Yugoslavia.

The relations between the Soviet Union and the eastern and central European countries were considerably looser than—except in respect to Yugoslavia—they became later. First it may be said that Yugoslavia sometimes pursued an even stiffer line than the Soviet Union. There was never an abler, more sincere and more relentless high priest of repatriation and of the apprehension of "traitors, quislings and war criminals" than Mr. Mattes. Occasionally the Russians were willing to compromise on details when Mr. Mattes was not: once the position was reversed. Notwithstanding the identity of their attitudes on most questions the private relations between the Russian and Yugoslav delegations could not be called close or cordial: Mr. Mattes and Mr. Tepliakov were not on the best of terms.

The Poles had not thrown off the last shreds of independence at that time. They had a bigger stake in the refugee question than any other country of origin. Some of the Russian proposals were not in their interests. A particularly fatuous amendment moved by Mr. Tepliakov to the effect that all expenses of repatriation should be borne by Germany, though no doubt its motive was to enable the USSR to avoid paying any contribution to the IRO, would have been a hindrance rather than a help to Polish repatriation. In a snap vote this amendment was passed with the communist member of the Polish delegation voting for it. But when the attention of the Polish delegation as a whole was drawn to it, their representative voted against it on reconsideration. Most members of the Polish delegation were personally humane and sincere in their attitude towards the refugees.

Czechoslovakia had little or no direct concern with the refugee question. Its own refugees had been speedily repatriated. Like Poland its delegation represented a political coalition. When we were hard put to it for votes on some critical amendments I noticed that the Czech representative who was sitting on the Third Committee in that part of the session was voting regularly with the Soviet Union on all issues. After attempting unsuccessfully to convince him that it was hardly in Czechoslovakia's interest to support all the Soviet amendments, I went to Mr. Masaryk and explained some of the issues that we were facing in the Third Committee, adding that I did not understand why the representative of Czechoslovakia had recently been taking sides invariably with the Russians on these issues. Mr. Masaryk looked surprised. "Is he doing that?" he exclaimed. He rose suddenly and left the room. During the rest of the session the Czechs abstained from voting on controversial issues and in the final plenary session of the Assembly they abstained when the decisive vote was taken.

Of the 48 meetings in the Third Committee of the Assembly in 1946 by far the greater number were given over wholly to the discussion of refugees and displaced persons. But even when the report was adopted on December 12, the discussion had not ended. For several hours in the plenary sessions it was resumed. This time Mr. Gromyko delivered the set piece for the Soviet Union in quiet, almost academic tones but in substance similar to that which his more entertaining colleague, Mr. Vyshinsky, had delivered at the outset to the Committee. Fortunately no attempt was made to move any further amendments and the Assembly vote adopting the constitution of the IRO and calling for ratifications was passed decisively, only Yugoslavia and Poland joining the Russians.

V

The Soviet Union did not join the International Refugee Organization. There are those who assert that it never intended to do so and who imply that the western negotiators were hood-

that the United States should join an international body one of whose functions would be to resettle elsewhere American citizens who did not wish to return to the United States? The remarks of some congressmen when a London magistrate promptly and quite properly released Mr. Gerhardt Eisler and permitted him to proceed eastward do not support an affirmative answer.

Possibly, in this intolerant age only the United Kingdom and the Scandinavian countries would be capable of the enlightened generosity which alone could inspire the government of a country to help a group of citizens hostile to it to transfer their allegiance to another country. However that may be, it is certain that the spirit of toleration in the USSR is too feeble and flickering to count in a question of this sort. Reasoning on such lines I argued in a memorandum in June 1946 on the financial aspects of the IRO that the countries of origin of the refugees should be required to contribute towards the expenses of maintenance and repatriation but should be exempted from the obligation to contribute towards the expenses of resettlement. This proposal was not accepted but I still hold that it would have been the best course to follow.

Finally there is one consideration that might have out-weighed all others and induced the Russians to join the IRO: that is, the simple desire to see what was going on in the organization and to influence its actions directly. Moscow had nothing to lose but its financial contribution by doing so and if it had brought in with it the other countries of origin it could have pressed for substantial representation on the Executive Committee and at least delayed decisions that were not to its liking. In this way it could have taken advantage of any of the supposed weaknesses in the constitution which Mr. Reston detects without specifying, and which, if they existed, were no longer important when the countries of origin were not there to exploit them.

The account of the negotiations in these pages should dispose of suggestions made after the event that the American and British negotiators were outmaneuvered by the Russians into making concessions that weakened the IRO, in the mistaken belief that by doing so they could induce the Soviet Union to join the organization. In the negotiations we were guided by a single aim: to obtain the approval of the United Nations Assembly for the constitution of an international refugee organization and its recommendation that all members of the United Nations should join it. After immense efforts the aim was achieved. It was to achieve it and not to persuade the Russians to join the IRO that concessions had to be made, none of which, however, encroached on the liberties of the refugees and their right to choose freely between repatriation and resettlement. We were always fighting against time. A temporary compromise in the Economic and Social Council in late September and a compromise on the form of limitation of debate in the Assembly in November enabled the work to be completed in time. It can fairly be said that subsequent experience has revealed no important weakness in the constitution of the IRO.

Nonetheless, we desired and made known our desire, that the countries of origin of the refugees, including the Soviet Union, should join the new organization. If they had done so the work of the western representatives on it would have been rendered more difficult. But we had sufficient confidence in the soundness and strength of our cause to be prepared to fight the issues over again, if necessary, on the Council and the Executive Committee of the IRO, leaving the outcome to be determined by the majority of the countries represented on the organization. Thus the record is clear: the responsibility for the failure of the countries of origin to cooperate after 1946 in the international solution of the refugee problem rests with them alone.

The great deterioration since 1946, not only in the relations between the west and the Soviet Union but also in the political life of Washington, has fostered the growth of a mythical view of the attitude and tactics of American negotiators in the late war and earlier postwar periods. It may be useful, therefore, in concluding, to emphasize that the principal American and British negotiators throughout 1946, Mrs. Franklin D. Roosevelt, Ambassador Winant and Mr. George L. Warren for the United States, and Mr. Hector McNeil, Mr. Beswick and Sir George Rendel for the United Kingdom were guided first of all by an unwavering pursuit of the interests of the refugees and displaced persons themselves. Whatever concessions might be made—and it is a naive or obtuse view of international affairs that supposes it possible to effect great enterprises without compromise—they must not endanger the liberties and welfare of the individuals for whom the negotiations were being held. Given this funda-

mental condition there was another duty. We were entering
on a new period of international negotiation. The representatives of almost all countries were gathered round the table. Beyond the immediate questions under discussion lay the grand
aim to do everything humanly possible to use the new international machinery for the peaceful and orderly adjustment of
international disputes on any question. During the war the main
affairs of the world had been ordered by a few great powers:
since it ended each nation, great or small, was exercising an equal
vote in the deliberations of international bodies. In these circumstances the duty of national representatives was not confined
to the discharge of immediate business: they had to consider the
effect of their words, the effect of the tone and temper of debate
generally, on the prospects for future international harmony.
The Soviet and some of the other eastern representatives approached international negotiations in a disconcerting manner.
On refugees their whole outlook was based on a different philosophy from that which has prevailed, not indeed exclusively, but
among a majority of people in the western countries. Our negotiators were talking with men whose mercy was not as our
mercy, nor their justice as our justice, nor their idea of compromise as our idea of compromise. It is therefore to our lasting
credit that, while firmly safeguarding the interests of the refugees,
our negotiators did not allow themselves to be provoked into
verbal retaliations in kind but were content to counter misrepre-
sentation with sober and dignified statements of fact and, so far
as they appealed to the emotions, rested their appeal on the infinite value of the individual and on the sense of compassion for
the homeless victims of a world catastrophe. In the international
tone and temper of 1951 the student of international affairs will
lose nothing by examining again the record of these discussions
in 1946 and noting the tone and temper in which the western
representatives then negotiated with the Russians and others
and laid the foundations for an international organization which
since then has re-established and given new hope to a million
people whom the war had rendered homeless and destitute.

NEGOTIATING ON THE BALKANS

Mark F. Ethridge was vice president and general manager of the Courier Journal *and the* Louisville Times *from 1936 to 1942 and has been publisher since 1942. He visited the Balkans for the Department of State in 1945, was appointed American Delegate to the United Nations Commission to Study Greek Border Disputes in 1947 and was Chairman of the United States Advisory Commission on Information in 1948.*

C. E. Black has been a member of the Princeton University Department of History since 1939. He was with the Department of State in Washington, D.C. and in Eastern Europe from 1943 to 1946 and accompanied Mark Ethridge on his mission in 1945. He was Advisor to the United States Delegation, United Nations Commission Concerning Greek Frontier Incidents in 1947. He is co-author (with E. C. Helmreich) of Twentieth Century Europe: A History *(1950).*

Negotiating on the

Balkans, 1945-1947

BY MARK ETHRIDGE AND C. E. BLACK

The story of the American-Russian negotiations concerning the Balkans after World War II is the story of the first important lessons learned by the United States about the postwar trend of Soviet policy. It was indeed a new trend in Soviet policy which was being developed during the first postwar years, despite the many old and tested elements which comprised it. It was new because the circumstances in which the Soviet Union found itself were unprecedented: for the first time since the defeat of Napoleon did central and western Europe lack the organization and power which for so long had served to counterbalance Russian influence.

Yet to say that Soviet policy after 1945 was a reconstitution of old and tested elements to meet the new opportunities of the postwar period, is not to say that its strategy and tactics could have been predicted with certainty. Many persons well-informed on Soviet affairs saw good reason to believe that the Soviet Union might of its own accord adopt a moderate policy after the defeat of Germany. It appeared indeed that the reconstruction of the vast areas of the Soviet Union destroyed as a result of the war would alone constitute sufficient reason for the Soviet Union to devote its main energies to domestic affairs for many years to come. It was primarily as a result of considerations such as these that American plans for the Balkans, as for Europe as a whole, provided for a minimum direct participation on the part of the United States in the implementation of a postwar settlement.

Such an estimate of Soviet policy was moreover well adapted to the other foreign and domestic demands on the United States Government. At the time of Germany's collapse, it still seemed likely that most of the United States military strength would have to be moved to the Pacific theater. Upon Japan's unexpectedly swift defeat, the great popular demand for an immediate return to "normalcy" led to the rapid demobilization of United States armed forces and to the sudden discontinuance of the Lend-Lease aid which had become one of the United States principal instruments in the field of foreign policy. If President Roosevelt before V-E Day questioned his ability to arouse sustained American interest in foreign affairs after the war's end, this task seemed well nigh impossible for his successor after the world-shaking events which culminated on V-J Day only a few months later.

Despite the paradoxical weakness of the resources at the disposal of American policy in Europe so soon after World War II, the general acceptance in responsible circles of the view that the Soviet Union would emerge from the war in a cooperative mood gave rise to the most optimistic expectations. According to this dominant American view, the Charter of the United Nations, which came into force on October 24, 1945, provided a framework within which the affairs of the Balkan states could be handled with due consideration for the interests of all parties. In this view, the Charter made ample provision for protecting the security interests of the Soviet Union in a region such as southeastern Europe. Through their participation in the United Nations, freely elected governments in the Balkans would be able to take advantage of the financial assistance of the International Bank for Reconstruction and Development and the International Monetary Fund, both of which came into existence on

December 27, 1945. Through the many other specialized agencies of the United Nations, in addition to the normal prewar channels, these states would find the means of solving their economic and social problems and would regain the road to a higher standard of living along which they had made such substantial progress between the two world wars. In the Balkan settlement which this optimistic view envisaged, as in the rest of Europe, the responsibilities of the United States and of the Soviet Union would be primarily those of leading members of the United Nations. American participation in Balkan affairs might well be greater than it had been before World War II, as would be that of the Soviet Union as well, but this participation would in any case take place within the framework established by the Charter. Such, in rough summary, was the view of those who saw the United Nations as the principal basis for a new international order.

This international order might indeed have been established in the Balkans had the great powers been in agreement as to ends and means, but such was not to be the case. The optimistic American view failed to take into consideration the long-standing factors of power and interest which dominate the eastern European scene, or at best it mistakenly assumed that these traditional behavior patterns could be easily abandoned in favor of the new and untried international order. That such an optimistic view was ever entertained may be explained in large part by the haze of distance and inexperience which has always tended to conceal the realities of eastern European politics from the relatively disinterested American eye. It may be explained in this instance more particularly, however, by the confidence in Soviet cooperation which the experiences of the wartime relationship inspired. To the leaders of American policy, who had been engaged in European affairs in a responsible way only since 1941, the friendly spirit of the Russians during the war appeared as the norm while the prewar Soviet attitude, never clearly understood, faded into the distant background. It was only gradually, and as a result of many painful experiences, that the truth of the matter became clear. It was in fact the wartime collaboration of the Russians which was the exception, and once the emergency was over the policy demanded by Lenin's and Stalin's interpretation of Marxism and of Russian national interests was resumed.

The Soviet leaders naturally saw the postwar situation in an entirely different light. Considering as they did that all non-Communist states were in principle enemies, they regarded the wartime collaboration against the Axis as scarcely more than an alliance with one group of enemies against a more immediately dangerous group. Once this policy had served its purpose, as had in their time the policies of vigorous participation in the League of Nations and of the Nazi-Soviet pact, it could be discarded with few regrets. Strong hints of this return to an orthodox Soviet policy were given in the speeches of Stalin, Molotov and other Russian leaders on the eve of the election held in February 1946, and Zhdanov's significant speech on "The International Situation" in November 1947, finally defined the Soviet-Western antagonism in unmistakable terms. The substance of the Soviet outlook as expressed in these and other statements of policy, was that as a result of World War II the position of the Soviet Union had been greatly strengthened as compared with that of the non-Communist powers. The defeat of Germany, Italy and Japan provided unrivaled opportunities for the expansion of Soviet power, and it was the duty of the Soviet Union to press this advantage to the full. In this operation the countries of eastern Europe played a particularly important role, since they had been liberated as early as the winter of 1944–45 by the Soviet Army and had immediately come under the influence of the Soviet way of life. Western commentators will continue to disagree whether the Soviet leaders have in fact been guided by Marxist doctrine, or merely use its terminology to justify policies motivated by the more conventional demands of Russian national interest. It can no longer be questioned, however, that the Soviet Union has pursued a policy of gaining complete dominance over the Balkan states.

In the light of this background, the problem of this chapter is to describe from the American viewpoint the negotiations which took place with the Soviet Union concerning the Balkan states during the first postwar years. The story starts with the wartime negotiations concerning the Balkan states culminating in the Yalta agreements, which were characterized on the American side by the preponderant view that the Russians would give precedence to domestic reconstruction and hence would not pursue an aggressive foreign policy. It ends with the formula-

tion of the Truman Doctrine in March 1947, which made resistance to Communist aggression the cornerstone of American
policy. The drama of this story lies in the process by which the
United States came to understand the nature of Soviet policy,
and in the significant role in this process of the negotiations concerning the Balkan states.

I

The Balkan states played a relatively small role in inter-allied
relations during the greater part of the war. As the Russian
armies began to reach beyond the Soviet frontiers, however, and
the western allies established themselves firmly on French soil,
the question of the political future of the Balkan states became
a matter of immediate concern. Yugoslavia and Greece were
represented by governments-in-exile which played more than a
nominal role in United Nations affairs, while Albania was largely
neutralized by geography and by political confusion. There remained the question of armistice terms for the three Axis satellites—Rumania, Bulgaria and Hungary—and it was to this problem that the Allies turned their attention in 1944.

Early in 1944 it seemed possible that the satellites might rise
up against their German allies and thus hasten the Axis defeat.
To this end the American, British and Soviet Governments issued a declaration to the three Balkan states and to Finland on
May 12th. This declaration warned them of "the inevitability
of a crushing Nazi defeat," and predicted that "the longer they
continue at war in collaboration with Germany the more disas-
trous will be the consequences to them and the more rigorous
will be the terms which will be imposed upon them." This attempt to mitigate the unconditional surrender terms met with
no success, but at least it served as an indication of cooperation on
the part of the Big Three on Balkan problems.

It was not until the Soviet armies advanced into the Balkan
region itself that concrete action could be taken with regard to
the satellites. In the negotiations of the resulting armistice terms,
the Russians had the advantage of being on the spot and of being
more fully informed on the local situation. At the same time,
they were able to use as a precedent the arrangement of the three
powers concluded in 1943 with regard to Italy. In Italy authority

was shared by the United Kingdom and the United States, while the Soviet Union had only a nominal role. In the armistice terms drawn up for the Balkan satellites this situation was now reversed, and the term "Allied (Soviet) High Command" was devised to indicate that the Soviet military authorities would act in the name of the victorious allies. Concluded in the course of the last year of the war—Rumania (September 12, 1944), Bulgaria (October 28, 1944) and Hungary (January 20, 1945)— these armistice agreements gave the occupying Soviet authorities broad political and economic powers. They not only supervised the redeployment of the armed forces of the defeated satellites and the administration of transportations and supplies, but also gave their governments political guidance. Soviet influence in the Balkans was based initially on Russian military preponderance in that region, but the armistice terms served to legalize and reaffirm this influence in the name of the entire United Nations coalition.

No less significant than this formal recognition of the Soviet position in the Balkans during the last year of the war, was the jockeying for spheres of influence among the allies which went on behind the scenes. It was becoming clear to many persons responsible for the United Nations policy that joint Allied administration of occupied areas would be impossible of attainment outside of Germany and Austria, and a trend inevitably developed to place the various conquered territories under the jurisdiction of the powers whose armies overran them as they pressed on towards Germany. This trend has already been mentioned in connection with the complementary position of western and Soviet authority in the Italian and Axis satellite armistice terms, respectively. At the same time, as regards the Balkans, a movement developed for a more formal assignment of spheres of influence pending the defeat of Germany. The British had long been concerned with the postwar status of the eastern Mediterranean region. Since this was an area of their special responsibility in Allied military councils, they had taken the initiative in the spring of 1944 in offering to recognize a controlling Soviet interest in Rumania in return for a corresponding recognition of British interest in Greece. For a while the United States had resisted this balance-of-power approach, on the ground that it would sow the seeds of great-power rivalry after the war. American objections were nevertheless overcome in the end by the personal intervention of Churchill, and a more comprehensive division of spheres was finally agreed to.

The final arrangements were made in Moscow in October 1944, by direct negotiation between the British and Soviet statesmen. It was agreed that the Russians would enjoy predominant influence in Rumania, Hungary and Bulgaria, while the United Kingdom would have a similar position of influence in Greece. In Yugoslavia, on the other hand, the two powers were to share influence on an equal basis. This agreement thus served to protect British interests in the Mediterranean, and it also drew a dividing line which may have served to reduce Western-Soviet frictions in this region during the immediate postwar period. Moreover it was not intended as a permanent settlement, but rather as one which was binding only for the transitional period pending the defeat of Germany. It was in fact negotiated at the time the armistice terms for the Axis satellites were being drafted, and these reflected the same tendency to acknowledge at least a temporary Soviet political predominance in the countries liberated by the Red Army. At the same time, it can hardly be questioned that this partition of the Balkans into two spheres of influence contained the seeds of many later difficulties. Particularly important is the fact that it was negotiated by the British and the Russians alone, without direct American participation. The American Ambassador in Moscow sat in on the negotiations only as an observer. From this circumstance and from western concessions on the armistice terms the Soviet statesmen may well have drawn the conclusion, despite official American assertions to the contrary, that the United States had no particular interest in the Balkans and that they need concern themselves only with British power. At the same time, the significance after 1947 of the firm western position in Greece and of the ambiguous status of Yugoslavia between east and west give the agreement of October 1944, a stature considerably greater than that of mere wartime expediency.

While the Soviet position in Hungary, Rumania and Bulgaria was being established by formal negotiations with the western allies, in Yugoslavia and Albania the initiative was taken by the partisan fighters. These vigorous guerrilla organizations, directed by Communist-led coalitions known as National Liberation Fronts, pursued aggressive tactics which placed them in a dominant position in their respective countries when the Germans were finally forced to withdraw. Tito in Yugoslavia and Hoxha in Albania outfought and outwitted their nationalist rivals to the extent that by the end of the war they were receiving material aid from the western allies as well as the political support of the Soviet Union. Similarly in Greece a National Liberation Front, better known by its Greek initials EAM, gained during the war the position of very extensive influence which it used so effectively in the early postwar years against the Greek Government and British forces. While in Yugoslavia and Albania the policies of the Soviet Union and the western allies were in substantial agreement by the end of the war, in Greece the Communist-led partisans served as an aggressive, unofficial instrument of Soviet policy at a time when the country was formally assigned to the United Kingdom as a sphere of influence.

The transition from wartime negotiations to the more permanent agreements for a postwar settlement was a gradual one, and it is frequently difficult to judge at what point the United Nations transferred their attention from the defeat of Germany which had for so long been their major concern to the establishment of a durable peace. So far as the Balkan region is concerned, it appears that the conference held at Yalta in February 1945, marks this turning point. It is therefore fateful that these discussions should have been held at a time when Soviet bargaining power in eastern Europe was so much stronger than that of the western allies. The Soviet statesmen possessed the important advantages conceded to them by the armistice terms with the Axis satellite states and by the British-Russian agreement of October 1944, and won for them by the partisan forces of Tito in Yugoslavia and Hoxha in Albania. They also knew that the war would soon be over and that their troops would be in firm possession of all of eastern Europe north of Greece and of much of central Europe as well. Moreover they may well have received the definite impression by this time that the United States had no particular concern for Balkan affairs, and that the United Kingdom would be satisfied if its traditional interests in the eastern Mediterranean received formal recognition.

The western allies were in no comparable position to bargain for influence in eastern Europe at this time. Their primary concern was the necessity of continuing the war effort against Japan as soon as Germany was defeated, and to this end of redeploying the major part of their military forces to the Pacific theater. Moreover the British were already aware of the economic straits which would limit their bargaining power in world affairs at the end of the war, while the American leaders were sensitive to the danger that opinion in the United States might well impose severe limits on a vigorous American policy as soon as the fighting was over.

Under these circumstances any specific and detailed agreement might have tended to work to the Russian advantage in the Balkans, as the terms of the armistice agreements with the Axis satellite states had already demonstrated. It is consequently significant that the western leaders now proposed a general statement of principles which served the purpose of establishing broad postwar objectives for United Nations policy in the liberated states. While it is difficult to determine the extent to which the western leaders foresaw the development of events, it is noteworthy that they adopted the course of obtaining Soviet agreement to broad policy objectives to which the latter might later be held accountable. In the statement agreed to at Yalta, entitled the "Declaration on Liberated Europe," the Big Three declared "their mutual agreement to concert during the temporary period of instability in liberated Europe the policies of their three Governments in assisting the peoples liberated from the domination of Nazi satellite states of Europe to solve by democratic means their pressing political and economic problems."

The Declaration went on to affirm the right of all peoples "to create democratic institutions of their own choice," and set forth the principal areas in which the liberated states would require assistance. Since the terms of the Declaration later became the subject of widespread controversy, and indeed became the principal issue in the Balkan negotiations, the text of the more important passages deserves quotation in full. The core of the Declaration was the pledge that, "the three Governments will jointly assist the people in any European liberated state or former Axis satellite state in Europe where in their judgment conditions require (a) to establish conditions of internal peace; (b) to carry out emergency measures for the relief of distressed peoples; (c) to form interim governmental authorities broadly representative of all democratic elements in the population and pledged to the earliest possible establishment through free elections of governments responsible to the will of the people; and (d) to facilitate where necessary the holding of such elections." Provision was further made for consultation on the part of the three governments whenever it appeared to be necessary for the discharge of the joint responsibilities set forth in the Declaration.

The Declaration on Liberated Europe has attracted much criticism since its publication on February 11, 1945. The principal criticism has to do with the vague and general character of its drafting, which gives it the appearance more of a hastily drawn up press release than of a negotiated instrument intended to bind the policies of three great powers in guiding the destinies of millions of liberated peoples during the difficult postwar period. Published accounts of the Yalta conference indeed confirm this impression of casualness as regards this particular Declaration, in contrast to the legal precision with which the Security Council voting formula was drafted. Moreover the text of the Declaration itself contains many terms, such as "democratic elements in the population" and "free elections," on the meaning of which Soviet and western opinion had been for many years in general disagreement. The facile use without any definition of such controversial terms would alone be sufficient reason to doubt the soundness of the document as a basis for joint action. At the same time it should be pointed out, as already noted above, that under the circumstances in which the western leaders found themselves a vague general statement pitched at a high level of hope may have served their purposes better than a precise document in which only limited gains might have been made for the western viewpoint.

The advantages to the Soviet Union of precise agreements relative to Balkan affairs at this juncture are well illustrated by the recommendation which the three governments made at Yalta with regard to Yugoslavia. It was recommended that certain members of the Yugoslav government-in-exile in London enter the National Liberation Front government led by Tito in Yugoslavia, and that certain members of the prewar Yugoslav parliament enter the Assembly of National Liberation established in Yugoslavia by the partisans during the war. While in form this solution appeared to represent a compromise between the Communist regime in Yugoslavia and the government-in-exile, in substance it meant a formal transfer of support on the part of the western powers from the latter to the former. The circumstances which subsequently led to the break between Tito and Stalin may not have been entirely unforeseen by the western leaders at Yalta, but at that time the decisions made with regard to Yugoslavia represented very substantial concessions to the Soviet point of view.

If the Declaration on Liberated Europe established the objectives of the western Allies regarding the postwar settlement in the Balkans, their ability to implement them in the face of Soviet resistance began before long to decline very rapidly. It is true that for about a year after the defeat of Germany, the United States and the United Kingdom continued to exert a considerable influence on Balkan affairs. Indeed, until the defeat of Japan in August it was by no means certain to what extent the United States would in fact withdraw from European affairs, and during this period Soviet policy in the Balkans exhibited great caution. Even after V-J Day, when the rapid demobilization of American armed forces and the abrupt discontinuance of Lend-Lease marked the end of the principal sources of United States bargaining power, a number of possibilities remained for the exertion of some influence on Soviet policy in the Balkans. The Soviet Union desired to obtain recognition for its clients, as well as agreement on the peace terms for the former Axis satellites, and the withholding of its accord on these matters remained an important American instrument of pressure.

The weakness of the western position in the Balkans was well illustrated by the Potsdam conference in July and August 1945, where the first attempts were made after the defeat of Germany to implement the program adopted at Yalta. The substance of American and British pressure at this stage was an agreement for a revision of the procedure of the Allied Control Commissions in Rumania, Bulgaria and Hungary. Certain restrictions which had been placed by the Soviet chairmen of the three Allied Control Commissions on the movement and supply of official American and British personnel were liberalized, and provision was made for greater western participation in the decisions of the Control Commissions. In practice this latter provision had little effect, since by this time the implementation of the Communist program in the Balkans had already been transferred to the hands of the local governments. The relaxation on travel restrictions was carried into effect, however, and was in fact extended to western journalists with temporary but significant results for western public opinion. Certain technical agreements in principle were also reached at Potsdam regarding the disposition of western-owned oil equipment in Rumania, and the broader question of the use of Allied property for satellite reparations.

While these minor agreements had little bearing on the balance of power in the Balkans, further provision was made at Potsdam for the negotiation of the outstanding issues in that region. This was the establishment of the Council of Foreign Ministers, which had as its "immediate important task" the drafting of peace treaties for the Axis satellite states. It was, indeed, the first meeting of the Council in London from September 11 to October 3, 1945, which revealed the crisis in American-Russian relations regarding the Balkans. The discussions at Yalta and Potsdam had been held in a spirit of wartime cooperation, and a substantial degree of agreement on broad objectives had been reached. In London the time had come to draft the permanent settlement, and the full extent of the divergence of policies now became apparent. The basic problem at London was not really the question of peace terms, since the main issues as regards territory and reparations had already been settled in the armistice agreements. It was rather the question whether, in the language of the Yalta Declaration, the Balkan states should have "governments responsible to the will of the people" established through free elections, or should become full-fledged satellites of the Soviet Union. In a larger sense, the Balkan problem thus became a test case in the struggle to win an international order in which sovereign states would participate freely in the United Nations, rather than a world dominated by two rival coalitions led by the United States and the Soviet Union.

It was at this stage in the negotiations that the Yalta Declaration on Liberated Europe came to occupy a central position, for it served as the basis for the American contention that peace treaties should not be signed with governments which failed to meet the standards set by that Declaration. The heated debates of Byrnes, Molotov and Bevin in London thus turned more on

Soviet policy in the Balkans than on treaty terms. The breakdown of the conference in so far as the Balkan problem was concerned resulted from the refusal of Molotov to admit that the representative character of the Rumanian, Bulgarian and Hungarian Governments could properly be questioned. For ten days the Foreign Ministers wrangled over these issues without being able to achieve agreement on anything more important than a few of the technical details of the proposed peace treaties. When the conference finally ended in failure, the Balkan problem was one of the principal subjects of disagreement between the Soviet Union and the western allies.

At the time the breakdown of the London conference occurred, during the first days of October 1945, the United States had not yet recognized any of the governments in southeastern Europe with the exception of Greece. At the same time the compromise at Yalta with regard to Yugoslavia had placed the United States in a position of being prepared to recognize Tito's regime as soon as it provided at least token evidence of its representative character. Such token evidence was provided by the elections of November 11, in which Tito received the overwhelming majority which Communists regimes are generally able to muster, and on December 22 the Yugoslav Government was recognized by the United States and the United Kingdom. In the case of Albania, under a Communist regime headed by Hoxha, a United States mission was sent there in May 1945, to prepare the way for diplomatic recognition. Recognition was in fact offered in November, but the Albanian Government failed to meet certain conditions set by the United States and the mission withdrew a year later without having established diplomatic relations.

Yugoslavia and Albania had not been enemy states during the war, however, and although Communist regimes had come to power the recognition of the former and the offer of recognition to the latter did not fall within the limits of the controversy at London of Byrnes and Bevin with Molotov. Such bargaining power as the western states possessed in this region related to the former enemy states of Rumania, Bulgaria and Hungary, for without diplomatic recognition and the conclusion of peace treaties they could not play their proper role in the community of nations as Soviet satellites. In the case of one of these states—Hungary—an early opportunity was offered to demonstrate the western point of view. In Hungary the Communists had not yet succeeded in gaining control of the goverment, and under vigorous leadership the moderate agrarian Smallholders party had succeeded in maintaining a precarious domestic balance. On September 22, in the midst of the Foreign Ministers' conference in London, Secretary Byrnes suddenly provided dramatic demonstration of the American viewpoint by offering to recognize Hungary in return for a pledge of free elections. Such a pledge was promptly offered and on November 2 the Hungarian Government was recognized. Two days later a general election was held in Hungary in which the Smallholders won 242 seats in the parliament, as opposed to 70 for the Communists, 69 for the Social Democrats, and 59 for the remaining parties.

In the meantime the question of the recognition of Bulgaria and Rumania remained unsettled. It was in these countries that the actions of the Soviet authorities and of the local Communist parties had been most flagrant, and they had consequently formed the focal point of the heated arguments of the Foreign Ministers at London. For the Soviet Union, the issue was the maintenance of its control through the local Communist parties of two countries of great strategic and political importance. For the United States and the United Kingdom, it was a question of assuring that the conditions of the Yalta Declaration be met before the two countries were recognized and the peace treaties concluded. Having decided to take a stand on this issue, on October 10, 1945, shortly after his return from London, Secretary Byrnes announced the appointment of the Ethridge Mission to conduct a survey of political conditions in Bulgaria and Rumania.

II

At London it was Molotov's frequent gibe that Secretary Byrnes was poorly informed regarding conditions in Bulgaria and Rumania, and the Secretary had indeed felt that his diplomatic representatives in the Balkans might have become too much engrossed in the details of their relations with the Communist regimes to see local conditions in their proper perspective. Moreover American opinion was scarcely prepared to support a vigorous challenge to Soviet influence at this time, and the Secretary believed that it would be necessary to build up a background of publicly acceptable evidence before such support would be forthcoming. The issues as to the representative character of the existing provisional governments and the degree of freedom which was likely to obtain in forthcoming elections had been so sharply drawn during the London debates, that a fresh and detailed factual survey appeared to offer the best means of documenting the western case.

It was because of these special circumstances that Secretary Byrnes decided to go outside the ranks of the Department of State, and to appoint as his special representative an experienced journalist and publisher. The assignment was originally envisaged as one of reporting rather than of negotiating, for the central function of dealing with the Soviet Government was naturally retained by the Secretary. Yet it soon became clear that the fact-finding tasks of the mission could be a powerful instrument of pressure, and in the course of the investigation direct discussions were held with Vyshinsky at Moscow. The investigation involved a trip between October 18 and December 3 covering some 13,000 miles, including over two weeks in Bulgaria, one week in the Soviet Union, and ten days in Rumania. The function of special representative of the Secretary brought the privileges and machinery of diplomacy to the support of the news-gathering techniques of the foreign correspondent, with the result that an extensive job of reporting was accomplished during the relatively brief period of the mission. With the invaluable assistance of the American diplomatic representatives on the spot, Maynard B. Barnes in Sofia and Burton Y. Berry in Bucharest, conversations were held in the two countries with over three hundred persons representing all elements and shades of opinion.

Priority was given to Bulgaria because of the urgency of the situation created by the forthcoming election scheduled for November 18. If this election could be held under conditions which provided guarantees of free participation for the democratic opposition parties, the Agrarian Union and the Social Democrats, a basis would be provided for the organization of a government which met the conditions of the Yalta Declaration. If this were not accomplished, the election would only confirm the Communist-dominated regime in power and prolong indefinitely the deadlock. In discussing the background of this crisis with the leaders of the government and opposition parties, the distinction between the commonly accepted facts as to the development of the political situation since the collapse of German power and the controversial issues which had more recently come to a head soon became clear.

In 1942 the leaders of anti-German opinion in Bulgaria had organized the political coalition called the Fatherland Front. This coalition included, in addition to the Communists, the progressive wing of the Agrarian Union, the Social Democrats, and the Zveno National Union. The Agrarians and Socialists had deep roots in Bulgarian politics, while the Zveno National Union was a more recent grouping of reserve officers and middle class leaders who wished to serve as a link (hence "Zveno") between rural and urban political forces in the interests of national unity. Apart from their opposition to the Axis, these four parties shared a preference for republican government, for friendly relations with Yugoslavia and Greece, and for one form or another of a welfare state. In addition to this Fatherland Front coalition, there was a more conservative group of leaders in the opposition camp who represented the Democratic party and the moderate wing of the Agrarian Union.

As German power in the Balkans began to decline rapidly in the spring of 1944, the pro-Axis Council of Regents and cabinet began to look for a way out. While the Bulgarian Government was at war with the United Kingdom and the United States, it was the only Axis satellite which had avoided breaking relations with the Soviet Union, and this circumstance served to complicate the situation. The first peace feelers were received from Bulgaria in February 1944, and conversations were immediately initiated among the Big Three. Negotiations were later undertaken directly with Bulgarian representatives, but they came to nothing because of the failure of their government to break relations with Germany and the inability of either western or Soviet forces at this time to influence decisively the military situation in Bulgaria. Thus no agreement had been reached by the end of August when the Soviet army began to approach the Bulgarian frontier across Rumania. Sensing that a crisis was at hand, the Regency appointed an anti-Axis cabinet on September 2 composed of moderate Agrarians and Democrats. Not even this regime ventured to attack the Germans, however, and on September 5 the Soviet Union suddenly declared war on Bulgaria. This unilateral gesture immediately placed the Soviet Union in charge of armistice negotiations and brought the advancing Red Army into close collaboration with the Communist partisans who had been biding their time in the Balkan hills. When the Fatherland Front seized power on September 9, the Communists gained the key positions in the government and promptly began to lay the foundations for obtaining exclusive control.

This Fatherland Front cabinet proved to be a pliable instrument of Communist influence, although at first the Communist role was nominally secondary. The Zveno group, headed by Kimon Georgiev, occupied the premiership and the nominally important ministries of foreign affairs, war and propaganda. The strength of this group lay in its influence with the army and in the technical experience of its key figures. The Agrarian Union was led by Nikola Petkov pending the return from exile of Dr. G. M. Dimitrov later in the month. Petkov occupied the post of minister without portfolio, and his followers held the ministries of agriculture, public works, and railroads. The strength of the Agrarians lay in the extensive support which they were able to rally in both rural and urban districts. The Social Democrats were led by Cheshmedjiev, and were given the relatively unimportant ministries of social policy and trade. The political influence of the Socialists rested on a small group of well-established trade unions, which at this stage had not yet succumbed to Communist infiltration. There was also an independent, Petko Stoyanov, who served as minister of finance. Of the sixteen posts in the cabinet the Communists held four, of which only two were important. These were the key ministries of interior and justice. The former controlled the police and the latter the courts, and these were soon forged into powerful political weapons. Along with the Fatherland Front regime on September 9, a new Council of Regents was placed in office. It was headed by the venerated independent leader Venelin Ganev. Of his two colleagues, one was a Communist and the other a member of Zveno. Eight year old King Simeon II, and his mother Queen Giovanna, played no political role.

Although the Fatherland Front had seized power by a *coup d'état*, there was reason to believe that the four parties together might have received the support of some 80 percent of the electorate if a free election had been held before the end of 1944.

Moreover the cooperation of these four parties had resulted in certain substantial accomplishments during the winter of 1944–45. The chief of these was the prosecution of the war against Nazi Germany. Under vigorous prodding by the Red Army, the Bulgarians fought their way up the Danube well into Hungary and claimed to have suffered losses of some 32,000. They also fulfilled the principal provisions of the armistice agreement which was signed in Moscow on October 28. Likewise in the domestic field important measures were initiated. A ten-point program announced on September 19 included such measures as social legislation, the legalization of civil marriages, credits for the peasantry, and other popular reforms. During the winter of 1944–45 Petkov, the Agrarian leader, Ganev, the senior regent, Stoyanov, the independent minister of finance, and many others, considered it likely that the Communists were not preparing to seize exclusive power. It was only in the course of the spring of 1945 that the intentions of the Communists became unmistakeable.

The caution of the Communists during the first months of the Fatherland Front was doubtless due primarily to weakness. They had first to organize the police and to infiltrate the army before they could openly challenge their colleagues in the coalition regime. Their caution was also due in some measure to the need for national unity while the military campaign against the Axis was still in progress, for the Russians were willing to subordinate their ultimate political aims to the more immediate goal of winning the war. Nevertheless keen observers had from the start noted that the Communists were establishing themselves in key political positions in the course of the winter, and it was not long before the public began to see signs of their intentions. The chief of these was the sentence passed after a spectacular trial on the wartime regents, cabinet officers and members of parliament who had served during the period of alliance with the Axis. Of these scarcely a dozen would have been regarded as war criminals worthy of capital punishment by the standards later applied at Nuremberg, yet on February 1, 1945, no less than one hundred of them were sentenced to death and shot on the same day. The savagery of this action shocked the nation and set the stage for what was to follow. Local "people's courts" throughout the country now took their cue from the capital city, and the brutality of their sentences added to the toll which illegal police action had already begun to take of innocent opponents of communism.

To this crescendo of terror against persons outside of the Fatherland Front was soon added a campaign to undermine the non-Communist members of the government coalition itself. As early as December 1944, effective steps had been taken to weaken Zveno influence in the officer corps of the army. In January, Dr. G. M. Dimitrov was forced to resign his key position as secretary-general of the Agrarian Union, and shortly thereafter he was placed under house arrest. In May he managed to escape from the police and find asylum in the home of the American minister, and it was only as the result of a major diplomatic effort that he was permitted to go peacefully into exile in September. In the meantime, Petkov was elected to replace him as party leader of the Agrarians, but before the end of July he and one of his Agrarian colleagues finally resigned from the cabinet. Two weeks later the remaining two Agrarian cabinet officers, along with the leading Socialist and the independent Stoyanov, also resigned. Thus less than a year after it seized power the Fatherland Front lost the support of the two parties which were believed to have the largest popular backing. By the end of August the cabinet included only the Communists and the Zveno group, neither of which had a broad popular base in the country, and a few minor Agrarian and Socialist party members who made a deal with the Communists in return for cabinet positions.

The issue which led to the resignations of the Agrarian and Socialist leaders was the central one which the Ethridge Mission had been sent to investigate—the question of free elections. It was possible to maintain that, when it seized power in September, the Fatherland Front had constituted an interim governmental authority "broadly representative of all democratic elements of the population" in the sense of the Yalta Declaration. The present controversy concerned the "establishment through free elections of governments responsible to the will of the people" which that Declaration called for. Elections had initially been scheduled for August 26, and the electoral law promulgated before the disintegration of the Fatherland Front had assumed that candidates of its four constituent parties would run for office on a single government list and hence made no provision for the registration of candidates of opposition parties. Moreover, arrangements had been made to allocate seats in the National Assembly among the four government parties in advance of the election by negotiation among those parties.

It was the extravagant claims made by the Communists in these inter-party negotiations, in addition to the increasing tempo of police terror, which finally convinced the Agrarian and Socialist leaders that they must withdraw from the government. Their withdrawal, however, upset all the plans for the August election. Since the Agrarians and Socialists were now in the opposition, they could not register as party candidates and hence could not properly challenge the Communists and the Zveno at the polls. Foreseeing that elections held under these conditions would certainly fail to meet the demands of the Yalta Declaration, the American and British Governments made a major diplomatic effort to convince Moscow that the election should be postponed and its procedure reconsidered. This determined action, taken shortly after V-J Day when the relations of the Big Three were still relatively cordial, produced remarkable results. Acting through the Allied Control Commission, the Russians declared that they found no objection to the postponement of the election. With it was postponed also the crisis in American-Russian relations over the recognition of Bulgaria.

The postponement of the August 26 election was a major setback for the Communists, and they retired to safe positions to prepare for the next test of strength on the new election date which was now set for November 18. It was in the course of the preparations for this election that the Ethridge Mission was in Sofia, and the electoral issues became the chief subject of the investigation. Since the August fiasco the electoral law had been amended to permit opposition groups to register candidates on party lists rather than merely as individuals. Moreover the three opposition papers now had considerable freedom, and only on the radio was no opposition criticism permitted. "Allow us one fault!" was the comment of Traicho Kostov, Secretary-General of the Communist Party, when questioned regarding the government's monopoly of the broadcasting system. Had this been the government's only fault the situation would indeed have been hopeful, but even Kostov was to find other faults with the regime when he was sentenced to death by his colleagues for treason in December 1949.

Despite these amendments to the electoral law, the Agrarian

and Socialist parties decided not to register opposition candidates for the November election. In several conversations, Petkov expounded the view of the opposition leaders that they could not trust the government's intentions. The regime still retained such powers of police coercion and would exercise such a strict control over electoral procedure, in Petkov's view, that such liberties as the Fatherland Front had recently granted could easily be canceled out when the election day came around. If the opposition leaders participated in this fraud, he concluded, they would not be left with much moral capital after the election.

It was by no means clear that the electoral boycott of the opposition was the best means of resolving the problem on an international level, since it by-passed the issue on which the United States and the United Kingdom were best prepared to take a strong stand. On a local level, however, the decision was understandable enough. Reliable reports of police terror continued to be received and, what was more important, Communist leaders were making thinly veiled threats as to what would happen after the elections to persons who voted the wrong way. This impression as to Communist intentions was strengthened by a long conversation on November 9 with George Dimitrov, head of the Bulgarian Communist Party and former Secretary-General of the Communist International. This conversation conveyed the definite impression that such concessions as the regime might make before the elections were only a ruse, and that the Communists had every intention of crushing all opposition as soon as they had won recognition and a peace treaty for their country by a token exhibition of tolerance.

An equally important impression left by this conversation with Dimitrov was that the decision regarding the Bulgarian election had been reached not in Sofia but in Moscow. George Dimitrov had returned to Bulgaria, for the first time after twenty-two years spent in exile, only two days previously. He had thus far guided the affairs of the Bulgarian Communists by means of frequent telegrams from Moscow, to the extent that the opposition press had given him the nickname of "Telegram George." In this conversation he clearly implied that the reason for his sudden return to Bulgaria was to strengthen the hand of a regime which was still shaken by the postponement of the August election. Discussions with other key personalities also indicated that little influence could be exerted locally. Colonel General Biryuzov, Deputy Chairman of the Allied Control Commission, expressed his official opinion that decisions regarding the implementation of the Yalta Declaration must be made by the three powers which signed it. His own instructions, he made clear, came from Moscow. Similarly Prime Minister Kimon Georgiev, the Zveno leader who was already overwhelmed by events which he scarcely understood and could not hope to influence, pointed to Moscow as the source of all political decisions in Sofia. Since the local authorities were in such general agreement that the decision lay in Moscow, it was decided that the Ethridge Mission should proceed to the Soviet capital to explore the possibilities with regard to the Bulgarian election. The Soviet Government accepted this procedure and sent a special plane to facilitate the journey.

When the Ethridge Mission landed at the icy Moscow airport on November 11, only a week was left before the date set for the Bulgarian election. The sole reason to hope for results from negotiations conducted at such a late hour, was that a continuance of the indefinite status of Bulgaria might appear as undesirable to the Soviet Government as it was to the American. If the Soviets were convinced that the United States would not recognize a government elected under existing conditions, a compromise might still be reached. Any such compromise would of course only postpone the date of a showdown in Bulgaria between the Communist-led Fatherland Front and the Agrarian and Socialist Opposition leaders, but there was reason to believe that the position of the latter might be strengthened by such a postponement.

Not only was there little time to spare, but there was a limited range of alternatives within which compromise was possible. The most satisfactory solution from the American point of view was for the election to be postponed long enough to permit the registration on separate party lists of the candidates of all four parties which had originally constituted the Fatherland Front. In the meantime, the government could be broadened by the inclusion of Agrarian and Socialist ministers, and measures could be taken to prevent the police and the courts from being employed as exclusively Communist instruments during the period of the election. Such a solution would approximate the conditions of representative government and free elections envisaged in the Yalta Declaration. A government reflecting the results of such elections could be recognized by the western democracies, and once a treaty of peace were signed the way would be open for a new approach to postwar relations with the Soviet Union in eastern Europe.

The task of handling Soviet interests in the Balkans had been assigned to Andrei Y. Vyshinsky, at that time Vice Commissar for Foreign Affairs, and a conversation with him on the evening of November 13 was arranged by Ambassador Harriman. One of the principal purposes of this exchange of views was to impress the Soviet Government with the firmness of the American position that the terms of the Yalta Declaration were not being fulfilled in Bulgaria, and this was done by presenting a full account of the findings of the mission. This account stressed in particular the extent to which the Fatherland Front had ceased during the first half of 1945 to be a representative provisional government in the sense of the Yalta Declaration, and the responsible role which the Communists had played with their ruthless methods. The impression created by the actions of Soviet military officials and by George Dimitrov's frequent communiqués from Moscow, that the Soviet Union was trying to gain a position of exclusive influence in Bulgaria, was also emphasized. Confronted with this frank report, Vyshinsky drew on his ready wit, and was almost genial in his own special way. He asserted that the American view paid too much attention to the complaints of the opposition leaders, for his own information was quite different. Excesses had doubtless been committed by both sides, but fundamentally conditions in Bulgaria were no different from those in any democratic country. Vyshinsky saw no relevance in the fact that the Bulgarian Chief of Staff had served for twenty years as an officer in the Red Army. If Dimitrov had sent telegrams from Moscow giving advice to the Fatherland Front, he had only been expressing his views as a private citizen as was his right. If the Fatherland Front was dominated by the Communists, so was the British Government dominated by the Labor Party.

After this fruitless exchange of views regarding conditions in Bulgaria had continued for over an hour, the question of the election scheduled for November 18 was broached. To a query whether the Soviet Government would be willing to join in advising another postponement, Vyshinsky replied that that would constitute an unjustifiable intervention in Bulgarian domestic affairs. When it was pointed out that the Russians had accepted postponement in August, Vyshinsky recalled that on that occasion the Bulgarian Government itself had asked the advice of the Allied Control Commission. Carrying the matter further, Vyshinsky was asked what the attitude of his government would be in case Bulgaria again asked its opinion with regard to postponement. This question would be considered, he answered, in the light of the circumstances under which it came up.

From this discussion it appeared that the Soviet Government was determined this time to push the election through, probably on the assumption that the United States and the United Kingdom were not prepared to withhold recognition indefinitely if faced with an accomplished fact. The one possibility which the conversation with Vyshinsky left open, was that Moscow might be willing to accept postponement if a request for advice on this question came from Sofia as it had in August. This was no more than an elaborate formality, since no request would be forthcoming in any event without Soviet consent, but it was a face-saving procedure which had proved successful three months earlier. With this possibility in mind, the Department of State sent a strong note on November 16 to the Bulgarian Government, informing it of the findings of the Ethridge Mission. The note went on to remind Sofia that an essential requirement for recognition by the United States was the holding of elections under the conditions defined in the Yalta Declaration, and concluded that there was no reason to believe that the elections scheduled for November 18 would result in a representative government.

This note was an eleventh-hour effort to avoid the deadlock which would inevitably follow if the election were held as scheduled. The United States would have to disregard the election and press for a reconstruction of the government on a representative basis, and eventually for new elections to meet the conditions of the Yalta Declaration. These possibilities did not concern the Ethridge Mission, however, but could be left to regular diplomatic channels. The election was in fact held on November 18 as scheduled, and the Fatherland Front was shortly able to announce the overwhelming victory which no one had doubted the Communists would be able to arrange. On the day of the election, the Ethridge Mission was already on its way from

Moscow to Bucharest to enter upon its second phase—the investigation of the political situation in Rumania.

The situation in Rumania was different from that in Bulgaria in several significant respects. The underlying factor was the heritage of enmity which had long characterized Russian-Rumanian relations, in contrast to the position of respect which Russia had traditionally occupied in Bulgaria. During the recent war Rumania had undergone partition in the period of Nazi-Soviet friendship, and had later participated actively in the Axis aggression on the Soviet Union. Rumanian forces had occupied a sizable portion of southern Ukraine up to the Bug River, including the important Black Sea port of Odessa, and had ruled with a heavy hand this territory which was christened Trans-Dniestria. The Russians reconquered this region in 1944, and as they prepared to enter Rumania the pro-Axis regime of Marshal Antonescu was overthrown on August 23 by a military *coup* organized by King Michael.

The development of political events after this point, as it emerged from discussions with political leaders of many shades of opinion, revealed the special character of the Rumanian scene. The first cabinet under General Sanatescu was broadly representative in the sense of the Yalta Declaration. This coalition, known as the National Democratic Bloc, included in addition to the Communists the three leading prewar Rumanian parties —the National Peasants, the National Liberals, and the Social Democrats. The Liberal party of Constantine Bratianu and Peasant party led by Iuliu Maniu and Ion Mihalache had long shared the center of the Rumanian political stage, and in the difficult years during which Rumania was caught in the vise of the Nazi-Soviet struggle they had avoided the temptations offered by foreign dictators. The Socialists were led by Titel Petrescu, and had a much smaller numerical following. They nevertheless had strong support in the small Rumanian working class, and as of the end of the war they had not been seriously infiltrated by the Communists.

The Rumanian Communists, on the other hand, had not in 1944 possessed even the limited local support which had permitted their Bulgarian colleagues to take the initiative from the start. The Communists played a limited role in the first Sanatescu cabinet, for neither the police nor the army were as yet under their control. These domestic instruments of power in non-Communist hands were more than counterbalanced by the Soviet forces in Rumania, however, and the Communists were left free to do as they pleased. Moreover their power position was in due course strengthened by the return of two divisions of Rumanian troops which had been captured by the Red Army and retrained to serve as a Communist militia. Under these circumstances the Communists were able to rely on strikes and street demonstrations as a means of indicating their dissatisfaction of the government of which they were a member, and since the latter was unable to retaliate these limited weapons proved very effective. On November 5 the cabinet headed by General Sanatescu was reorganized as a result of Communist and Soviet pressure, and on December 6 a new government was formed by General Radescu, another non-party officer. As early as November the Communists had organized a leftwing coalition known as the National Democratic Front within the larger National Democratic Bloc, and this group now became their principal political instrument.

In this new National Democratic Front, the Socialists were the most numerous group. By the end of 1944 the Socialists were rapidly losing their freedom of action, however, and it was the Communists who dominated the policies of the coalition. Affiliated with the Communists were two groups which had been created for the purpose of extending Communist influence, the Plowmen's Front and the Patriotic Union. The Plowmen's Front was headed by Petru Groza, a wealthy landowner from the province of Transylvania, and was designed to compete with the Peasant party for the support of the Agrarian population. The Patriotic Union, an even smaller organization, was designed to gain support for the Communists among professional people and artisans. Disturbances organized by the National Democratic Front against General Radescu increased in extent and frequency, and were cited by the Russians as an excuse to demand that King Michael appoint a government which could "keep order". Vyshinsky himself went down from Moscow on February 27, 1945, to superintend the operation, and the king was finally pressured into accepting the Vice Commissar's "advice". On March 6 Groza was appointed prime minister at the head of a

National Democratic Front regime without the cooperation of either the National Peasant or the National Liberal parties.

This Groza Government now became the chosen instrument for the furtherance of Communist aims, and it was a good deal further from the norm agreed to at Yalta than the Bulgarian Fatherland Front had been at the start. All the principal positions were held by Communists, including the ministries of interior, justice, propaganda, public works and communications. The Socialists were permitted to occupy the relatively secondary ministries of labor, mines and education, while an allegedly non-party general was sponsored by the Communists as minister of war. Tatarescu, a former member of the Liberal party and once a prime minister under King Carol, served as vice premier and minister of foreign affairs. Tatarescu was a clever opportunist, but his war record had made him an easy object of blackmail by the Communists and he was consequently at their disposal.

The real leaders of the Rumanian Communist party did not hold cabinet positions at this time, but operated behind the scenes. The reasons for this were partly that the party was still in the process of being organized and required their full attention, and partly that they were members of minority groups who would not have attracted much support as public figures. Emil Bodnaras and Ana Pauker were respectively members of the Ukrainian and Jewish minorities in the province of Moldàvia, while Vasile Luca stemmed from the Hungarian minority in the province of Transylvania. Ana Pauker was delegated to present the views of the party to the American representative, and on November 22 in her comfortable suburban villa she discussed the Communist line with regard to current Rumanian problems. Since the question of holding elections was not an immediate one in Rumania, the principal issue was the representative character of the Groza Government. In the view expressed by Mrs. Pauker, the Maniu Peasants and the Bratianu Liberals had not adopted a sufficiently firm attitude towards the pro-Axis regime during the war, and were opposed to the close relations with the Soviet Union and the radical domestic program which the Communists supported. When asked how in this case the Communists could collaborate with Tatarescu, whose past record was certainly more anti-Soviet than that of Maniu or Bratianu, Mrs. Pauker replied that Tatarescu had recently altered his views. He now saw the necessity of supporting the Communist program, and it was therefore possible to work with him. While a wide variety of issues was covered in this conversation with Mrs. Pauker, the substance of her viewpoint was that acceptance of the Communist policy formed the only basis on which representatives of the other parties could be brought into the National Democratic Front.

The reason that the Rumanian Communists were able to adopt such an uncompromising attitude despite their lack of support within the country, was that the Russians themselves played a more active role in Rumania than they did in Bulgaria. Not only were larger contingents of the Red Army present in Rumania, but the Soviet officials intervened more directly in the domestic affairs of the country. While Molotov had assured the USSR's allies in a formal declaration on April 2, 1944, that the Soviet Union had no intention of altering the social structure of Rumania, his subordinates in fact participated actively in the implementation of the Communist program. The principal Russian instrument for exerting pressure was the armistice agreement, which as has been noted gave the Allied (Soviet) High Command wide latitude. By regulating the prices of the goods destined for delivery under the armistice terms, and the supplies to be provided for Soviet forces in the country, the Russians gradually brought the Rumanian economy to its knees. Further pressure was brought to bear through a trade agreement concluded in May 1945, and through the creation of Soviet-Rumanian corporations controlling oil production, transportation, and banking in which participation was only nominally equal. When to these economic instruments of pressure were added the direct interference of Soviet police and party agents and the general prestige of the Soviet Union as the local representative of the victorious United Nations coalition, it was not surprising that the Rumanian Communist leaders should have felt that they could dictate the terms on which they would collaborate with the Peasant and Liberal parties.

The balance of political forces in Rumania at this juncture was well illustrated by the position of King Michael. The twenty-four year old monarch had won the respect of the country by his vigorous leadership in throwing off upon the approach of the

Red Army in 1944 the pro-Axis regime which he had inherited from his father in 1940. He had moreover shown more courage and independence than the veteran political leaders in resisting Soviet pressure. He had indeed found it necessary to accept the Groza regime in March after the forceful representations of Vyshinsky failed to evoke any substantial countermeasures on the part of the western allies, but he had continued to work for a re-establishment of parliamentary procedures. When the allies at Potsdam broached the question of resuming diplomatic relations with the former Axis satellites, the king called upon Groza to resign in order to make way for a more representative government which could win the recognition of all three allied powers. Upon Groza's rejection of this demand, the king withheld his signature from all decrees and official papers and appealed to the allied powers to assist him in obtaining an acceptable government. A flurry of diplomatic notes was the only result of this appeal, however, and there ensued a constitutional crisis in which the cabinet governed without the consent of the king. The popular strength of the king was nevertheless sufficiently great, that neither the local Communists nor the Russians were prepared at this time to assume the responsibility for removing him.

The situation in Rumania in November 1945 was thus more difficult than that in Bulgaria in that there was no commonly accepted political program such as that of the Fatherland Front which might serve as the basis for a compromise, if the western allies were able to exert sufficient pressure on Soviet policy. The very weakness of the Rumanian Communists forced them to rely more exclusively on direct Soviet support than did their Bulgarian colleagues, and hence made compromise more difficult. As far as the prospects for free elections were concerned, Rumania was in an earlier stage of development than Bulgaria and hence there was more opportunity for affecting the course of events. An electoral law was being considered at this time, but the Communists were not yet sufficiently strong to attempt a single-list plebiscitary election on the Soviet model. The prospects that an eventual election would be free if conducted by the National Democratic Front as organized under Groza, were nevertheless not bright.

It is also interesting to note that a common pattern of Communist behavior emerged from the reception accorded to the

American mission in Bulgaria and Rumania. The outstanding feature of the Communist approach in each country, and in Moscow as well, was an insistence that the Yalta Declaration was being implemented in every respect. It was still over a year before the Cominform was to unveil "People's Democracy" as a transitional form of government designed to transform the satellites into socialist states of the Soviet type, and in the autumn of 1945 the view was consistently expounded that the Communists were eager to cooperate with agrarians, liberals, and socialists. If the latter refused to participate in Communist-led coalitions, it was implied that they were in some way undemocratic or even treasonable. Since the Fatherland Front and the National Democratic Front were thus masquerading as democratic coalitions, they welcomed the special representative of the United States Secretary of State with flowers, banquets, and cheering crowds.

On one occasion in Bulgaria thousands of labor union members in marshalled enthusiasm achieved such abandon, that they tried to lift the official limousine onto their shoulders. Another time a cheering crowd in front of Sofia's Hotel Bulgaria almost became a riot when opposition groups attempted a counter-demonstration. The Rumanian leaders were no less alert, and requested to be informed of the hour of the mission's arrival so that they might arrange an appropriately "spontaneous" popular demonstration. This time, however, circumstances prevented the staging of what would undoubtedly have been a skillful performance. That this spirit of hospitality was firmly coordinated with official policy, became clear when the mission went to Moscow. Travel to the Soviet capital, when it was thought that the American representative might be prepared to offer concessions, was provided in a deluxe special plane. After the fruitless discussion with Vyshinsky, return passage was made available in a crowded, bucket-seat transport plane.

III

The final report of the Ethridge Mission was submitted to the Secretary of State on December 8, 1945, in a form suitable for publication as originally intended. It summarized the numerous and more detailed interim communications and reports which had been made in the course of the investigation, and marshalled the findings with respect to the principal issues at stake. The report asserted explicitly that the governments of neither Bulgaria nor Rumania were broadly representative of all democratic elements, and that in fact they were authoritarian regimes which excluded the representatives of large segments of democratic opinion in both countries. The report was equally pessimistic regarding the prospects for the free election of governments responsible to the will of the people, which the Yalta Declaration had stipulated. It stressed the fact that the election held in Bulgaria on November 18 had provided no opportunity for the expression of views other than those represented by the single list of candidates of the Fatherland Front, and found no reason to expect better conditions in elections which might be held in Rumania.

Referring briefly to the broader aspects of the Balkan problem, the report recommended that elections with separate party lists and protected by adequate civil liberties, such as those recently held in Hungary and Austria on November 4 and 25 respectively, be taken as the norm for the two Balkan states. The elections in Hungary and Austria had been held with Soviet consent, and although the Communists had lost heavily in each case the Soviet Union had accepted the results. In making this suggestion, the report recognized the very real considerations of security and national interest which motivated Russian policy in the Balkans. Recollections of the ravages of the Rumanian army in the Ukraine naturally influenced the Soviet attitude, as did the desire to protect the communications of the elements of the Red Army stationed in Germany. The Russians were also interested in the developments in Greece and concerned with the question of the Turkish Straits. At the same time it did not appear that these considerations should outweigh the importance of an agreement of the three governments regarding the implementation of the Yalta Declaration. Since the Russians had agreed to separate lists and substantial civil liberties in Hungary and Austria, a vigorous western policy should be able to obtain the acceptance in Bulgaria and Rumania of comparable terms.

The report of the Ethridge Mission was thus sharply critical of Soviet policy in the Balkans, and its publication as originally planned would have been something of a shock to the prevailing view of American opinion which was still optimistic regarding the prospects of cooperation with the Soviet Union. This might have strengthened the hand of the administration if, as seemed to be the case when the London conference broke up in October, the time had indeed arrived when open political conflict could no longer be avoided. The situation had undergone a change since then, however, for at the end of November the Soviet Government accepted a proposal of Secretary Byrnes that the Foreign Ministers should meet in Moscow for further discussions. Since agreement as to peace treaty procedure was generally regarded as the first objective of American policy at this stage, it seemed best not to disturb the affirmative outlook of American opinion so long as any hope remained that a settlement could be reached through friendly negotiation. It was therefore decided that the report on the Balkans should not be published, but should instead be used as a basis of discussion with Stalin and Molotov.

When the next round of negotiations by the Foreign Ministers took place in Moscow, the Balkan problem was considered together with issues concerning peace treaty procedure, the plan for a commission on atomic energy, and the settlement in China, Korea and Japan. More than ever, in view of the recent failure in London, the western stand on the Yalta Declaration now had to be considered in the light of the total situation. The outcome of the Moscow conference was that the Russians accepted the idea of holding a peace conference on condition that negotiations were kept firmly in the hands of the Big Three, and agreed also to the establishment of a commission on atomic energy in the United Nations framework. As regards the far eastern issues, no substantial sacrifice was made in the American viewpoint. To the general western public these seemed like real gains, for it was still hoped that once a formal peace settlement had been agreed to the processes of economic recovery would restore the political balance.

As it turned out, however, these Soviet concessions to the western viewpoint regarding the procedure for the peace settlements had been purchased at the price of a substantial increase in Soviet bargaining power in eastern Europe. The compromise reached at Moscow regarding Bulgaria and Rumania provided that the Communist-dominated regimes of Georgiev and Groza should be broadened by the admission of an additional two representatives of the democratic opposition parties in each country. In the case of Rumania, a pledge of free elections was also required. This latter pledge was readily given and two of the lesser members of the Peasant and Liberal parties were admitted to the government, with the result that United States recognition was granted on February 4, 1946. Rumania now proceeded to ignore the substance of its pledge, and when carefully controlled elections were finally held on November 19, 1946, the Communist-led coalition won by an overwhelming majority. The Moscow compromise proved to be even less effectual in Bulgaria. There the results of the election of November 18, 1945, had hardened party lines, and when it came to implementing the Moscow compromise two opposition party members could not be found who were willing to enter the cabinet. The United States therefore withheld recognition, and for almost two more years it continued to use the pressure of non-recognition.

By the time the great powers turned their attention in the summer of 1946 to drafting peace terms for the former Axis satellite states, the United States had thus surrendered in all the Balkan countries excepting Hungary and Bulgaria, the substance of the hopes held out in the Yalta Declaration. The failure to agree to terms of recognition with Albania had arisen from circumstances outside the scope of the Yalta Declaration, while in Yugoslavia and Rumania recognition had been granted under conditions in which the substance of representative government and free elections could not be implemented. When it came to drafting the peace treaties in Paris in the summer and autumn of 1946, it became increasingly clear that these negotiations would offer no opportunity to win back the concessions which had already been made to the Soviet point of view. As a result of prolonged efforts, which finally achieved success at the meeting of the Foreign Ministers in New York in January 1947, Secretary Byrnes negotiated acceptable compromises on such matters as the status of Trieste and the withdrawal of Soviet occupation forces. The peace treaties which were signed in Paris on February 10, 1947, marked no advance, however, in the western effort to establish representative government based on free elections in eastern Europe. The peace treaties did indeed contain articles on the enforcement of human rights, but the provisions for their implementation were no more effective than those of the Yalta Declaration.

By 1947 it was the accepted Soviet doctrine that no insurmountable obstacles existed to communizing the states of eastern Europe, and they now unveiled their program for the systematic transition to communism which goes under the name of "People's Democracy." The extent of Communist self-confidence at this stage was well illustrated by the vigorous assistance afforded by Albania, Bulgaria and Yugoslavia to the Communist guerrillas in Greece. Under these circumstances, the United States effort to hold Bulgaria to the Yalta Declaration by the pressure of non-recognition was no longer consistent with the large concessions made in neighboring states. Sensing this weakness, the Bulgarian Government launched an all-out attack on the Agrarian Union headed by Nikola Petkov. New elections held in October 1946, had yielded over one quarter of the seats in the Assembly to the opposition in spite of governmental threats of retaliation, and now that the peace treaty was signed the Communists were prepared to liquidate the non-government parties. On June 6, 1947, Petkov was arrested, and on September 23 he was hanged. In the meantime the Agrarian Union was dissolved and all pretense of political liberties was abandoned. That the Bulgarian Government could afford to take this action without fear of retribution, was shortly demonstrated when the United States extended on October 1st the recognition which it had withheld for so long.

Thus the year 1947, which also saw the arrest of the opposition leaders in Rumania and the rout of the Smallholders in Hungary, marked the failure of the American efforts to preserve a degree of political freedom in the Balkan states through the implementation of the Yalta Declaration. The substance of this freedom had been bargained away in the hope that such concessions might win Soviet cooperation in what appeared to be broader and more significant fields of international endeavor. By the time it was clear that such cooperation would not materialize, it was no longer possible to revert to a policy of implementing the Yalta Declaration. New policies were needed to redress the balance of power, and these made their appearance in 1947 in the form of the Truman Doctrine and the Marshall Plan. With the development of these policies American-Russian relations in the Balkans entered a new phase.

It was a slow and devious process by which western, and more particularly American, opinion became convinced after World War II that the Soviet Union was determined to pursue a policy of unlimited political aggression. Many events contributed to this process, and the significance of the negotiations regarding the implementation of the Yalta Declaration in the Balkans is that they provided one of the earliest indications of this trend in Soviet policy.

The principal lesson of these negotiations is that in dealing with the Soviet Union there is no substitute for power. The exhaustion of western Europe at the end of the war, the preoccupation of the United States with far eastern problems, and in particular the delusion of informed American opinion that the Soviet Union would be too preoccupied with domestic concerns to pursue an aggressive foreign policy—all these factors help to account for the weakness of the western bargaining position in 1945. Much other evidence, from Greece in 1947 to Korea in 1950, was eventually accumulated to convince western opinion that Soviet policy involved the use of vigorous power in many forms and could in the last analysis be met successfully only by the exertion of equally vigorous and diversified power. In the immediate postwar period this important fact was little understood in government circles, however, and the Balkan negotiations played a role of great importance in helping to arouse official American thinking to a fuller recognition of this fact.

Apart from this larger lesson, the Balkan negotiations also demonstrated that general political agreements are of little value if the terminology is not strictly defined. The negotiations concerning the language of the United Nations Charter offer an example of the degree of success which can be achieved by careful drafting, and even there opportunity has been found for much subsequent disagreement. In the case of the Yalta Declaration on Liberated Europe, there was no evidence of such careful drafting. On the contrary, terminology in regard to democratic political procedures was used concerning which there was a long tradition of disagreement between the Soviet Union and the west. No effort was made in this document to spell out the criteria by which elections were to be judged "free" or governments "representative," and as a consequence Soviet propaganda was frequently able to make a plausible case before world opinion for its point of view.

The inability of the United States to secure the implementation of the Yalta Declaration was only the first in a series of retreats in the face of the expansion of Soviet power. The failure to appreciate Soviet intentions from the start resulted in the loss of much ground and of many lives, but at least it can be said that the lesson of this failure appears to have been learned. The United States is now in the process of assembling the instruments of political, economic, psychological, and military power within the framework of a growing coalition of states. There is reason to believe that in due course this country will be in a position to exert that form of power, so lacking in the Balkan negotiations in 1945, which will permit the achievement of American objectives by means short of war.

NEGOTIATING ON ATOMIC ENERGY

Frederick Osborn is a corporation executive. He was appointed Chairman of the President's Advisory Committee on Selective Service in October, 1940, and Chairman of the Joint Army and Navy Committee on Welfare and Recreation in March, 1941. He was appointed to the temporary rank of Brigadier General in 1941 and promoted in 1943 to the temporary rank of Major General and resigned from the Army in 1945 after having served as head of the morale branch and as Director of the Information and Education Division. He was appointed United States Deputy Representative on the United Nations Atomic Energy Commission in 1947 and served in that capacity until the end of January, 1950.

Negotiating on Atomic

Energy, 1946-1947

BY FREDERICK OSBORN

On June 14, 1946, the United Nations Atomic Energy Commission met in New York to negotiate a treaty for the international control of atomic energy. The General Assembly of the United Nations, with affirmative votes of the Soviet Union and the Soviet satellites, had given the Commission instructions to "Make specific proposals:

(a) for extending between all nations the exchange of basic scientific information for peaceful ends;

(b) for control of atomic energy to the extent necessary to ensure its use only for peaceful purposes;

(c) for the elimination from national armaments of atomic weapons and of all other major weapons adaptable to mass destruction;

(d) for effective safeguards by way of inspection and other means to protect complying states against the hazards of violations and evasions."

The Commission included among its members a number of men of outstanding ability and sincerity. It would have been hard to pick an international group more highly qualified for their task. They were competent and ready to negotiate. The atmosphere was one of expectation.

It was a time when certainly the majority of Congress and of our people still hoped that we could cooperate with the Soviet Union. They could agree with Mr. Stimson when he wrote about atomic energy to the President on September 11, 1945: "The chief lesson I have learned in a long life is that the only way you can make a man trustworthy is to trust him; and the surest way to make him untrustworthy is to distrust him and show your distrust." [1]

At Yalta President Roosevelt had gambled for world peace based on moral relationships. Perhaps he knew before his death that he had lost. But in June 1946 the people and most of their leaders did not yet realize it. In the light of later events the President was blamed for the failure. But if he had not tried it is likely that he would have been blamed even more.

Even today, when under its own inexorable inner imperatives the police state dictatorship behaves in such a way that our minds know we cannot deal with them, our hearts cannot take it in. We still feel that friendliness, frankness, some new approach, might bring them around. Looking back we cannot blame the American delegates for their hopefulness at the first session of the Atomic Energy Commission of the United Nations in June 1946.

Mr. Baruch said in his opening statement:

> "The United States proposes the creation of an International Atomic Development Authority, to which should be entrusted all phases of the development and use of atomic energy, starting with the raw material and including
> "1. Managerial control or ownership of all atomic energy activities potentially dangerous to world security.
> "2. Power to control, inspect, and license all other atomic activities.
> "3. The duty of fostering the beneficial uses of atomic energy.
> "4. Research and development responsibilities of an affirmative character intended to put the Authority in the forefront of atomic knowledge and thus enable it to comprehend, and therefore to detect, misuse of atomic energy. To be effective, the Authority must itself be the world's leader in the field of

---

[1] *On Active Service in Peace and War*, by Henry L. Stimson and McGeorge Bundy, Harpers, New York, 1945, p. 344.

atomic knowledge and development and thus supplement its legal authority with the great power inherent in possession of leadership in knowledge."

Then followed the offer of the United States:

"When an adequate system for control of atomic energy, including the renunciation of the bomb as a weapon, has been agreed upon and put into effective operation and condign punishment set up for violations of the rules of control which are to be stigmatized as international crimes, we propose that:
"1. manufacture of bombs shall stop;
"2. existing bombs shall be disposed of pursuant to the terms of the treaty;
"3. the Authority shall be in possession of full information as to the know-how for production of atomic energy."

These proposals seemed fair, even generous, at the time. In the two years of negotiation which followed they were clarified, and elaborated by specific proposals drawn in large part for the purpose of defining and limiting the powers of the authority, assuring each nation of its equitable share in the world's uranium resources, preventing any disproportionate drawing down of uranium ores from mines in any particular country, preventing the production of dangerous atomic materials in excess of those needed for peaceful uses, and making the prohibition of atomic weapons effective.

How is it that the Soviet Union has not only rejected these proposals as a whole and in every part, but after two years of discussion and attempted clarification stoutly maintains that this plan is a conspiracy of the Anglo-American bloc to interfere with and control the economic life of other nations, to threaten the world with atomic destruction and to monopolize the uses of atomic power?

There is nothing in the atomic background to explain this extraordinary result.

The United States had developed the atomic bomb in the hopes that it would bring a quick end to the war and in the knowledge that the Germans were working on it. So far as we know, there has been no criticism on the part of the Russians, or of anybody else, of our development of the bomb.

The bomb was dropped on Hiroshima and Nagasaki in the belief that it would assure an immediate Japanese surrender, thus saving an estimated million American lives, and perhaps several million Japanese lives. The considerations which led to our use of the bomb are set forth in Mr. Stimson's book, *On Active Service in Peace and War.* They are wholly convincing to those who know Mr. Stimson and who do not read or judge them by the points of view which have developed since that time. General Marshall has further clarified these considerations by pointing out (in talks with the author in February 1947) that towards the end of the war there existed in Japan a unique situation which might never arise again. Three years of fighting had demonstrated that the Japanese soldier would fight suicidally for his Emperor and would not surrender unless told to do so by the Emperor himself. The Emperor was aligned with the political groups who wanted to make peace. But the extreme military and naval party might at any time have staged a *coup* and taken over the Emperor, making him, in effect, their prisoner, issuing such orders as they chose, and no others. If this had happened, surrender of Japanese troops would have been extremely unlikely, since the war party would have held on for a long time, hoping to get better terms by a protracted resistance, and, in any event, having nothing to lose.

Many "liberals," and of course all fellow-travelers, have held that the dropping of bombs on Japanese cities was morally reprehensible, but this does not seem to be a majority opinion, even in this country, and it seems absurd to hold that such a "moral" feeling exists among the men in the Kremlin, whatever use they may make of it for propaganda purposes.

We do not believe that the failure of negotiations on international control can be laid to any moral failure on the part of the United States in making or using the bomb, nor to the steps taken by the United States after the bomb was used.

When President Truman announced the bombing of Hiroshima on August 6, 1945, he included in his statement a reference to the legislation which would be required and said: ". . . I shall give further consideration and make further recommendations to Congress as to how atomic power can become a powerful and forceful influence towards the maintenance of world peace." On the same day, Secretary of War Stimson said in a public statement: "Every effort is being bent toward assuring that this weapon and the new field of science that stands behind it will be employed wisely in the interests of the security of peace-loving nations and the wellbeing of the world."

Three days later, on his return from Potsdam, President Truman said in a radio broadcast: "We must constitute ourselves trustees of this new force to prevent its misuse, and to turn it into channels of service to mankind. It is an awful responsibility which has come to us."

In a message to Congress on October 3, 1945, President Truman asked for immediate action on two fronts—the domestic and the international. He stated that discussion of the international problem could not safely be delayed until the United Nations Organization began functioning and was "in a position adequately to deal with it." Therefore, discussions would be initiated first with the United Kingdom and Canada, then with other nations, "in an effort to work out arrangements covering the terms under which international collaboration and exchange of scientific information might safely proceed." On the same day the first atomic energy bill was introduced in Congress. The subject was under debate for almost ten months. The final legislation, the McMahon Bill, was signed by the President on August 1, 1946. It met substantially all the requirements listed in the letter which the President had sent to Senator McMahon on February 1, 1946, of which two paragraphs are particularly worth noting:

> "2. The Government must be the exclusive owner and producer of fissionable materials. . . .
> "The disadvantages of Government monopoly are small compared to the danger of permitting anyone other than the Government to own or produce these crucial substances, the use of which affects the safety of the entire nation. . . ."

The foregoing quotations are of special interest in view of the decisions of the United Nations Atomic Energy Commission almost a year later when they declared, in effect, that the disadvantages of international monopoly are small compared to the danger of permitting anyone other than the international agency to own or produce these crucial substances, the use of which affects the safety of the entire world.

The act for the development and control of atomic energy reads as follows in regard to international arrangements:

"Sec. 8. (a) Definition.—As used in this Act, the term "international arrangement" shall mean any treaty approved by the Senate or international agreement hereafter approved by the Congress, during the time such treaty or agreement is in full force and effect.

"(b) Effect of International Arrangements.—Any provision of this Act or any action of the Commission to the extent that it conflicts with the provisions of any international arrangement made after the date of enactment of this Act shall be deemed to be of no further force or effect.

"(c) Policies Contained in International Arrangements.—In the performance of its functions under this Act, the Commission shall give maximum effect to the policies contained in any such international arrangement."

In the meantime, Prime Minister King of Canada and Prime Minister Attlee of the United Kingdom had met in Washington with President Truman on November 10, 1945. On the 15th of November they signed the Agreed Declaration, in which they said: "We are prepared to share, on a reciprocal basis with others of the United Nations, detailed information concerning the practical application of atomic energy just as soon as effective enforceable safeguards against its use for destructive purposes can be devised." They advocated a Commission of the United Nations which would make "specific proposals," forecasting the language used by the General Assembly itself when it set up the Atomic Energy Commission.

Finally, in December 1945, the Foreign Ministers of the Soviet Union, the United Kingdom and the United States met in Moscow and agreed on a proposal for setting up a United Nations Commission on Atomic Energy, with the terms of reference which had been used in the Agreed Declaration on November 15th. But at this Moscow conference the Soviet Union for the first time gave an indication of what its attitude would be in the future. Secretary Byrnes reported (broadcast from Washington, December 30, 1945): "The Soviet Union offered only a few amendments to the proposal submitted by us. These amendments were designed to clarify the relations of the Commission to the Security Council. With some revisions we accepted them." In the Security Council lay the protection of the veto. The Soviet Union was already looking to that protection.

These, in brief summary, were the official actions which preceded the first meeting of the Atomic Energy Commission on June 14, 1946, just ten months after the dropping of the first bomb on Japan. It is hard to find in these preliminary steps anything which might explain the later behavior or decisions of the Soviet Government. Up to the time of the opening of negotiations in the United Nations Atomic Energy Commission, the Russian attitude towards atomic energy control was passive and acquiescent.

I

Mr. Baruch's own story of his negotiations with Andrei Gromyko would be fascinating and highly instructive. No one but Mr. Baruch could write it, and the following brief outline of events from June to December 31, 1946, is given only to provide a necessary background for the negotiations which followed:

There are two obvious points which may have had a bearing on the later behavior of the Russians, though they lead one to opposite conclusions. In the first place, the Acheson-Lilienthal Report was published before Mr. Baruch's appointment was confirmed, and in the circumstances he very wisely laid down the whole of the American position on the first day of the negotiations. Some people have suggested that this made the Russians suspicious of us from the start. Negotiations are not usually started in that way. The second point is that the Soviet Union almost immediately brought in its own proposal, namely, that there should be at once a convention prohibiting the manufacture, possession and use of atomic weapons. It did not at first even bring up the question of means to enforce such a convention. The speed with which this proposal was presented, in the first few days of the negotiations, makes it almost certain that it had been planned long beforehand. The Soviet delegates never acted without definite instructions, and their instructions never were given them hastily.

Ever since their proposal was introduced in June 1946 the Russians have consistently held to the position that there should be a treaty outlawing the atomic weapon, but have never accepted the type of controls which, in the opinion of the other delegates, would be effective. The advantages of their own plan would be obvious to the Kremlin. Public opinion in the democracies would force the United States and the United Kingdom to observe the prohibition. After ratifying such a treaty, no Congress would appropriate money for atomic weapons. All the world would know that the Soviet Union was safe from atomic attack. But the iron curtain would hide from the world what was going on inside the USSR. They could, in the words of Mr. Vyshinsky, develop atomic energy for moving mountains, and thus pose a most frightening threat to all the other nations, while, at the same time they were claiming to be the first to develop atomic energy for the benefit of their people. In five years the Soviet Union has not changed its position. It continues to tell the world that the United States will not agree to the prohibition of atomic weapons and only the USSR wants peace. It is hard now to believe that this position wasn't determined well before the first day of the negotiations.

The essence of Mr. Baruch's proposal was that the prohibition of atomic weapons without at the same time providing effective means of enforcement would only increase suspicion and distrust and make war more likely. Enforcement could be effective only if an international agency had, among other powers, managerial control or ownership of all atomic energy activities potentially dangerous to world security. The Soviet Union was opposed to this point of view from the start, but during the first six months it did not take any final position, and when the vote came on the First Report on December 31, 1946, it simply abstained. It had left the ground open for putting in a series of amendments to the Report.

Mr. Baruch resigned after the adoption of the First Report. In March 1947, Secretary of State Marshall appointed Frederick Osborn Deputy United States Representative on the United Nations Atomic Energy Commission, to serve under Warren Austin, then Chief of the United States Delegation to the United Nations.

The strong and able leadership of Mr. Baruch had given some of the delegates from other countries a feeling of pressure and insufficient time for the consideration of all possible alternatives. A number of the countries felt that, given more time, they could perhaps make important contributions to the development of the plan. In the conferences which were held before the Commission reconvened, the French and Canadian delegates, who combined an intimate experience of the previous negotiations with a knowledge of the field and a high degree of personal competence, took a leading part. As the work proceeded, General A. G. L. McNaughton, the representative of Canada, gradually, and by common consent, became the leader of the group. Of transparent integrity, great powers of self-control, and a tenacious grip on the fundamentals, he was ideally suited to the role. As head of the Canadian Delegation, and with an intimate knowledge of the Canadian atomic energy program, as well as from his own personal qualities, he carried more weight than any one else on the Commission. François de Rose, of the French Delegation, spoke of him as the conscience of the Commission. It was a correct designation.

Gromyko appeared to recognize McNaughton's position on the Commission. But at times he appeared deeply puzzled by it. The fact that the members of the majority group on the Commission were friends who enjoyed each other's confidence did not mean that they always agreed. Once when McNaughton and the American delegate were engaged in quite a violent argument over some point in the plan, I remember glancing at Gromyko and seeing an extraordinary expression of bewilderment on his face, as though he were trying to figure out whether or not the whole thing was being staged for his benefit. It was apparently impossible for him to believe that there could be such a thing as free discussion. Certainly, no Soviet delegate other than Gromyko ever thought for a moment that the majority delegates did anything except on orders from the United States. In a very real sense, the Soviet delegates were victims of their own indoctrination. We will not be able to understand their behavior in the negotiations if we allow ourselves to think of them in terms of the individual Americans and western Europeans whom we know and understand.

The Commission reconvened on March 19, 1947. It assigned to the "working committee" the task of studying the amendments to the First Report proposed by the Soviet representative, and assigned to Committee 2 the work of developing specific proposals from the general principles laid down in the First Report.

The meetings of these two committees were held on alternate dates, and the work proceeded concurrently. But the discussion of the Soviet amendments started first, was actively pushed, and was finished before the completion of the work on the Second Report. The Soviet delegates were insistent on the immediate discussion of their amendments. They had waited for them for almost three months, and they represented definite instructions from the Kremlin. Their position on these amendments was always clear and unswerving, in great contrast to their position on the proposals of the Second Report, where, except for their continuous attacks on the motives of the Anglo-American group, they often seemed at a loss to know what to say.

These Soviet amendments at first reading seemed fairly innocuous to an inexperienced negotiator, such as the present writer. But when the Secretariat printed them in parallel columns opposite the appropriate sections of the First Report and we really studied them, they began to look not only tough but sly.

The First Report was, in effect, a set of general principles, but it was tightly drawn. All of the majority delegates felt that in approving their governments had not signed anything that they would not be able to go through with when it was drawn up in detail. They were naturally anxious not to put their governments in a position which might embarrass them at any later date, and there is no doubt that they were afraid of compromises which might result in later misunderstandings. While they did not enter the debate on these amendments without suspicions of Soviet motives, they were hardly prepared for the methods with which the Soviet delegates proposed to cripple the First Report without admitting for a moment what their changes really meant.

There were twelve amendments in all. They were drawn in relation to an early draft of the First Report, instead of in relation to the final draft as it was voted. This was a cause of considerable embarrassment to the Soviet delegates. They appeared embarrassed also by the fixity of their orders, which apparently permitted no compromise, but absolute insistence on the Soviet position without change. Three of the amendments would have given the Security Council power of veto over the decisions of the international agency, not directly in so many words, but by using the words, "administered within the framework of the Security Council" (Amendment No. 2), or, "Serious violations shall be reported immediately by the Commission to the Nations parties to the convention and to the Security Council" (Amendment No. 9), instead of using the language of the First Report, which read: "Serious violations of the treaty shall be reported immediately by the international control agency, to the nations parties to the treaty, to the General Assembly, and to the Security Council." It is perfectly clear, in the light of later events, that the Soviet delegates were from the start determined not to allow the General Assembly to play any part in considering violations of the control treaty, but, instead, intended to keep all these matters in the hands of the Security Council, where the USSR could block any action by invoking the rule of unanimity. But the Soviet representatives never admitted this purpose during the debate, and a number of times almost carried their point before the other delegates realized the trap that was being laid for them.

The Soviet amendments also attempted to provide for two treaties instead of for one, as called for in the First Report. Amendment No. 1 read: "Immediately after the entry into force of an appropriate convention or conventions." This precipitated a long discussion which seemed to have to do merely with the use of words, as the Russians insisted on the use of the word convention instead of the word treaty as used in the First Report. But when the majority agreed to use the words "treaty or convention," the Soviet delegate insisted on adding "or treaties or conventions," and it was evident that the separation into two treaties, one on prohibition and one on control, was what he really had had in mind all the time. This was shown again in Amendments No. 2 and No. 3. The First Report in section 5 called for "an effective system for the control of atomic energy . . ." and in section 6 said, "That international agreement to outlaw the national production, possession, and use of atomic weapons is an essential part of any such international system of control and inspection." The Russians proposed in Amendment No. 2, "That an effective system of control . . . be established by an enforceable multilateral convention. . . ." And in Amendment No. 3, "That an international convention outlawing the production, possession and use of atomic weapons is an essential part of any such system of international control of atomic energy." When the Soviet amendments were first presented, there did not seem to be any great difference between Amendments No. 2 and No. 3 and the corresponding sections of the First Report. But as the discussion went on it became pretty clear that the

Russians were trying to get back to their original proposals for two treaties, one on prohibition and one on control, or at least to leave the door open for continuing the argument, by their insistence on the words "treaties or conventions" instead of the words of the First Report "treaty or [as later agreed to] convention."

Coupled with the idea of two treaties was their tenacious insistence that the treaty on prohibition should go into effect first, before the treaty on control. This was covered in their Amendment No. 12, which read: "With a view to the earliest possible implementation of the findings and recommendations stated, and also of the General Assembly Resolution of 14 December 1946 on 'Principles Governing the General Regulation of Armaments,' the Security Council recognizes the urgency of considering draft conventions on the prohibition of atomic and other major weapons adaptable to mass destruction."

It seems quite evident that at this stage they desired to continue the negotiations. They did not make a final issue of the matter of two treaties or one. If they could not amend the First Report to provide for two treaties, they wanted the door left open to an endless debate on this subject later on.

So long as they could keep open the possibility of two treaties they were willing to go along with the section of the First Report which provided that "The treaty or convention should embrace the entire programme for putting the international system of control and inspection into effect and should provide a schedule for the completion of the transitional process over a period of time, step by step, in an orderly and agreed sequence leading to the full and effective establishment of international control of atomic energy." The Amendment (No. 11) which the Soviet Union offered to this section of the Report appeared to have intended only a slight rephrasing, and Gromyko himself said at the time that there were no serious differences between the two. It was only when, at a later date, the Soviet representatives found themselves blocked in their attempt to get two separate treaties, one on prohibition and one on control, that they repudiated this section on stages. With a single treaty, both control and prohibition would have gone into effect "step by step," each step to control being accompanied by a corresponding step towards prohibition. But with two treaties, as in the Soviet plan, the treaty on prohibition would have gone into effect within three months after ratification, as the Russians first proposed, with the treaty on control still to be negotiated, or, as they later proposed, "simultaneously," that is, the treaty on control would go into effect along with the treaty on prohibition when they both were signed and ratified. Under any of these proposals, the treaty on prohibition would certainly have been implemented within three months, while it would have been impossible to establish even the semblance of control within such a brief period. Lacking effective international control, there would have been no assurance that the Soviet Union had ceased making bombs and destroyed its stocks at a time when other nations were entirely without these weapons. The United Nations repeatedly rejected the Soviet proposals, but the Soviet Union would not consider any others.

All of this is very clear today. It was not so clear at the time, and the refusal of the majority to reopen the question of two treaties or one seemed to many onlookers an unnecessarily uncompromising position. It is a tribute to both Soviet propaganda and to the American sense of fair play that at this time it was much easier for *The Bulletin of the Atomic Scientists* to print articles accusing the majority delegates of stubbornness than to print anything to show why it would be dangerous to agree to put prohibition into effect before controls were actually operating.

Amendment No. 8 provoked a long discussion. It provided "for the destruction of stocks of manufactured atomic weapons and of unfinished atomic weapons," in contrast to the corresponding section in the First Report which read, "Providing for the disposal of any existing stocks of atomic weapons and for the proper use of nuclear fuel adaptable for use in weapons." "Disposal" meant that the bombs would no longer be in the hands of nations, but either destroyed or turned over to the United Nations. "Destruction" of atomic weapons was an almost meaningless phrase, because it was understood throughout the debate that the destruction applied only to the bomb casings or detonating mechanisms. All of the delegates, including those of the Soviet Union, agreed that the nuclear fuel which was the actual explosive should not be destroyed, because it had, potentially, too great a value for peaceful purposes. But, of course, it was the nuclear fuel which was expensive and took a long time to make, and constituted the unique danger. The bomb mechanisms could be recreated in a short time, at a relatively small expense, and in secrecy, no matter how strict the control, which would not be the case with the elaborate processes necessary to the production of nuclear fuel. It would be in a very real sense a fraud on the public to say that the bombs had been destroyed, when actually the explosive was available and the mechanism could be made almost overnight.

All this was made abundantly clear in the course of the debate. But the Soviet attack lost none of its fury. In a series of speeches which exceeded in bitterness anything that had gone before, they accused the United States and the "Anglo-American bloc" of refusing to destroy their bombs, of having made a hypocritical offer which was now unmasked and, of course, of threatening the world with atomic weapons. To a majority of the delegates these statements seemed only propaganda, and this fact, together with the violence of the Soviet language, had much to do with the other delegates ultimate approval of the United States' position that the amendment should not be accepted. But with the general public the Soviet talk about destroying atomic bombs was quite effective. For a long time afterwards this charge was the basis for criticism of the United States and the other majority delegates. Undoubtedly many people got the idea that the United States was refusing to destroy its bombs and that, while the Soviet Union was willing to make a deal on atomic energy, the United States was not.

The debate on the Soviet amendments continued from March into the summer. It did nothing to clarify the mind of the public about Soviet intentions, but it left the majority delegates with some very definite impressions which undoubtedly colored their attitude during the balance of the negotiations. It was clear that the Soviet delegates were acting under explicit instructions as to the detail of their work, so that even in the smallest matters they had to refer back to Moscow. A number of their speeches were evidently written in Moscow and sent with instructions that they be delivered without change. There could be no give and take under such circumstances. It was clear that the Russians would not admit the intent, or even discuss the meaning of their proposals. After three months of such experiences, the other delegates came to look on any new Soviet proposals with grave suspicions. To a very real extent they became hardened to Soviet name calling, and learned that it was often wiser to reply briefly, or even not to reply at all, than to become involved in arguments which seemed to have no purpose except delay or the attempt to catch one up on some poor use of words.

While the debate on the Soviet amendments was going on in the Working Committee, a far more important discussion was taking place in Committee No. 2.

Even before the first meetings of Committee No. 2, the majority delegates had discussed among themselves whether it would be possible to do any constructive work in the regular committee meetings at Lake Success if the Soviet delegates chose to continue the harassing methods they had employed previously. The delegates of France, the United Kingdom, Canada and Belgium, who had been with the Commission during the writing of the First Report, pointed out that the only way it had been possible to write any part of the Report, had been to hold relatively informal meetings where the Russians had had no chance to air their views in public, and had felt no need of making a record for themselves with their bosses in the Kremlin. It was accordingly agreed that the majority would propose a series of informal meetings to be held in a small office rented by the United Nations in New York City, at which there would be no regular interpreter and no record other than a brief summary of actions taken, which would be kept by a single member of the Secretariat. It was planned that these meetings would be attended by all the members of the Commission, that the Chairman of the Commission would act as presiding officer and that he would, with the consent and advice of the others, appoint sub groups who would be charged with writing the various sections of the proposed Second Report.

This plan was presented in detail at the first meeting of Committee No. 2 held at Lake Success on April 10, 1947. The Soviet delegate did not strongly disapprove of the plan, but he did take the very explicit position that since the specific proposals were going to be based on the general framework of the Commission's First Report—and the Soviet Union had not approved the First Report—the Soviet delegate could not take part in the development of these proposals, but would sit in as an observer.

The general procedure having been formally approved at Lake Success, the first informal meeting was held in New York on April 28th. During May, the United States delegate presided, since the United States delegate was chairman of the Commission that month. Sub groups were established, charged with preparing specific proposals covering various areas of the proposed Second Report according to a subject list which had been prepared by the United States Delegation and previously presented and approved at the April 10th meeting of Committee No. 2 at Lake Success. The sub groups were composed of three to eight members. Sir Charles Darwin of the United Kingdom headed the group charged with the section on research; General Mc-Naughton of Canada headed the group charged with the section on location and mining of ores; Dr. Wei of China headed the group charged with the section on preparation of source materials; General Kenneth Nichols of the United States headed the group charged with stockpiling, production, distribution of nuclear fuels, design and construction of reactors; and François de Rose of France headed the group charged with the section on inspection and operational and developmental functions.

The Soviet Union had assigned its technical advisor, Dr. Skobeltzyn, to sit in as an observer on these informal meetings. Every effort was made to get Dr. Skobeltzyn to take part in the work of one or another of the groups, but in each case he refused, falling back on the decision which had been made at Lake Success that the Soviet representative would sit in as an observer only.

The sub groups were exceedingly active during May and the early part of June. They met in the offices of the various delegations, wherever convenient, worked often late into the night, and did an extraordinarily competent job. In most cases the chairmen of the different groups assumed the major responsibility for the preparation of the specific proposals. This was particularly the case with General McNaughton's chairmanship of the group working on the location and mining of ores, and with Mr. de Rose's chairmanship of the group working on inspection. Both men of a high order of ability, they produced outstanding reports. I had not myself seen the drafts of the section on the location and mining of ores before it was brought before a general meeting of the group for discussion, and I remember the pleasure and interest with which I listened to General McNaughton's presentation and to some of the quite unexpected ideas he had incorporated in the draft.

By the end of May most of the sub groups had brought their papers in for informal discussion by the New York group, after which the respective chairmen were to give them a final redrafting prior to their going to Lake Success for presentation and formal discussion by the Committee. At an informal meeting held in New York a number of these papers were presented in fairly complete form and for the first time it was evident that the Commission was going to be in a position to put out a Second Report which would contain sound and carefully written specific proposals. Dr. Skobeltzyn was sitting in, in his position as observer, flanked by the two younger members of the Soviet staff who usually accompanied him wherever he went. As the discussion developed, one of these young men handed Dr. Skobeltzyn a paper. When he opened and read it, he became highly excited and interrupted with the demand that he be given the floor at once. The Chairman suggested that the delegate then speaking might complete his remarks, but Dr. Skobeltzyn insisted he be given the floor. The other delegate withdrew and Dr. Skobeltzyn then spoke quite excitedly. He demanded, first, that a verbatim record be made of what he was about to say. When this was arranged (fortunately a stenographer-interpreter was present, although no record was being made of any other talks) Dr. Skobeltzyn launched into an extraordinarily bitter attack on the meetings and the people taking part in them. He said that the meetings were illegal, conducted according to unauthorized procedures, and represented a treacherous attempt of the tools of the ruling clique to develop their sinister purposes, secretly and without participation of the Soviet Union, and that he, for one, repudiated any part in the proceedings; all of this delivered with much vehemence. When he was through he handed to the men sitting behind him the paper they had given him. None of the other delegates who were present at this outburst made any reply. The procedures we were following had been approved in great detail in the formal meetings of the committee at Lake Success. Dr. Skobeltzyn had been urged in the strongest possible terms to take part in the work of the sub groups and had been present in all the meetings of the group as a whole. It was the feeling of the other delegates that this outburst was due to Skobeltzyn's sudden realization that the work had advanced further than anything he had reported to Moscow, and his fear that he would be criticized for having permitted so much of a constructive nature to be done.

Dr. Skobeltzyn's outburst was the beginning, and, in a sense, the end of Soviet participation in the constructive work of the Commission. The proposals which had been elaborated in New York were taken out to Lake Success to be discussed and voted on. The Soviet delegate found them unacceptable and put every obstruction in the way of their being brought to a vote. At first he charged that the proposals had been developed illegally, but, after the first few meetings, dropped this tack and concentrated more on criticism of the proposals themselves. His criticisms were usually based not on what the proposals actually contained, but on what he said they contained. There were the usual endless attacks on the motives of the majority delegates, on their having been "coerced" by the United States, on the proposals being simply "an attempt to extend the monopoly of the United States."

The proposals were incorporated in the Second Report of the United Nations Atomic Energy Commission, which was developed in committee during the late summer of 1947, in the face of every sort of delay and obstruction by the Soviet delegate. The Report was not, however, completed in time for presentation to and debate by the General Assembly in the fall of 1947.

During the first six months of 1948 every effort was made to develop in detail the proposals of the Soviet Union, to see if some common ground could be found with respect to the specific proposals. Nothing came of this effort, however, largely because the Soviet delegate was unable, or unwilling, to discuss the proposals themselves in detail, so that it was almost impossible to get any clear idea of his actual views. The matter of quotas was an interesting example of this difficulty. It is worth describing at some length because of its subsequent use for propaganda purposes by the Russians.

The Second Report provided in the section on the location and mining of ores that the mines in various areas of the world should be drawn on according to quotas, based on their relative size; the material to go into the pool administered by the international agency. In this way each nation could be assured that uranium ores located in its territories would not be depleted at a higher rate than the ores of other countries. The quotas thus defined were to be fixed by the international agency, in accordance with its need for uranium. This seemed an eminently fair arrangement.

In an entirely different section of the Second Report, that having to do with making or using dangerous atomic materials, provision was made that quotas to be assigned each nation for the peaceful use of atomic power on an equitable basis should be written into the treaty. The methods for determining an "equitable basis" was left to be worked out at a later date but there were strong indications in the Report that an "equitable basis" would mean a basis bearing some relation to size, industrialization, and actual needs of any given nation. These quotas would not be subject to arbitrary decisions of the International Control Agency.

When the proposal was first introduced by the French that the quotas for peaceful use should be fixed in the treaty, Gromyko displayed considerable interest and said it was something the Russians would like to discuss. A year later, however, he had apparently received different instructions from the Kremlin, for from that time on, the whole handling of quotas was under constant attack by the Soviet Union. Over and over again in the meetings of committees, of the United Nations Atomic Energy Commission and later in the General Assembly, the Soviet delegate read excerpts from that section of the Report having to do with the mining of ores, and attacked the other nations for proposing similar quotas for peaceful uses. It was useless for the other delegates to read patiently from the Report itself and to point out that the quotation used by the Soviet delegate did not refer to quotas assigned for peaceful uses, but to an entirely different matter relating to mining. The Soviet delegate remained oblivious to the facts presented him, and continued to draw a picture of injustice which, by simple reading of the Report, was demonstrably without foundation. Yet to those who did not follow the debate closely it must have appeared that the majority position on quotas was unfair.

During the two years in which the specific proposals of the Second Report were under discussion, the Soviet position seemed to harden, almost from month to month. At the start they had expressed their interest in an equitable plan of quotas; at the end they were attacking the quota proposals without even being willing to read what they were. When the First Report was presented, Gromyko went along with the plan for putting the treaty into effect step by step (the so-called stages). At the end of two years this was one of the bitterest points of opposition. From the start, the USSR had claimed that the proposed international agency was endowed with too much arbitrary power. The French proposal for quotas to be written into the treaty, and the British proposal that no nuclear fuel should be made except for use in peaceful power plants actually under construction, were designed to reduce the authority of the international agency. These changes were accepted by the United States and formed a part of the Second Report. These charges did limit the authority of the international agency, making it clearly the servant of the nations for which it was trustee. Its decisions would be subject to an appeal to the courts if it went beyond the clearly defined limits of its powers. It was a very substantial change from the First Report, but the Soviet delegate never admitted that any concessions had been made.

It would be hard to believe that the Soviet delegates did not understand what they were doing when, as was frequently the case, they refused to admit the existence of whole sections of the Second Report which were placed before them. They must have known that their position was not an honest one. It is harder to know what was going on in the minds of their masters in the Kremlin. There were many times when it seemed to us that the information sent back to the Kremlin by the Soviet delegates themselves was incorrect. They were telling the men in Moscow the things they thought they wanted to hear. In many cases they were, in effect, relaying back the propaganda put out from Moscow and reiterated in some naive or fellow-traveler source in this country. It is just possible that the Politburo sincerely believed that the proposals of the majority were insincere and dangerous to the Soviet Union. Nothing is impossible to minds so suspicious and so isolated, equipped with such limited information. It is perhaps more likely that the members of the Politburo were determined from the start that nothing should be done to raise the iron curtain, and instructed their delegates not to get themselves into a position of agreeing to open up the Soviet Union to the outside world, or the outside world to the Soviet people.

In June 1947, while the proposals of the Second Report were being developed, the Soviet delegate announced to the Commission the second set of Soviet proposals. The circumstances of the announcement were rather interesting. Gromyko let it be known that he had an important document from Moscow, and for three days before the meeting of the Commission at which it was to be disclosed his spirits were unusually high. Everyone noted the cheerfulness and deep satisfaction with which he presented the proposals. It was as though he had been pent up for months for lack of instructions and at last felt he was doing something constructive. The Soviet proposals were subjected to a debate which lasted almost a year. The final analysis of the Commission was that they offered nothing new or constructive, that they would not provide effective means for enforcing the prohibition of atomic weapons, and that they would increase rather than diminish distrust between nations. As the criticism of the Soviet proposals developed, Gromyko's cheerfulness vanished. He became morose and increasingly bitter in his attitude in the Commission. Towards the end of his stay he spent an increasing proportion of his time in procedural delays and attacks on the motivation of the other delegates, a mode of operation which his successor, Mr. Malik, was peculiarly well fitted to carry out.

II

During all the discussions on atomic energy the Soviet delegates maintained a remarkably hostile attitude. It was clear that what they said was dictated to them from Moscow, and a good many of us came to the conclusion that they emphasized the hostility because they wanted to be sure they would never be reported to the Kremlin as being lukewarm in their efforts. The verbatim records of the debate would show what they actually said; but the reports of their colleagues would give a further proof of their zeal. We have already noted Dr. Skobeltzyn's defensive harangue in Committee No. 2 when he found that the work of the committee had progressed further than he had previously realized. There were many other similar outbursts whose only purpose seemed to be to give the individual a strong record with which to defend himself.

The behavior of the Soviet delegates to each other at times seemed to indicate that they were afraid of each other and of what each might say about the other. Skobeltzyn was quite evidently afraid of Gromyko.

Part of their hostility found expression in their repeated charge that the United States was run by a small group of conspirators in Wall Street. We took this at first as part of their propaganda line. Later we came to the conclusion that they were personally quite sincere in this belief. Government by conspiracy was the only kind of government they could imagine. They knew nothing else. Such an attitude would, of itself, make them difficult to deal with. When Gromyko was going back to Moscow at the end of his term here, I met him in the lounge and asked him whether we couldn't sit down together and go over atomic energy matters before he left. I told him that we had worked together for three years on this problem; that I was sure he was sincere in his desire to find a solution, and believed he thought me sincere; that I might be able to give him a better idea of my government's position in such a talk than in the public debates in the Commission. He looked at me quietly for a moment and then said, "Mr. Osborn, you may be sincere, but governments are never sincere." We never had our talk.

If their hostility were confined to the larger powers, it might have been thought an attempt to win over the smaller ones. But this apparently was not the case. A number of times Vyshinsky actually went out of his way to humiliate representatives of the various powers before the whole Assembly. In Paris in 1948, when the debate opened on atomic energy, both Senator Rollin of Belgium and M. Ramadier of France made speeches suggesting that there must be some compromise. We thought that Vyshinsky would use their offers for propaganda purposes. But, instead, he turned on them with extraordinary fury, accusing them of being tools of the United Kingdom and the United States. Again, in the Assembly in New York in 1949, the representative of Lebanon made a sincere proposal for compromise. It seemed a very dangerous move, because it would have made controls ineffective. We were concerned that Vyshinsky would take it up. But our concerns were groundless, for he replied at once, and angrily, that the representative of so small and unimportant a country as Lebanon had an unmitigated gall to think he could take part in a debate on so important a subject.

We were forced to the conclusion that the Soviet delegates were more interested in propaganda than in negotiations, and that their propaganda was directed almost entirely to the emotions of the people on their side, rather than to the intelligence of their audience.

A statistical content analysis of the debates seems to confirm these impressions. Dr. Lilian Wald Kay of the Psychology Department of New York University took the verbatim records of the 26 meetings of the Working Committee of the Atomic Energy Commission held in 1947, and the summary reports of the eight meetings of the Ad Hoc Political Committee of the General Assembly held in 1949, and analyzed the length and content of the various speeches.[2]

The time taken up by the various delegations in the meetings was as follows:

	1947	*1949*
Four powers	36%	21%
USSR	37%	21%
Remaining delegations	27%	58%
	100%	100%

Thus the Soviet delegates talked as much as, or more than, the delegates of the four other major powers combined. Since the satellites were great talkers, always following the lead of the USSR and in a diminishing hierarchy of time consumed, the time taken up by the remaining delegations in the table above was probably divided on about an equal basis, between the Soviet bloc and the 48 other members of the United Nations.

As to content, one of the most interesting analyses was the count that was made of attacks on the motives of the other delegates. In this category, the Soviet Union contributed twelve out of fifteen such attacks in the 1947 meetings and 53 out of 65 in the 1949 meetings. Most of the others were, I believe, contributed by Soviet satellites. Attacks on motives were not a usual method of debate with the others. But to the Soviet Union it seemed the final argument. "The United States and the United Kingdom delegations, anxious to prevent the prohibition of

2 Kay, Dr. Lilian Wald. Discussion Techniques in a series of United Nations Debates. Meeting of the Eastern Psychological Association at Worcester, Mass. April 22, 1950. Also unpublished papers.

atomic weapons, were using every pretext to oppose the U.S.S.R. proposals." (November 8, 1949.)

The Working Committee meetings were concerned with accepting or rejecting the ideas which would eventually go into a treaty. The following table shows the comparative negativism of the Russians:

Ratio of Accepting to Rejecting Statements, 1947

Delegation	Accept: Reject (General)	Accept: Reject (Specific)	Accept: Reject (Total)
Australia	4:1	1.5:1	2.6:1
Belgium	5:1	1:1	3.5:1
Brazil	7.5:1	12:1	13.5:1
Canada	6:1	2:1	2:1
China	8.5:1	3:1	5.8:1
Colombia	4:0	3:0	7:0
France	15:1	2.3:1	4.2:1
Poland	1.5:1	8:1	2.4:1
Syria	1:1	2:1	1.3:1
USSR	5:1	.4:1	.5:1
United Kingdom	7:1	2.5:1	4:1
United States	2.2:1	2.9:1	2.4:1

It was the custom in the Working Committee to change or rotate the chairmanship every month. The chair was expected to act impartially, take little part in the discussion, and when he did state his country's position, to make it clear that he was speaking not as chairman but as a representative of his country. Mr. Gromyko was the only one who, while chairman, argued his country's case without, as it were, stepping down from the chair. The following table shows the analysis of chairman behavior during the seven months of Working Committee meetings during 1947:

Behavior of Chairman

Delegation in the Chair	Number of Meetings	Chairman's acts per Meeting	Delegate's acts per Meeting
USSR	2	22	28
United Kingdom	4	26	3
United States	4	16	6
Australia	8	20	3
Belgium	4	20	0
Brazil	2	22	0
Canada	2	33	2

The statistical analysis of these meetings confirms the conclusions of the non-Soviet delegates. The Soviet delegate talked four times as long as any other delegate; the Soviet delegate, and only the Soviet delegate, constantly attacked the motives of the other delegates or their countries; when the Soviet delegate was chairman he interfered with the discussion far more than did any other chairman, and when he took part in the argument, did not dissociate his role as chairman from his role as delegate.

This behavior may have resulted from ignorance; it may have been the result of a very real and deep seated suspicion of his foreign "adversaries" (the Soviet delegates always acted like men who were being conspired against); his intransigence may have been the result of his own fears and sense of inferiority; or, it may have been a studied behavior taught him in the communist schools for diplomats. But whatever it is that makes him tick, his behavior is not of a sort to win friends or give the impression that he is taking a serious part in a negotiation.

III

Throughout these three years of negotiations the Soviet delegates repeated over and over again a few quite simple statements: "The United States refuses to agree to the prohibition of the atomic weapon"; "The United States proposal for control is an attempt to continue the monopoly of atomic energy in the hands of the United States"; "The other nations have been coerced into accepting the United States plan"; "The Soviet Union has agreed to accept international control and inspection."

It was very obvious to anyone who listened to the debate that none of these statements was true. Prohibition without means for enforcement would not have any reality. As one of the delegates properly said, an explosive which could remove mountains could also remove cities. The offer of the United States to turn over all its atomic facilities, materials and information to an international agency, and to give up its weapons in exchange for effective control, could hardly be considered an attempt to extend a monopoly. As to the charge of coercion, the other nations indignantly denied it, not once but many times, in the committees and in the General Assembly, and pointed out that no other proposals had been made which would provide any sort of effective controls. And when the Soviet delegates said that the Soviet Union accepted international control and inspection, they were defending a position in which, after weeks of exhaustive debate, the other delegates found no reality.

These statements of the Soviet delegates were proved, and obvious, falsehoods. But their constant reiteration had a certain effect. The delegates of the other nations did not believe them. But after hearing them repeated in almost every speech by the Russians or their satellites over a period of months and years, the other delegates stopped refuting them. It was hopeless, it only prolonged the debate, and gave the Soviet delegates renewed opportunities to repeat the falsehood. But they still got headlines in the American and other newspapers, and a considerable section of the American intelligentsia believed them. They must have had a very great effect on the vast Communist audiences who read them in the Communist press and heard them over the Communist radio, without ever hearing the refutation. *Pravda* and *Isvetzia* printed the speeches of Gromyko and of Malik in great detail, but they never printed any part of the able replies of McNaughton or de Rose or Cadogan.

For their own purposes the Soviet method of propaganda was exceedingly shrewd. Even on the delegates of the other nations it had a sort of numbing effect. It is true that it consolidated the opposition and made us view every Soviet move with suspicion. But it seemed to be the Soviet aim to arouse the open hostility of the other delegates.

IV

The negotiation which we have been describing took place over a period of three years. Eleven men (or twelve when Canada was not on the Security Council) took part as principals. Two of these men, the representative of the Soviet Union and the representative of the Soviet satellite (first Poland and then the Ukraine) differed markedly in their behavior from all the others. The Soviet representative was quite evidently under specific instructions both as to what he was to say and as to his conduct. He was at all times to question the motives of the others; he was to try to split the other nations apart from each other, but never to conciliate the smaller nations, to whom he was always to be arrogant and truculent; he was never, under any circumstances, to concede a point except on specific instructions from the Kremlin, and then only in the exact language given him; and, finally, he was to talk as much as all the others put together, to delay, to confuse, and never to admit his true intent or to tell the truth. The representative of the satellite was under his orders, and was to repeat the same thing in much the same words but at somewhat less length, and with new variations of bitterness and accusation.

Gromyko, Malik, and Skobeltzyn could all be very charming socially, and on all the many formal social occasions when they met with the other delegates seemed to take a certain pride in showing us this side of their characters. But their behavior in the meetings of the Commission was entirely different. It was stylized to the extreme. It showed careful training. Of the three men, only Skobeltzyn ever came close to a departure from it, and he was an elderly scientist who had spent much time in Paris. The few times he seemed to be making a departure from the approved Soviet style, he was quickly put back on the track by Gromyko, or by one of his aides.

At no time did any of these men give any honest clarification of their proposals; at no time did they indicate any possibility of compromising any issue, though there were plenty of times when they made compromise proposals, patently fraudulent to the other delegates, for purposes of propaganda. At no time did they discuss the proposals of the other delegates on their merits.

In contrast to the behavior of the delegates of the Soviet Union and its satellites, the other nine or ten delegates behaved as one might expect any high-grade group of serious men to behave in similar circumstances. They were sincere, stuck to the issues, did not attack anyone's motives, discussed the various proposals on their merits, strongly upheld their own points of view, accepted compromise, and took responsibility for decisions within the considerable latitude allowed them by their governments. They were there to reach a solution to a problem: the international control of atomic energy. The Soviet representatives were there to make certain proposals, and to make propaganda if the proposals were not accepted.

Was this a negotiation? Certainly it was not in any ordinary sense of the term. I think that at the end of the three years all of us came to believe that we had not been negotiating, except among ourselves. That was the basis for the final recommendation of the Commission: that the Commission should discontinue its sessions until its six permanent members found that there was a basis for agreement.

If there is a lesson to be learned from these meetings with the Soviet Union over a period of three years, it is this: that the word negotiation should not be used to define meetings in which only one of the parties is actually attempting to negotiate. Such a "negotiation" must inevitably fail, and it is not always easy to make it clear to the public who was to blame for the failure.

CHAPTER NINE

NEGOTIATING ON CULTURAL EXCHANGE

*Ernest J. Simmons is Executive Officer of the Department
of Slavic Languages and Professor of Russian Literature at the
Russian Institute in Columbia University. He received his undergraduate and graduate training at Harvard University and
taught there and at Cornell before going to Columbia. He visited
Russia four times between 1928 and 1937 for research purposes.
He is former Editor of the* American Slavic and East European
Review *and presently is General Editor of Columbia Slavic
Studies and the author of many articles and books of which the
principal books are:* English Literature and Culture in Russia
(*1935*); Pushkin (*1937*); Dostoevski, the Making of a Novelist
(*1940*); Tolstoy, a Biography (*1946*); *Editor,* U.S.S.R.: A Concise
Handbook (*1947*).

Negotiating on Cultural

Exchange, 1947

BY ERNEST J. SIMMONS

Culture has been common tender the world over in both ancient and modern civilizations. Ideas, scientific discoveries, literature, art forms, works of art and artists themselves know no national boundaries. Whatever the pride of race or nation in indigenous culture; no manifestations of genius are so international as those which enrich the human mind and spirit with man's loftiest creations of the beautiful or his deepest probings into the nature of things. Every nation has drawn upon preceding cultures or those of its neighbors in developing its own. The early culture of the United States was nourished by that of the United Kingdom, and in later years its growth was indebted to the contributions of innumerable talented foreigners who settled among us from the various countries of Europe. In fact, only in recent years can we be said to have achieved a position of real independence in artistic, scientific and intellectual matters, and in turn we are beginning to influence cultural developments among the peoples of Europe. We have always made

a virtue of our cultural borrowings and lendings, for the free
interchange of ideas and persons and the gifts of genius between
nations has ever been an American principle of international
life.

In certain respects the growth of Russian culture in its early
stages of borrowing bears a resemblance to that of the United
States. In the medieval period strong Byzantine and Scandinavian
influences in Russian literature, art and architecture may be
observed. And in the seventeenth and eighteenth centuries there
existed in Russian upper-class circles almost a slavish devotion
to western European culture and thought. Only with the wonder-
ful flowering of literature, art and music in the nineteenth century did Russian culture begin to attract the admiration and
even the imitation of the west. Over all these years, despite the
often antagonistic attitude of the tsarist government, Russian
intellectuals and artists were relatively free to travel to the centers of learning and culture of the west, and a great many cul-
tured foreigners visited the Soviet Union. There were times when
foreign scholars held honored positions in Russian universities,
when foreign architects designed their buildings, and foreign
manners, customs, clothes and cultural tastes profoundly influenced the way of life of the Russian landed gentry. And in the
more practical matters of economy, manufacturing, mining,
railroad building and military organization, the USSR has been
indebted to the west. In its widespread attacks since the war on
"cosmopolitanism" both at home and abroad, with a consequent
distorted nationalist rejection of all significant foreign influence
on native genius, the Soviet Union is willfully misrepresenting
the whole history of the development of Russian culture.

Though with few exceptions American-Russian diplomatic
relations before 1917 had been friendly, there had been no extensive cultural interchanges. Both the liberal and radical Russian intelligentsia found inspiration in our democratic ideals and
government, and in certain cases they were influenced by our
libertarian writers. Further, the principal works of many of our
better known authors of belles-lettres were frequently translated
into Russian and much admired. In turn, the great Russian
novelists of the nineteenth century ultimately found a wide reading public in the United States. But educated circles in neither
country knew very much about the life and culture of the other.

There was no systematic study of the United States in Russian universities, and in our own the situation with regard to the study of the Soviet Union was no better.

I

The Soviet Revolution of 1917 thrust the USSR upon the attention of the world as no other event in its long history. In the early years of the Soviet Union foreign intervention and lack of recognition on the part of the major nations engendered a rooted hostility to the outside world that was to have fateful consequences. The fact that this new regime was dedicated to the economic life of Marxism, opposed to capitalism, and with the further mission of promoting communism throughout the world, only served to deepen this hostility. It would perhaps be idle to speculate on what the future might have been if the great nations at that time had adopted an attitude even of neutrality to the young Soviet regime. In any event such an approach might have softened the intransigence of the Soviets, and if it had been accompanied by some economic aid, it might have deprived the leaders of the revolution of the possibility of creating that atmosphere of permanent insecurity in the Soviet Union which has contributed so much to the total control of a whole nation. However, historical hindsight can be a fallacious instrument of evaluation when the determinants of events depend so much upon human imponderables in the struggle for political power.

Clearly cultural interchanges between the Soviet Union and the outside world were extremely difficult in such an atmosphere of accumulated enmity and bitterness. On the other hand, there were certain factors during the early years of the Soviet regime which opened the way for various exchanges.

The success of the enormous reconstruction effort involved in the First Five-Year Plan (1928–32) depended a great deal upon foreign aid to the Soviet Union. And no doubt it was partly with the intention of creating the proper atmosphere for foreign trade and assistance that Stalin at this time announced his doctrine of building socialism in one country, in order to disarm the old fears of the capitalist nations of world revolution.

In this situation American technical aid and industrial equipment played a significant part in the accomplishments of the first

two Five-Year Plans, despite the fact that at the outset we had
not yet recognized the Soviet regime. To be sure, our own de-
pression at this time stimulated our interest in such a market,
especially when we soon learned that the Soviets were punctual
in meeting their financial obligations. As a consequence the
annual average of American-Soviet trade grew from under $37,-
000,000 in 1921–25 to about $95,000,000 annually over the next
five years. American Locomotive, General Electric, International
Harvester, the Ford Motor Company and many other industrial
and engineering concerns not only sold their products to the
Soviet Union, but instructed Russians in American plants and
in the Soviet Union how to make these and other products. A
large number of American scientists, technicians and foremen
were employed by the Soviets as advisors and workers during the
First Five-Year Plan. Colonel Hugh L. Cooper and his associates
were instrumental in the designing and building of the huge
Dneprostroi Dam, the machinery for which was furnished by
American firms. Mr. John Littlepage was a chief technical advisor to the Soviet gold-mining trust, and Mr. Ralph Budd, President of the Great Northern Railway, directly aided Soviet engineers in reorganizing the country's railroads and transport.
Further, American concerns played an important role in the
whole development of the Soviet automotive industry, and the
petroleum and sugar industries. Mr. Peter Bogdanov, head of
Amtorg, remarked that in 1930 alone there were 600–700 American engineers in the Soviet Union, and he took this occasion to
thank publicly the many American companies and experts for
their aid in the reconstruction of his country.[1]

At that time and later there were frank Soviet admissions on
the extent of American help and on the high regard for our
science and production methods. In 1932 Stalin declared: "We
observe the United States with interest, since this country ranks
high as regards science and technique. We should be glad to
have American scientists and technicians as our teachers and in
the technical field to be their pupils." [2] In a conversation with
Eric Johnston in 1944, Stalin was also reported as saying that
about two-thirds of all the large industrial enterprises in the

[1] See *Cultural Relations between the United States and the Soviet Union*, Department of State Publication 3480, April 1949.
[2] Z. Suchkov, "Soviet Industry and the U.S.," *Review of the Soviet Union*, February 2, 1934, p. 45.

Soviet Union had been built with United States material aid or technical assistance.

In a real sense the experience of these years supported the viability of the principle of the coexistence of the socialist and capitalist systems. In fact, over the ten years from 1928 to 1938, the cultural impact of the United States on the Soviet Union was considerable and not unsympathetically received. To be sure there was no end of criticism of the United States, and the American stereotype of the fat, silk-hatted capitalist was the endless butt of Soviet humor. But there was a warm and widespread admiration for our efficiency, technical skills and industrial production. Such achievements were the unquestioned models for Soviet engineers and workers, and the good-natured portrayals of Americans in Soviet plays and novels reflected approval of these positive virtues while condemning the economic system that nurtured them.

In the Soviet schools American political, social and economic history was taught, always from the Marxian point of view, but nevertheless with some brief made for the progressive aspects of our development as a nation and people. Not a few of the works of progressive modern American authors were on the reading lists of literature courses in the Soviet schools in those days. In fact, American literature, past and present, was popular reading material in the Soviet Union, and the total number of published copies of such translations ran into surprisingly high figures. Many American tourists were able to obtain visas to visit the Soviet Union after 1933, and even a few American students were allowed to enroll in the universities. In general, it can be said that over these years the Soviet Union did not make a virtue of ignorance of the United States, however much it may have cheerfully anticipated the collapse of our way of life.

During the corresponding period in the United States we can hardly be said to have made a virtue of knowledge of the Soviet Union or to have taken any forthright steps towards promoting cultural relations. The sixteen years of non-recognition rendered official overtures for cultural exchanges difficult if not impossible, and after recognition in 1933 the Soviet Union and communism became such strident political issues in the United States that there was little hope for improved relations in the area of intellectual, educational and cultural matters. So deeply

rooted had become our suspicions of the ultimate intentions of
the Soviet Union, which were in no sense allayed by the persistent propaganda maintained against the capitalist system, that
little encouragement was found for the introduction of studies
on the Soviet Union in our educational institutions. Knowledge
of the achievements of Soviet culture among the general public
was limited pretty much to scattered translations of belles-
lettres, the popularization of new musical compositions, the showing of Soviet films, Soviet participation at the World Fair in New
York and the rather frequent public meetings and exhibitions
arranged by certain American organizations devoted entirely to
the cause of the Soviet Union. This was the situation that existed
up to the entrance of the Soviet Union into World War II in
1941. It can be truthfully said that at this point the people of
these two powerful nations were woefully ignorant of the human
aspirations, culture and way of life of each other.

II

With the United States and the Soviet Union as allies in the
titanic struggle against Nazi Germany, it would appear that circumstances had at last created a climate more favorable to closer
cultural relations. And at the outset there were many hopeful
signs that the alliance would serve to bring about a deeper and
more sympathetic understanding and intercourse between the
two peoples and governments. The magnificent resistance of the
Soviet armies to the enemy inspired much admiration among
Americans, and at the time of the capitulation of the Germans
at Stalingrad a wave of enthusiasm for the Soviets swept the
United States. Russian War Relief contributed millions of dollars worth of medical and other necessary supplies.

At about this time the study of the Russian language in our
colleges and universities began to increase by leaps and bounds,
and our learned foundations, recognizing a national need for
more widespread education and research in this field, granted
thousands of dollars to aid this effort, to set up special studies of
the Soviet Union and to translate its best scholarly productions.

While the United States was mounting its own gigantic war
mobilization, it sent in an endless stream to the Soviet Union, at

a heavy cost to itself in ships and men, lend-lease material amounting ultimately to $9.5 billion. Whole plants were shipped to the Soviet Union, including the latest machinery and the technicians to supervise the erection of the plants. Vast electric generating equipment was sent over; four huge refineries containing the most advanced aviation gasoline process; 1,900 locomotives, 427,000 trucks and enormous quantities of other supplies.

At first there appeared some disposition on the part of the Soviet Government to conceal this kind of aid from its people, but eventually some publicity was given to it, and Stalin himself later paid public tribute to the vital nature of such American assistance in the Soviet war effort.

Though the delay in the opening of the second front tended to sour the friendly attitude of the Soviet Government and people towards its ally, there were numerous official and popular demonstrations of good will and friendship for the United States over the war years. In a report to the Moscow Soviet on November 6, 1941, Stalin stressed the existence of democratic liberties and trade unions in the United States. And in its program of instructions issued by the Commissariat of Education to all teachers of history in the Middle Schools in 1942, they were advised to point out to their pupils that "the friendship of the peoples of the U.S.S.R. and the U.S.A. is based on old historical traditions. In this respect, it is sufficient to recall at least the friendly position of Russia at the time of the American struggle for independence, Russia's aid to the Northern States in their war against the slave-owning South, the peaceful resolutions of the questions concerning the territorial claims of Russia on the shores of the Pacific, etc." And throughout the Soviet Union there were many exhibitions and lectures dealing with American literature, music, painting and culture in general.

In fact, so favorably did we regard the situation that Ambassador Averell Harriman, after the Moscow Conference of October 1943, pointed out to Mr. Molotov that if relations between the two countries were to be enduring they must be based on sympathetic understanding and friendship. He formally requested Soviet approval for distribution in the USSR of two bimonthly magazines designed to explain to the Russian public the nature of the American war effort and the prominent features of American life. And he submitted additional proposals for direct contact with Soviet news editors for the exchange of information and the dissemination of Americans news; the publication of a daily news bulletin for the use of the embassy and diplomatic missions; the distribution of American films to the American Soviet Film Committee; and that VOKS (the All-Union Society for Cultural Relations with Foreign Countries) should serve as a contact for cultural purposes.

Mr. Molotov answered this request on December 31, 1943 in a letter in which he acknowledged the importance of an exchange of material and ideas in the fields of radio and motion pictures. Out of this effort came the permission to distribute to a limited number of Soviet officials and institutions the daily Radio Bulletin as issued by the State Department to all United States Missions abroad and, ultimately, the publication of *Amerika,* a magazine in Russian designed to inform the Soviet people about American life and culture. In general certain advances were made during the remainder of the war in obtaining Soviet cooperation for developing mutual understanding of the two peoples through various cultural media. But it cannot be said that the attitude of the Soviet Union in these respects was in any real sense a cordial one and it did not result in building a firm foundation for future cultural relations after the war.

III

The successful conclusion of the war in Europe and the preliminary talks bearing on the organization of the United Nations filled the peoples of the world with the expectation of prolonged peace after the frightful carnage and devastation. The United States and the Soviet Union had emerged from the strife as the two most powerful nations in the world. There was a clear recognition on the part of the United States Government that the future peace of the world would depend in a large measure on maintaining cordial relations with the Soviet Union, and we fully realized that such relations must be based upon a free interchange of ideas and persons and cultural products. So persuaded were we of this great need that the government ultimately attempted to implement it by law, the objective of which was "To promote a better understanding of the United States in other countries, and to increase mutual understanding between the people of the United States and the people of other countries." [3]

Despite the failures of the past, this widespread hope for better relations with the Soviet Union was also reflected in popular sentiment in the United States at the end of the war. There existed the feeling that the new world responsibilities of the Soviet Union would at least temper its doctrinal hostility to the capitalist system and awaken its leaders to the desperate need for peaceful coexistence in the community of nations. The conviction of the average thinking American citizen at that time was well expressed by Raymond B. Fosdick, President of the Rockefeller Foundation, who declared: "Our relations with Russia are too immediately important, too freighted with all sorts of possibilities, to be left to the mercy of uninformed emotion, whether ecstatic or denunciatory. What is required is a determination to be accurately informed, to see things as they are. It may not be possible to bridge the ideological chasm, but certainly a wider and deeper knowledge on our part of Russian ideas and motivations, and a reciprocal attitude on the part of the Soviet Government, will afford a basis of mutual understanding on which the two nations can live together in the same world." [4]

Some of these hopes for improved cultural relations seemed on the way to realization in the flurry of activities during 1946. As early as 1945 an announcement was made in the Soviet Union that a Foreign Committee had been established in connection with higher institutions of learning to facilitate the freest exchange of students, teachers and scholarly materials between the USSR and other nations. [5] And in October 1945, shortly after the end of hostilities in the west, the Department of State expressed its desire to establish a firm basis for postwar cultural relations with the Soviet Union. It requested the United States Embassy in Moscow to ascertain the earliest date on which the Soviet Government would consider sending the Red Army Chorus or similar groups to tour the United States. The Department of State further requested information on the possibilities of arranging an exchange of ballet dancers, theater companies

---

[3] Public Law 402, 80th Cong., 2d sess. (United States Information and Exchange Act of 1948).

[4] *The Rockefeller Foundation: A Review for 1945*, New York, 1946.

[5] See *Soviet News*, No. 1287, London, October 1945.

and orchestras, and of holding reciprocal exhibits of art, architecture and handicraft as a means of improving the mutual understanding between the two peoples. The Soviet authorities failed
to respond to this overture.

Shortly after this attempt, on November 13, 1945, Ambassador
Harriman conveyed to Deputy Foreign Minister Vyshinsky that
the Department of State would appreciate knowing whether
the Soviet Government objected in principle to initiating an
exchange of students between the two countries in the academic year 1946–47. No reply was made by the Soviet Government.

Meanwhile, throughout 1946 various American individuals,
groups and institutions sought direct cultural contacts with the
Soviet Union. Several leading colleges and universities asked
permission to send members of their staffs to the Soviet Union or
to arrange for professional exchanges, or to set up tuition scholar-
ships for Soviet students to study in the United States. The American Council of Learned Societies contemplated sending ten or
twelve research workers to the USSR. In February 1946, Princeton extended invitations, through the Soviet Embassy in Washington, to a number of distinguished Soviet scholars to attend
the University's bicentennial celebration, and the Rockefeller
Foundation invited two prominent Soviet professors to this country. Though the number cannot be accurately indicated, there
is reason to suppose that many American students applied personally to Soviet embassy and consular officials for visa permits
to visit and study in the Soviet Union. No success emerged from
all these various efforts.

In the realm of music the Boston Symphony Orchestra extended an invitation to Mr. Eugene Mravinsky of the Leningrad
Philharmonic to be its guest conductor on any one of several
dates, but no answer was received. And in May and again in
July of 1946, Dr. Serge Koussevitzky of the Boston Symphony,
who had played a prominent part in Russian War Relief, proposed to Soviet authorities that his famous orchestra be allowed
to travel in the Soviet Union at its own expense for two weeks
and give a series of concerts, the proceeds to be donated to whatever local benefits the Soviet Government might designate. No
acknowledgement was made of this offer. Nor was any answer
given by VOKS to an invitation to send over a Soviet ballet

company to participate in the International Dance Spring Festival to be held in New York.

In August 1946, Dr. E. D. Young proposed to the Soviet Ministry of Health to provide it with a complete penicillin plant and to discuss a mutual exchange of scientists, especially in the medical field, but again no answer.

Meanwhile further efforts were made at setting up student exchanges. American authorities designated certain Soviet institutions in which veterans under the GI Bill might study, but Soviet authorities failed to make provisions for their admittance into the country. And in July 1946, two officials of the Department of Commerce, Mr. Ernest C. Ropes and Dr. Lewis Lorwin, discussed in Moscow with the Soviet Ministry of Higher Education an invitation from Cornell University to four Soviet students to do graduate work and at the same time offer instruction in Russian. After a long wait the Deputy Minister of Higher Education, Mr. A. Samarin, announced that the Ministry regarded the proposal favorably but could not make arrangements for the academic year 1946–47. However, he suggested no other year and did not refer to the matter again. And no interest was shown in the offer of Mrs. La Fell Dickinson, President of the General Federation of Women's Clubs, who had been invited to the Soviet Union, to establish a scholarship for a Soviet girl to study in America. And the request of Professor Richard Foster Flint of Yale to the Soviet Academy of Sciences to engage in field work with Soviet geologists was rejected by the Soviet Government which replied to the American Embassy that the Academy of Sciences would not be working in the districts which would be of interest to Professor Flint. Later visas were also denied to other distinguished applicants, among them Dr. George Schadt, Director of the New England Laboratories, who was interested in an exchange of information on clinical pathology; Mr. Reeves Lewenthal, representative of the Association of American Artists, who wished to acquire information about Soviet art; and Dr. Elliott P. Joslin, well-known specialist on diabetics.

Despite these many and significant failures shortly after the war, certain successes were achieved in promoting cultural interchanges during 1946. Visas were offered for visits to the Soviet Union to the well-known dramatist Lillian Hellman, Mr. John Strohm, President of the Association of United States Agricultural Publications, Dr. Edwin Smith of the American-Soviet Friendship Council, and a bit later to Mr. Fred Myers, Executive Director of the American-Russian Institute, and Professor Percy Corbett of Yale University.

On the occasion of the 220th anniversary of the Russian Academy of Sciences in 1946, a group of prominent American scientists were invited to attend the ceremonies. They were asked to give reports and were very cordially treated. And on the Soviet side a limited number of young technicians were sent over to the United States to receive instruction in machine tooling and radio manufacture, and a group of fifteen Russian students, working for the Ministry of Foreign Trade, were allowed to continue their studies at Columbia University where they had come during the war years. Further, a group of Soviet astronomers, headed by Professor A. A. Mikhailov, Chairman of the Astronomy Council of the USSR Academy of Sciences, toured the United States for six months during 1946 and visited our universities and observatories.

In the early summer of 1946 a good-will gesture that was much discussed in our press was the visit of three well-known Soviet authors and journalists, Ilya Ehrenburg, Konstantin Simonov and Mikhail Galaktionov. They toured the United States for ten weeks as guests of the Department of State and attended the convention of the American Society of Newspaper Editors, which they were invited to address. Later Ehrenburg and Simonov repaid the hospitality accorded them with vicious attacks on the United States.

The surgeon-general of the United States Public Health Service invited, for November–December 1946, four prominent Soviet doctors, including the eminent Dr. Vasili V. Parin, former secretary-general of the USSR Academy of Medical Sciences, to make an inspection tour of hospitals and twelve main cancer research centers, where all the experimental advances were shown to them. Shortly after, however, this trip appears to have brought Dr. Parin under suspicion, for he seems to have vanished from the Soviet scene.

IV

In terms of the initial expectations, the actual successes in promoting cultural relations over 1946 were gratifying but still quite meager. However, new hope arose when, on December 21, 1946, in the course of an interview with Mr. Elliott Roosevelt at the Kremlin, Stalin answered the questions: "Do you favor a broad exchange of cultural and scientific information between our two nations? Also, are you in favor of the exchange of students, artists, scientists, and professors?" with an unequivocal "Of course."

Ambassador Walter Bedell Smith at Moscow seized upon this opening. In February 1947, he wrote Foreign Minister Molotov that the view expressed by Stalin is:

> ". . . gratifying to me since, as you know, I have strongly advocated such exchange to broaden the base of contact which is necessary in order that the people of each of our nations may understand and appreciate the cultural life and objectives of the other . . . I am encouraged by Generalissimo Stalin's expression of views to bring to your personal attention a number of proposals for exchange of the nature referred to above, which have recently been made through this Embassy by organizations and institutions in the United States, and which are waiting Soviet agreement to be put into effect." [6]

Ambassador Smith then went on to list a whole series of recent cultural proposals from the United States, already mentioned in the preceding pages of this chapter, and about which no positive reaction at all had been obtained from the Soviet authorities.

Though no reply was made to this communication, in April Ambassador Smith conveyed to Deputy Minister of Foreign Affairs Vyshinsky the further proposal that the United States would be happy to welcome the visits of some fifty Soviet scholars in various fields of science and culture "to confer with American scholars in the same fields on matters of mutual professional interest," [7] and that it would appreciate similar invitations by the Soviet Union to American scholars.

The only reaction to this proposal was a demurrer on the part of the Soviet authorities that visiting scholars would be com-

[6] Quoted in Cultural Relations between the United States and the Soviet Union, cited above, p. 14.

[7] *Ibid.*

pelled by the United States to register as agents of a foreign power under the provisions of the Alien Registration Act. This objection no doubt was prompted by the fact that a recent visiting Soviet delegation to the American Slav Congress was requested to register under the Act because their activities were construed as political by the Department of Justice. However, no visiting Soviet students or scholars, or Soviet citizens who had been invited by the United States Government had been requested to register under the Act. Nevertheless, Ambassador Smith quickly obtained a ruling from the attorney general to the effect that foreign students and scholars traveling to the United States to engage in educational pursuits would not be asked to register under the Act provided that they limited their efforts to cultural activities.

Despite this removal of any possible objection, the only reply that Ambassador Smith received on the invitation to fifty Soviet scholars to visit the United States was an acknowledgement of its receipt and the information that it would be forwarded to the appropriate authorities for consideration. The Soviet Ministry of Foreign Affairs did eventually enter into communication with the American Embassy on the long series of cultural proposals listed in Ambassador Smith's letter to Mr. Molotov, but the net results were outright rejections, evasions or specious excuses for failure to accept these offers.

V

Clearly the considerable efforts that had been made by the Government of the United States and by various institutions and individuals to promote cultural relations with the Soviet Union after the war had met with little success. These failures had not unduly surprised American experts on the Soviet Union who had expected little from these efforts, but hopeful signs kept appearing on the horizon which seemed to indicate that if the proper approach could be found some progress might be made. Another such sign was the interview of Mr. Harold Stassen with Stalin on April 19, 1947. To quote the TASS account of the meeting: "Stassen would like to know whether J. V. Stalin hopes for a wider exchange of ideas, students, teachers, artists, and tourists in the future in the event that collaboration (i.e., economic and commercial collaboration) is established between the U.S.S.R. and the U.S.A. J. V. Stalin replies that this will be inevitable if collaboration is established. An exchange of goods will lead to an exchange of people." Mr. Stassen returned to this matter later in the interview in saying, according to the TASS version, "the press, trade and cultural exchange are the spheres in which the two systems must find ways of setting to right their mutual relations. J. V. Stalin says that this is true." [8]

Of course, this difficulty was no doubt at least part of the crux of the whole matter—the two countries had not entered into full-scale postwar commercial and economic relations, and the failure of the Soviet Government to accept wholeheartedly American cultural proposals was a reflection of this fact. To be sure, there were other reasons of a much deeper and more serious nature, but it never seemed to occur to the Soviet authorities that a free cultural interchange of people, ideas, literature, music and art was at least one of the factors that would help to encourage better commercial and economic relations with the United States.

Yet Americans who were interested in promoting cultural relations with the Soviet Union were still loathe to give the matter up entirely, and Stalin's statement to Mr. Stassen had inspired a slight new hope. The pattern of previous negotiations had been through official government channels, or direct requests by individuals and institutions through the Soviet Embassy in Washington or the American Embassy in Moscow, or directly by mail to Soviet organizations such as the Academy of Sciences or VOKS. The different approach was now considered of sending a scholar, who knew Russian, to Moscow to deal directly with Soviet cultural authorities.

Accordingly, in the winter of 1947 the American Council of Learned Societies invited the writer of this chapter to undertake such a cultural mission to the Soviet Union if a visa could be obtained; a trip made possible by a grant-in-aid by the Rockefeller Foundation to the American Council of Learned Societies. It was felt that my own long interest and activity in attempting to promote cultural relations on an educational level between the two countries might win a hearing for me in the Soviet Union.

In the process of obtaining my visa, I had talks with the Soviet Ambassador to the United States, Mr. Novikov, with the Consul

[8] *Ibid.*, p. 13.

General at New York, Mr. Lomakin, and with the Soviet representative to the Security Council of the United Nations, Mr.
Gromyko. I told them of my mission and felt that I received
some encouragement from all of them. In the course of my interview with Ambassador Novikov, he indicated that his government desired better cultural relations with the United States;
that it did not wish to send students to the United States until
it could do so on a reciprocal basis, which it was unable to do
then because of the poor conditions in his country owing to the
war, but he hoped that there would be an improvement shortly.
He did say, however, that the Soviet Union was now being accused of maintaining an iron curtain, and he wondered, should
it allow American students to come there to study, if his government would not then be accused by our press of communizing
these students. However, after a long wait, my application for a
visa was successful, and the very fact that I was granted one at
all, which is usually not done without an acceptance on the part
of the Ministry of Foreign Affairs of the applicant's reasons for
applying, gave me a slight feeling of hope that some of my requests might be favorably received by Soviet officials.

Rather than confine myself solely to discussing the improvement of cultural relations in general terms I felt that a series of
concrete proposals in this respect from a limited number of colleges and universities would serve to anchor the subject in solid
performance. Accordingly, officers of the Rockefeller Foundation
and the American Council of Learned Societies kindly circular-
ized a number of colleges and universities, interested in the
study of the Soviet Union, with the purpose of my mission and
requested statements on any concrete projects that they wished
me to undertake. The replies were extremely interesting in the
light they threw on the seriousness of the study of Russia and
the Soviet Union in most of these institutions and on their
willingness to make important commitments in order to improve
their cultural contacts with the Soviet learned world. From these
replies I culled five concrete proposals, selecting largely those
which did not involve a *quid pro quo* arrangement, which I
felt, in the circumstances and on the basis of past experience,
would endanger the chances of success. I further received a series
of important proposals from Mr. Luther H. Evans, Librarian of
Congress. My mission then had two objectives: 1) to explore the

possibilities of improving cultural relations in general and at the same time to propose for action a series of definite projects involving educational and cultural exchanges; 2) to investigate the state of Slavic studies in the Soviet Union.

I arrived in Moscow on July 15, with about a month in which to conduct my business there. All past experience indicated that the best plan of procedure would be to work through VOKS, for few Soviet individuals and institutions in the educational field will meet and discuss cultural proposals on a practical level with a foreign specialist without the sponsorship of VOKS. And VOKS can be endlessly helpful in facilitating such meetings. To be sure, final results can hardly be achieved without the full support also of the Ministry of Foreign Affairs, but it seemed advisable at first to work through the regular cultural channels, for to have appealed at the outset to high officials in the Ministry would have required the intercession of our Embassy, whereas the best advice was to keep the mission, as far as was possible, where it properly belonged—on a non-governmental basis.

I visited the vice-president of VOKS, Mr. Karaganov, on my second day in Moscow. He received me cordially enough, for I was well known to him through my professional work in Russian and Soviet literature. He had also apparently received communications about the general purpose of my mission from Soviet representatives in the United States and the Ministry of Foreign Affairs. We discussed a number of matters concerning American-Soviet cultural relations, and he asked me several questions about the American Council of Learned Societies—its organizational structure, importance in educational work, etc. I then told him of the purpose of my mission and outlined the projects I had to offer. He seemed interested, especially in the proposals of the Library of Congress, and he asked me to send him a detailed memorandum.

The next day I sent in the requested memorandum to Mr. Karaganov. It read as follows:

Subject: CULTURAL RELATIONS

I have been sent over to the Soviet Union by the American Council of Learned Societies with the purpose of furthering cultural relations between American and Soviet educational institutions. I was also requested to report on the development of Slavic studies, particularly in the literary and philological fields, in the main centers of Slavic studies in the U.S.S.R. With this mission in mind, various important American universities and the Library of Congress were requested to submit concrete proposals, which they were prepared to implement in furthering cultural relations with the Soviet Union. In a preliminary conversation with Mr. Karaganov of VOKS, I was requested to submit these proposals in writing. These proposals are listed below. I have taken the liberty to add several requests for aid which will be of real service in enabling me to fulfil my cultural mission in Moscow and elsewhere.

PROPOSALS

Library of Congress:

1. The Librarian of Congress, Mr. Luther H. Evans, proposes a combined Soviet-American bibliographical enterprise, a co-operative effort of the librarians of both countries, to compile a bibliographical list of historical, political, economic, and cultural relations between the United States and pre- and post-revolutionary Russia. Such a list does not exist at present. American and Soviet scholars would benefit alike from such an enterprise. This all-embracing list should be annotated and cover monographic as well as periodical literature.

2. This project might be connected, for preliminary exploratory purposes, with the offer of the Librarian of Congress to receive two representatives of a Soviet research library for the purpose of spending six months in the Library of Congress. In return, it is hoped that two members of the staff of the Library of Congress would be invited to spend six months in the Moscow Lenin Library.

3. The Librarian of Congress also proposes that the following gaps in the Soviet material now being received by the Library of Congress be filled:

(a) The provincial press.

(b) Local publications—books published outside such large centers as Moscow, Leningrad, etc.:

(1) All kinds of bibliographical tools, including *Knizhnaya Letopis'; Letopis Zhurnalnykh Statei; Letopis Gazetnykh Statei,* and the main bibliographical publications of the individual Soviet republics.

(2) Publications of the national academies of the various Soviet republics (periodicals as well as monographs).

(3) Serial publications of the various Soviet educational institutions—universities, industrial colleges, medical, technical, military, law and art schools, research institutes, observatories, schools for training librarians, archivists and teachers, schools for the teaching of foreign languages, schools of diplomacy, etc., etc.

4. The Librarian of Congress agrees to consider the restoration of part or all of the Yudin collection to Soviet authorities, who have a strong interest in it because of its association with Lenin, provided, however, that arrangements can be made to replace the volumes in a form not less serviceable than that which they now are, and that reimbursement be made for the costs of such replacements.

Visiting Soviet Professors to American Universities:

1. The Russian Institute of Columbia University in New York wishes to invite a Soviet professor in any one of the following fields: Russian history; Soviet economics; Soviet law; Soviet international relations; Soviet literature. The incumbent would serve as a regular member of the staff of the Russian Institute for one or two semesters and would enjoy all the privileges of the University. It is hoped that he would be a man of outstanding distinction in this field and he would have to lecture in English.

2. The Department of Slavic Languages of Columbia University wishes to invite a Soviet professor of Russian literature to serve in the Department for one or two semesters. He would be expected to teach courses and direct graduate study in any of the three following divisions: Old Russian Literature; 18th Century Russian Literature; 19th Century Russian Literature. He would be required to lecture *only in Russian.* It is hoped that professors of such distinction as Derzhavin, Gudzii, Blagoi, Tomashevski, etc., etc., would be interested in such an invitation.

3. The Dean of Yale University in New Haven, William C. DeVane, has tendered through me an invitation to a distinguished Soviet professor of Russian literature and philology at the graduate level. This invitation is for the academic year 1948–49, and would be for a year or a longer period.

4. The Dean of the University of Chicago, Richard P. McKeon, would welcome a distinguished professor from the Soviet Union to teach for a year at the University of Chicago, preferably in the field of Russian culture. It would be desirable for the visiting professor to lecture in English. Dean McKeon would also welcome graduate students from Soviet Russia and would arrange scholarship assistance for them.

5. The Far Eastern Institute of the University of Washington, Seattle, would welcome a visiting professor of Russian literature for a year or six months. Representations to this effect have already been made to the Soviet Ministry of Education through VOKS.

6. A number of American universities and colleges such as Stanford, Northwestern, Kansas, Bryn Mawr, etc., etc., would welcome having Soviet professors give several lectures in Eng-

lish on their respective fields if they were already on the staffs of other American universities as visiting professors.

REQUESTS FOR AID

In carrying out my cultural mission here, I would be very grateful if VOKS would arrange for me the possibility to meet:

1. The Soviet Minister of Education, Mr. Kaftanov.
2. The Director of the Lenin Public Library.
3. The Head of the Academy of Sciences, Mr. Vavilov.
4. The Director of the Lenin Institute.
5. Professors in the general field of Russian literature and Slavic philology, such as Derzhavin, Bogatyrov, Blagoi, Tsyavlovski, Gudzii, Tomashevski.
6. The Head of the Foreign Section of the Writers' Union.

Professor Ernest J. Simmons,
Representative of the
American Council of Learned Societies

VI

Five days later, after considerable prompting on my part by telephone, Mr. Karaganov invited me to come to VOKS again and discuss the memorandum. He said that he had divided it up into several parts and sent them to the various Soviet officials for consideration and that now I would have to wait for their answers. I reminded him that my stay in the Soviet Union was limited and that I would appreciate his expediting the matter as much as possible. To my question as to whether he would arrange for the conferences I had requested, he replied that he had tried to arrange for a meeting with Mr. Kaftanov, Minister of Education, but that he was away for a few days, and that he would try again. As for Mr. Vavilov, head of the Academy of Sciences, he could not be certain that he would agree to meet me. Obviously, something had happened between my first and second interviews with Mr. Karaganov to lower the temperature of his interest in my mission, probably a talk with the authorities in the Ministry of Foreign Affairs.

At his request, we then discussed the whole matter of book and periodical exchanges. He said that VOKS would like to receive copies of our popular periodicals—*Life, Time, Newsweek, Saturday Review of Literature, Harpers, Atlantic Monthly, Nation, New Republic*—and especially literature and books on art, music, theater, cinema and science that had appeared during the war years. I mentioned the possibility of centralizing the whole matter of the exchanges of such materials, indicating the difficulties that American organizations have had in the past in dealing with a variety of Soviet institutions, but he declared his conviction that Soviet institutions would get less material under any system of centralization. On the whole, he said, the Lenin Library was a center for the exchange of books in general; the Library of the Academy of Sciences for scientific works, the Medical Library for medical books, etc. When I suggested, however, the possibility of an over-all exchange of books between the Lenin Library and the Library of Congress, he was interested and asked me to ascertain if the Library of Congress would agree. (I cabled the Library of Congress on this score.) I also described to him the translation project of the American Council of Learned Societies, and asked him if he wished to submit any titles for consideration. He suggested that we canvass the scientific works of all the Stalin laureates.

I did not hear from VOKS again until five days later, when I was informed that a conference had been arranged with the director of the Marx-Engels-Lenin Institute, Professor V. S. Kruzhkov. I wished to find out about developments in this important Institute, since I had been last there ten years ago. I also felt that it might be important to interest its director in my proposals, particularly the offer of the Library of Congress to return the Yudin collection, which Lenin himself had made use of.

We had an interesting and profitable discussion on scholarly matters, and Professor Kruzhkov brought me up to date on recent important acquisitions of the Institute, which has over a million volumes, and on the new publications that the Institute is undertaking, especially the new edition of Lenin's works. He proved to be much interested in the Yudin collection and said that he would talk with VOKS about it. In our general discussion of cultural relations he volunteered the opinion that the time was simply not ripe for an exchange of professors and students. VOKS had an official observer at this interview, and on the way out I engaged her in conversation. Among other things she complained bitterly of the way the United States Government had treated the group of recent Soviet visitors, delegates to the Slav Congress in America, by requesting that they register under the

Alien Registration Act. "We are proud," she said, "and though it is possible that this law might apply to visiting Soviet historians and economists, we do not see how it could apply to Soviet writers and artists visiting your country." I took this as more or less a reflection of the official attitude of VOKS on this incident.

Upon not hearing from Mr. Karaganov for several more days, I phoned him to ask for any news on my memorandum. He told me that the Lenin Library was considering the pertinent section of my memorandum and he hoped soon to arrange an interview for me on the matter. Concerning other sections of the memorandum, he could add nothing new, nor could he tell me anything definite about the interviews with various other officials which I had requested. I then reminded him once more of my time limitation, saying that I had now been in Moscow fifteen days without any results, and I informed him that if I did not have some concrete results soon, I would take steps to present my proposals directly to the Ministry of Foreign Affairs. That same day I informed the Embassy of the situation, and Ambassador Smith agreed that if I did not get results within a few days he would endeavor to arrange an interview at the Ministry of Foreign Affairs.

Five days later I took the occasion to meet Mr. Karaganov at a gathering. He asked me with some assurance if the Lenin Library had got in touch with me. When I informed him that it had not, he said he would look into the matter at once. To my query as to whether or not Mr. Kaftanov, Minister of Education, and Mr. Vavilov, head of the Academy of Sciences, would see me, he replied that Mr. Kaftanov was much too busy, and that Mr. Vavilov had just left for his vacation. The implication was clear: if Mr. Karaganov had informed Mr. Kaftanov and Mr. Vavilov about my proposals for Soviet professors to visit and teach in the United States, and these two gentlemen had found it impossible to see me, the obvious answer to the proposals from these quarters was "no". Finally, Mr. Karaganov asked me if I had seen the president of VOKS, Mr. Kemenov. I replied that I had written a letter to Mr. Kemenov about the purpose of my mission and had never received a reply, but that I would be happy to meet him. Mr. Karaganov said that he would try to arrange a meeting, and then he added that he himself would like to see me for a good long talk before I left the country. I said I would be delighted, and reminded him that I would be leaving Moscow on August 14th.

I called Mr. Karaganov's office several times in the next few days about the projected visit with the director of the Lenin Library, and meanwhile I had provided the Embassy with material for an *aide mémoire* on the proposed interview at the Ministry of Foreign Affairs. On August 9th I was informed by VOKS that I had an appointment with the acting director of the Lenin Library, Madame Kamenetskaya—the director, Olyshev, was off on his vacation. The acting director had before her the section of my memorandum dealing with the proposals of the Library of Congress, and from our subsequent conversation it became clear that she had given these proposals careful consideration, no doubt in consultation with some one from the Ministry of Foreign Affairs. Her answers were all prepared.

On point No. 1 of the memorandum—the suggestion of the Library of Congress for a combined Soviet-American bibliographical enterprise to compile a bibliographical list of historical, political, economic and cultural relations between the United States and pre- and post-revolutionary Russia—she said that the Lenin Library was already working on extensive bibliographical projects in connection with their Five-Year Plan expansion program, and hence they simply could not spare any bibliographical experts at this time for the proposal of the Library of Congress.

On point No. 2—the proposal for exchange visits of two representatives of a Soviet research library to work in the Library of Congress for six months and two representatives of the Library of Congress to work in the Lenin Library for the same period of time—she replied that they would be unable to do this because of the reasons she mentioned in connection with the first proposal—all their experts were now needed for their large expansion program.

On point No. 3—the request of the Library of Congress for various items that it is not now receiving from the Soviet Union—she asserted that the Lenin Library was limited in the amount of materials that they had for exchange and that there were many other libraries which they had to service in this respect. However, she added that she would do everything possible to send the specific items mentioned in the memorandum. She pointed out that some of the items mentioned, such as the provincial papers, the Lenin Library could not always procure for itself. I asked her if this were also true of *Knizhnaya Letopis'*, and she replied that they were often lacking in extra copies of this bibliographical item. She also admitted, when I asked, that *Knizhnaya Letopis'* did not list all published items, particularly the smaller ones, and that the figure of 60 percent of the total publication for this list was about right.

On point No. 4—the offer of the Library of Congress to restore the Yudin Collection under certain conditions—she flatly answered that, though they would be interested in certain items in the collection which Lenin may have used, they were definitely not interested in obtaining the whole collection. I was reminded of a statement made to me by a foreign minister in Moscow from one of the satellite countries: "The Soviets do not always make it easy for you even in the matter of giving them gifts."

I then mentioned the possibility of an over-all exchange or a complete exchange in specified categories between the Library of Congress and the Lenin Library, for I had in the meantime received an answer to my cable to the Library of Congress which requested me to explore this matter. The acting director repeated that the Lenin Library was very limited in the materials they had for exchange purposes; that though they get three copies each of all books published, these are needed for their own purposes and for exchange basis with libraries in general. She concluded that she preferred to leave the exchange basis with the Library of Congress as it was and to try to improve it as much as possible.

Of course, I offered up arguments to these various answers of the acting director to the points in my memorandum, but it was clear that these answers had been officially decided upon and that she did not have the authority to take any other stand.

In concluding this part of the conversation, I suggested that if there were any items in the memorandum which they wished to raise in the future, I hoped they would get in touch directly with the Library of Congress. The acting director promised to do this.

On the same day (August 9th), I had an interview at the Ministry of Foreign Affairs arranged by Ambassador Smith. A few days before the Ambassador had met with Vice-Minister Vyshinsky on another matter. At the end of this meeting, the Ambassador told me, he had pointed out to Mr. Vyshinsky that in the past he had brought to his attention a number of proposals designed to improve cultural relations between their two countries and that in no single case had he received favorable action by the Soviet Government. He added that he no longer felt it consistent with the dignity of his government to pursue these matters any further. However, he continued, Professor Simmons, representing the American Council of Learned Societies, was now in Moscow with a series of important cultural proposals, and that he would consider it a personal favor if Mr. Vyshinsky would agree to discuss these matters with Professor Simmons. Mr. Vyshinsky replied that he would be glad to do what he could, though at this time he was very busy, owing to the fact that Mr. Molotov was away.

Nevertheless, it took further prodding on the part of the Embassy before it was informed that an appointment had been arranged at the Ministry of Foreign Affairs, but with Vice-Minister Y. A. Malik and not with Mr. Vyshinsky.

The *aide mémoire* prepared for this occasion contained the following introductory remarks:

> The attention of the Ministry is invited at this time to a series of concrete proposals relating to cultural exchanges which have been brought before the Soviet authorities by Professor Ernest J. Simmons, a representative of the American Council of Learned Societies, who is presently in Moscow.
> Dr. Simmons, Executive Officer of the Department of Slavic Languages at Columbia University, undertook at the request of the American Council of Learned Societies a cultural mission to the Soviet Union. The American Council of Learned Societies is a member of the International Union of Academies, and with it are associated twenty-four learned societies and organizations in the fields of the Humanities and Social Sciences.

There next followed a listing of the several cultural proposals exactly as described in the memorandum, included elsewhere in this chapter, which was presented to VOKS, and a brief account of the activities and interviews arranged by VOKS in connection with this memorandum. The *aide mémoire* then concluded:

> It will be recognized by the Ministry that Professor Simmons is a representative of the highest organs of learning in the United States, that his proposals outlined above carry the weight of authorities interested in developing real cultural relations between the United States and the Soviet Union, and the outcome

of his present mission will be a matter of great concern to scholarly and educational circles in the United States. For this reason the Embassy of the United States attaches special importance to the request that the Ministry aid in making Professor Simmons' mission successful.

The conference took place in the Soviet Ministry of Foreign Affairs on August 9 at 6 p.m., and was attended by Ambassador Smith, Professor Simmons, Vice-Minister Malik and his interpreter.

Ambassador Smith began by offering a brief résumé of the recent efforts of the American Embassy to improve cultural relations with the Soviet Union. He indicated that it was of vital importance, especially at this time, to endeavor to maintain cordial cultural relations between the two countries. And it was in this spirit, he added, that, despite the lack of success in recent efforts, he had requested the Soviet Ministry of Foreign Affairs to see Professor Simmons and discuss with him a series of concrete proposals designed to promote better cultural relations between the two countries, and that he would be gratified if these proposals were favorably entertained. He concluded by saying that Professor Simmons was a representative of the highest American educational organizations, and particularly of the American Council of Learned Societies. Ambassador Smith then requested Professor Simmons to describe the projects that he had come to the Soviet Union to propose.

The Russian interpreter translated faithfully these remarks of Ambassador Smith. Mr. Malik replied that he, too, wished to say that his government was interested in maintaining cordial cultural relations with the United States, and that he would be happy to listen to Professor Simmons, of whom he had heard a good deal. This statement was translated.

I then spoke to Vice-Minister Malik in Russian. I said that I was pleased that the Vice-Minister had some knowledge of my efforts in educational circles to promote better cultural relations between the United States and the Soviet Union, and that in many respects this had been one of my main endeavors over the last fifteen years. I told him that I had been asked by the American Council of Learned Societies to come to the Soviet Union with a series of definite cultural proposals. I described the tremendous growth of interest in the Soviet Union in American educational circles since the war. Before the war, I said, there had been scarcely more than a half dozen universities where Russian was taught, and hardly more than a hundred students studying the language, but that since the war there were more than a hundred colleges and universities where the language was taught and more than thirty thousand students studying it.

Mr. Malik expressed surprise at this information and some gratification, but he added that there were of course many more students than that studying English in the Soviet Union.

I continued and said that there were also now many students studying the social sciences and humanities in the United States with direct reference to the Soviet Union. I added, however, that American educators felt that the learning of these students specializing in the Soviet field would be incomplete if the best of them were not allowed to finish their studies by spending some time in the Soviet Union.

Vice-Minister Malik interrupted to say that at the present time, and especially since the war, there were a hundred student applicants for every available place in Soviet institutions of higher learning. Accordingly, he added, it was extremely difficult for the Soviet Union now to accept foreign students.

This statement was translated, and Ambassador Smith said that he could appreciate the crowded situation, but that it was common knowledge that the Soviet Government had received in its universities students from some of the eastern European countries, and that he hoped that the Soviet Union would take even four or five Americans as a gesture of good will. Mr. Malik replied that he hoped this could be done in the future.

I continued by saying that before I came over, the American Council of Learned Societies and the Rockefeller Foundation had canvassed a number of the most important American universities with the request that they report to me any proposals they might wish me to convey to the Soviet authorities with regard to my mission of promoting better cultural relations. I said that the replies to this request were very interesting, for they indicated the keen desire of these institutions to improve their offerings in the study of the Soviet Union. Out of these replies, I said, had come five definite invitations from major American universities to Soviet professors of Russian literature and culture, and Soviet economics, jurisprudence, international relations and Russian history; that these men would be gladly received on the staffs of these universities as visiting professors for a semester or two; that it was hoped that they would be distinguished authorities in their fields, but that, with one exception, they would be required to lecture in English.

To this request, which I said was in the memorandum which VOKS had requested me to submit, Vice-Minister Malik replied that for much the same reasons which he had indicated in the matter of American students coming to study in the Soviet Union, the Soviet Government would find it very difficult to send professors to the United States. That is, because of the tremendous demand in educational circles, they desperately needed their professors for their own students. He added, however, that in the future perhaps such invitations could be accepted. Mr. Malik then said that he had heard from one Soviet professor who was going for a trip to the United States that he had a "great psychological fear" of this visit because of the things that might happen to him in connection with the American Alien Registration Act; that he had tried to comfort this man by saying that even Americans at times had to submit to this. This statement was translated and Ambassador Smith replied that he had taken the trouble to obtain an authoritative ruling for the benefit of Soviet authorities, to the effect that any Soviet visiting student, professor or scientist to the United States need have no fear that he would have to submit to this Act in his regular activities as a student, professor or scientist.

Mr. Malik repeated, however, that Soviet visitors to the United States would nevertheless have such a "psychological fear" of what might happen to them because of this law. I rejoined that in the light of what the American Ambassador had said, I found it hard to imagine that any visiting Soviet professor to the United States would possibly suffer from any psychological fear.

I went on to list the four proposals of the Library of Congress, which I indicated, would be found in detail in the *aide mémoire*. I said that Mr. Karaganov of VOKS had arranged for me an interview with the acting director of the Lenin Public Library, in order to discuss these projects, and I briefly described the proposals. I then added that there was still a fifth proposal, namely, that the Library of Congress was willing to explore the possibility of an over-all exchange, or an over-all exchange in a number of categories, of all books that were published in both countries. I concluded by saying that I had discussed all these matters relating to the proposals of the Library of Congress with the acting director of the Lenin Public Library, and that the results appeared to me to be entirely negative.

Vice-Minister Malik seemed a little surprised at this and said that they wanted the largest possible book exchange with the United States. However, he had nothing concrete to offer on these proposals of the Library of Congress. He added, however, that he had information to the effect that the Soviet Union was in no sense getting in return as many books as they were sending to the United States, and that he hoped that this situation would improve.

I told him that there were many difficulties involved in the smooth operation of book exchanges and particularly in the purchasing of Soviet books. I pointed out that communications with the Soviet Union on these matters often went unanswered, and that it was my impression that the difficulty could be largely solved if it was possible to centralize the whole matter in the Soviet Union. I had mentioned this to Mr. Karaganov of VOKS, I said, but that he had replied that such centralization would probably result in the Soviet Union getting fewer books from the United States. But I pointed out that the Four Continents Book Store in the United States, an agent of the Soviet Government, was able to buy on the ground large quantities of American books for the Soviet Union with comparative ease, whereas it was difficult for American institutions and individuals to carry out all the purchases of Soviet books they desired without any agency directly representing them in the Soviet Union.

The conference ended at this point, with Vice-Minister Malik, at my request, promising to provide answers to the various proposals discussed at this meeting and indicated in the *aide mémoire* which was left with him.

Though I remained in Moscow until August 14, no answer on the several proposals presented to the Ministry of Foreign Affairs was received by our Embassy prior to my departure, and no effort was made by Mr. Karaganov, Vice-President of VOKS, to arrange the meeting he had suggested with the president of

VOKS, Mr. Kemenov, or to have the final talk with me that he had mentioned, though he knew precisely the date of my departure, and I had taken the precaution to inform his office once again of this fact. The only response to the proposals discussed by me was a short *aide mémoire* from the Soviet Ministry of Foreign Affairs, dated August 22, indicating that the proposals had been forwarded to the proper Soviet organizations for study.

VII

Certain conclusions can be drawn from this and similar failures at negotiating cultural relations with the Soviet Union. Incidentally, British experiences in this respect have largely paralleled those of the United States. Culture in the Soviet Union is political, and there is a direct correlation between all cultural manifestations and Soviet domestic and international policies. In short, the determination of cultural policies rests entirely with the government. The mildly improved cultural relations with the United States immediately after the war in 1946 and early 1947 undoubtedly indicated that Soviet domestic and international policy at the time were still in a state of fluctuation. Between the time I was granted a visa in early April 1947, by the Soviet Ministry of Foreign Affairs for the purpose of making cultural proposals and my arrival in Moscow in July, Soviet policy in reaction to the Truman Doctrine had been formulated. And a new "line" in cultural policy was then laid down to correspond with this domestic and international policy. Though there had been rumblings of an attack on western culture as early as the speech of Zhdanov against the magazines *Zvezda* and *Leningrad* in August 1946, it was not until the summer of 1947 that the violent condemnation of virtually everything western and particularly American broke out in all its fury. When an AP correspondent sent in a despatch to the effect that I had arrived in Moscow and described the purpose of my visit, the despatch was returned from the censor with the phrase deleted that I had come with proposals designed to improve American-Soviet cultural relations. The Soviets are usually consistent in these matters. At a moment when they had begun an all-out ideological war against American culture, they probably saw little sense in entertaining favorably the proposals of a representative of that culture. It was further clear on every side that no matter with whom you negotiated in the Soviet cultural world, the final decision rested with the Ministry of Foreign Affairs.

Since this time, as is well known, the Soviet denunciations of all forms of American art, science and learning have reached a screaming crescendo in the Soviet press, on the stage, in the cinema and in thousands of public lectures. And the State Secrecy Act of June 1947 provided severe penalties for Soviet citizens divulging information which is regarded in other countries as perfectly normal data for publication, and a decree promulgated in December 1947, forbade any Soviet institution other than the Ministry of Foreign Affairs and the Ministry of Foreign Trade from having any relations with representatives of foreign nations. Attacks have even lately appeared in the Soviet press condemning Americans who seek cultural relations with the Soviet Union as people who are concealing ulterior and evil motives.

Obviously, there can be no further hope of negotiating cultural relations with the Soviet Union for the time being. A thin façade of relations will be maintained by the Soviets for the understandable purpose of obtaining the vast quantities of American printed matter and information which they very much want through library exchanges and their official agents here, a situation in which we are at a great disadvantage in our efforts to procure similar Soviet materials. And in any possible future development of a free interchange of ideas, peoples and cultures, there will always be the obstacle of Soviet fear of standing comparison with American achievements. At any rate, such a future development will be possible only when the Soviet Government becomes convinced that it will be in their own interests to achieve it. If such a time ever comes, they will make it abundantly clear, and then there will be no great difficulty in negotiating cultural exchanges with the Soviet Union.

Philip E. Mosely has been Professor of International Relations at the Russian Institute of Columbia University since 1946 and Director of the Institute since the spring of 1951. Educated at Harvard and Cambridge, he taught at Princeton University, Union College and Cornell before going to Columbia. From 1942 to 1946 he served as an officer of the Department of State in various capacities including that of Advisor to the United States Delegation at the Moscow Conference, 1943, Political Advisor to the American Delegation on the European Advisory Commission, 1944–1945, at the Potsdam Conference, 1945, and at the meetings of the Council of Foreign Ministers at London and Paris in 1945 and 1946. He was the United States Representative on the Commission for the Investigation of the Yugoslav-Italian Boundary in 1946. He is the author of Russian Diplomacy and the Opening of the Eastern Question in 1838 and 1839 *and of many articles on the history and politics of Eastern Europe.*

CHAPTER TEN

Some Soviet Techniques

of Negotiation

BY PHILIP E. MOSELY

There is a deep-seated tradition in western diplomacy that an effective diplomat should be a two-way interpreter. He must present his own government's policy forcefully to the government to which he is accredited and defend the essential interests of his country. If he is to give intelligent advice to his government, he must also develop a keen insight into the policies of the government with which he deals and become skilled in distinguishing basic interests and sentiments which it cannot disregard from secondary ones which it may adjust or limit for the broader purpose of reaching agreement. Occasionally, as instanced by Woodrow Wilson's criticism of Walter Hines Page, it has seemed as if individual ambassadors became too much penetrated by the viewpoint and interests of the country to which they were sent and less able to press contrary views of their own governments.

No such problem of delicate balance in functions arises to plague the Soviet negotiator. This has been especially true since the great purge of the Commissariat of Foreign Affairs in 1938–39 and the replacement of Litvinov by Molotov in 1939. The new foreign affairs staff was recruited among the middle ranks of Soviet officials, whose entire training had been based on rigid adherence to centralized decisions and who had rarely had informal contacts with life outside the Soviet Union. The present-day Soviet representative can hardly be called a "negotiator" in the customary sense. He is rather treated as a mechanical mouthpiece for views and demands formulated centrally in Moscow, and is deliberately isolated from the impact of views, interests and sentiments which influence foreign governments and peoples. Probably the Soviet representative abroad, through fear of being accused of "falling captive to imperialist and cosmopolitan influences," serves as a block to the transmission of foreign views and sentiments, rather than as a channel for communicating them to his government.

This does not mean that Moscow is cut off from the flow of public-opinion materials from abroad. On the contrary, it probably receives a very large volume of material, especially clippings of all kinds. On occasion Andrei Vyshinsky quotes triumphantly from some small local newspaper or some relatively obscure "public figure" to prove that the "ruling circles" in the United States are hatching some "imperialist," "war-mongering" plot. This practice arouses bewilderment or uneasy merriment in American listeners, whose ears are attuned to the cacophony of conflicting views. In the Soviet way of thinking, the citing of such sources is perfectly logical since it is assumed that nothing happens "accidentally" and therefore all expressions of opinion are of equal value in exposing the underlying pattern of hostile intention. Incidentally, the diligent Soviet gathering of opinion data appears to rely primarily upon newspapers and their editorial expressions; from the indirect evidence available it seems that very little attention is paid to radio material and to the much more potent role of radio-commentators in molding the thinking of the public.

The large amount of opinion material imported daily from abroad appears to be analyzed and digested in Moscow with two purposes in mind. One is to prove that, despite protestations of humanitarian and peace-loving intentions, the adversary is actually preparing an aggressive war of conquest. Thus, isolated expressions of a willingness to go to war in the near future or statements of ability to wage war are gladly built up into a confirmation of the "imperialist" and "aggressive" aims of the "ruling circles" in the United States. Other material is cited to prove that "the broad masses" in the enemy country are opposed both to war and to all preparation for defense, but are thwarted in giving effect to their attitude by the "dictatorship of big capital."

Some students of Soviet policy believe—in my opinion, far too hopefully—that this two-fold use of foreign press material is directed primarily towards molding public opinion within the Soviet Union, in satellite or, rather, "captive" states, and among the Communist or Communist-influenced faithful elsewhere, and that the Soviet leaders at the center of power have available an objective and factual analysis of foreign events and currents of opinion as a basis for their decisions. No doubt, the *Politburo* has available many facts and reports which do not enter into the controlled flow of information available to their subjects. And on occasion Stalin, less often Molotov or Vyshinsky, has shown an awareness of facts or opinions widely known abroad yet not imparted to their own people. On more rare occasions they have shown a willingness to make small concessions to those interests, alien as they are to the Soviet way of thinking.

At Potsdam President Truman and Secretary Byrnes presented with great earnestness the resentment felt by Americans at the complete censorship which was being exercised over news reporting from the former German satellites,—Hungary, Rumania and Bulgaria,—with the connivance or by the orders of the Soviet occupation authorities. They protested that, since the United States was among the victors and was represented on the Allied Control Commissions, American opinion could not understand why American correspondents were prevented from reporting freely on developments in those countries. While Generalissimo Stalin undoubtedly continued to regard conscientious western correspondents as "spies" and as a nuisance to be tolerated as little as possible, he accepted President Truman's arguments based on the power position of the victor and agreed, after relatively unacrimonious dispute, to the United States proposal for assuring western correspondents of freedom to gather and transmit news from the three satellites. The leader of the Soviet regime could accept the western contentions in this matter, particularly as they left untouched the central power positions of Soviet policy, while subordinate agents would have felt impelled, in harmony with the Soviet concept of centralized manipulation of "opinion," to reject them with vehement accusations of ill-will.

I

In opening negotiations with any Soviet representatives except Stalin the first problem is to discover whether the representatives have any instructions at all. To discover what those instructions, if any, are requires sitting out the whole course of the negotiation, with its demands, insults, and rigidities and its always uncertain outcome. By comparison, western representatives are often allowed to exercise a certain amount of discretion. They may facilitate the ultimate attainment of a workable compromise—a generally shared goal of both sides—by giving their "opposite number" some fairly clear intimation of the "hard" and "soft" spots in their instructions. A still further development of this flexible approach to the desired goal of adjustment, one based on a high level of inter-governmental and inter-personal trust, is to discuss in detail, at various stages in their formulation, instructions which are in process of preparation. For example, a staff officer may be able to tell his counterpart what recommendations on a given matter he proposes to make to his superiors and similarly to learn what ones will be made by his "opposite number" in the other government; if his recommendations are overruled "higher up," no reproach is made to him and no official reference can be made to his confidence.

A thorough knowledge on both sides of the respective instructions as they are being worked out enhances the mutual understanding of the interests and forces which underly the positions taken, eliminates many secondary points of friction and leaves the larger unagreed issues in clearer view. This pattern of "continuous" negotiation, preceding and following the principal and formal negotiation, requires continuing consultation and reporting at at least three levels,—the expert or "recommending and drafting" level, the intermediate or "Assistant Secretary" level, and, finally, the "ministerial" level. Where, in addition to the ministry of foreign affairs, various other ministries or executive departments, dealing with military, financial and other matters, are also concerned, there may emerge parallel three-level consultations with those departments on the same informal basis.

A similarly informal and highly effective approach is provided by the "working party," a technique which was first cultivated within the British civil service to deal with interdepartmental problems below the level of the cabinet and the cabinet secretariat, and which has been applied very successfully in inter-allied and even wider international negotiations. Under the "working party" technique the staffs of experts are given a broadly stated problem to work out, on which each national staff brings to bear a broad picture of the aims and interests of its own government. In the course of its work, facts are established, alternative solutions are considered, and an agreed recommendation may be reached, for presentation to the principal negotiators on both sides. Under this procedure the various staffs operate as experts as much or more than as national representatives, and it is understood that neither side is bound by anything said or tentatively drafted until the report and recommendations as a whole have been considered and approved "at a political level."

These and similar techniques or habits of "continuous negotiation" provide the daily adjustment or lubrication of policy among like-minded and like-purposed western powers. They are, of course, not practiced by the Soviet government in its dealings with the west. Soviet experts and diplomats cannot participate in an informal day-to-day exchange of information, comments and tentative recommendations concerning policy. Until Moscow has sent instructions they can say nothing at all, for they may fail to express the exact nuance of thinking or intention which has not yet been formulated at the center, and transmitted to them. After Moscow has spoken they can only repeat the exact formulation given to them, and no variation may be introduced into it unless Moscow has sent the necessary further instructions. The "western" habit of continuous negotiation is baffling to the Soviet diplomats, who cannot understand that their western colleagues have both the opportunity and the responsibility for presenting and even advocating policies within their own gov-

ernmental operations and that, within a broadly agreed pattern
of interests and purposes, they have considerable leeway in finding the most effective, and usually informal, methods of influen-
cing their "opposite numbers" in foreign ministries or embassies.

The frequently noted "woodenness" of Soviet negotiation apparently applies in relations with satellite or captive regimes, at
least with their governments. Thus, President, then Premier,
Gottwald, outwardly the principal leader of the Communist
Party of Czechoslovakia, was called on the carpet in Moscow, in
early July 1947. He was told by Stalin in person that his government must withdraw its acceptance of the invitation to participate in the conference which was about to meet in Paris to prepare the groundwork for the Marshall Plan of economic aid to
European economic recovery. Gottwald had assumed that the
government of Czechoslovakia was free to accept this invitation
and that the Communist members of the cabinet were free to
vote for its acceptance. His dismay, on being confronted with
Stalin's absolute and vehement veto, points to the absence, at
least at that time, of informal and day-to-day exchanges between
the two governments. Similarly, the period preceding the June
1948 break between Moscow and Belgrade was clearly marked
by the failure of informal communication between Soviet and
Yugoslav policy-makers as well as by the failure of the Soviet
embassy to inform Moscow of the probable effects of an attempt
to overthrow the leadership of Marshal Tito.

The important network of informal communication among
the "western" powers, as well as the moderate latitude given to
their representatives, makes for a swift pace of negotiation which
arouses bewilderment and suspicion among their Soviet colleagues. Since western foreign ministries are receiving daily a
flow of confidential comment on foreign views and intentions,
they are forearmed with current analyses and can often give
necessary decisions rapidly. "Western" diplomats also have a
substantial latitude to work out agreed positions and drafts, at
least on secondary and procedural matters. Thus, their minor
differences are often resolved with what seems to their Soviet
colleagues like suspicious speed.

Not believing in or not understanding the system of informal
communication and limited individual latitude, the Soviet representatives readily fall back on the theory of "American dicta-

tion." It is easier for them to assert that the United States government has exerted political, military and financial pressure to force its will upon other governments than to take the trouble to analyze the complex and, to them, unfamiliar and unbelievable system of informal communication which usually lies behind the "automatic majorities" assembled around United States proposals. They are incredible when told that such pressure is exerted only rarely and that more often agreement is reached through give-and-take of views, by which no side gets its full position and each gets a part of it.

Sometimes the sole instructions with which a Soviet delegation enters a conference are that it is not to commit itself to anything or sign anything. Oddly enough, the outcome may be fairly pleasant and even profitable. When the British and American governments decided to call a conference, held at Bretton Woods, for the creation of postwar institutions of financial and economic cooperation, the Soviet government at first decided to refrain from participation in it. Probably it saw, at best, no direct gain to itself through setting up international machinery to promote monetary stability and the flow of international investment. At the worst, in accordance with the Soviet philosophy of history, it must have regarded such efforts as a futile and undesirable attempt to stave off the long-predicted "general crisis of capitalism." When the Soviet government received the intimation that its refusal even to attend the Bretton Woods conference would discourage the tenderly nurtured growth of interallied cooperation and would provide Goebbels with valuable propaganda material, it reversed its position regarding participation in the conference, but not with respect to joining in arrangements and obligations which might emerge from it, and sent a small but able delegation. Having no direct responsibility for the outcome and probably having no need to annoy "the center" in Moscow with requests for instructions, members of the Soviet delegation could devote their very considerable ingenuity to helping the progress of the conference, by making many minor but useful suggestions as they went along.

The usual experience with "uninstructed" Soviet delegations has been the reverse of this. In some negotiations it became clear, after delivery by it of numerous charges and accusations, that the Soviet delegation had no instructions except to "report back." In 1944, with the beginning of the liberation of western Europe, it became urgent to make provision for the orderly restoration of inland transportation, both by land and water, and it was hoped that these provisions would be applicable to all European belligerents except the Soviet Union and the United Kingdom. Some countries had been stripped of rolling-stock and barges; others held plundered equipment in large quantities. Undestroyed repair facilities would be very unevenly distributed upon the cessation of hostilities; some countries would have considerably more than the necessary minimum of new rails, rolling-stock and bridging material, while others would have none at all. And efficient allocation of urgently needed materials, which Great Britain, Canada and the United States were preparing to supply, required the establishment of some European-wide agency for arriving at agreed but voluntary decisions on these matters. During the greater part of 1944 American, British and Soviet delegations negotiated in London for the establishment of an emergency European Inland Transport Organization.

At least the American and British delegations negotiated with each other and with the Soviet delegation, with great zeal and energy, but the Soviet delegation failed to "negotiate back." The western representatives explained over and over again that not only each great power but each member government would be free to accept or reject the recommendations of EITO, but that it was hoped that agreed recommendations, based on a joint study of the facts, would usually be reached. The Soviet delegates reiterated endlessly that their government could not agree to leave these decisions to any experts. Obviously, the concept that governments would merely ratify the "decisions" reached by experts was both unfamiliar and inconceivable to them. While the western negotiators felt that the "European" character of the proposed organization was a positive factor, the Soviet delegates seemed to regard it with great suspicion, which was merely confirmed when the British delegation expressed a hope that currently neutral countries would also join EITO after the conclusion of hostilities. As the discussions with the Russians continued, the American and British drafts were clarified and gradually began to merge into a single draft, more or less "by attrition." Naturally, this only increased the uneasiness of the

Russians, who could not conceive of any representative daring to modify the sacrosanct text which had been handed down to him.

Days and weeks went by with constant meetings. When the Soviet representatives criticized some aspect of the American or British draft, the other delegations promptly offered some revision which appeared likely to meet that particular criticism. So many versions of the various articles flew around the table that the Russian interpreter was frankly unable to render them to his own delegation. Without attempting to grasp the fine nuances as between successive drafting texts the Soviet delegate proceeded to repeat this or that general criticism, accusation or suspicion after each one of them. Firm in a consciousness both of good intentions and of a practical, functional approach to a vital problem, the western delegates urged on their Soviet colleagues the importance of the early creation of EITO, in order that it could begin urgently needed planning for the recovery of the transportation system. To this the Russian representative blandly retorted that "planning" was not possible under capitalism, anyway.

After several weeks of "negotiation" the American delegation came to the conclusion that the Soviet delegation was unable to present any proposals of its own or to accept any British or American proposals. On the other hand it was free to raise and repeat any number of criticisms of the other drafts, provided it did not allow itself to be pinned down to approval of any individual provision or textual wording. It was clear that the Soviet delegation had long since given up any effort to record in Russian or to transmit to its own government any of the numerous modified drafts which had been submitted by the other two delegations during the course of the negotiation. It was quite probable that the Soviet delegation had been hustled off to London with no proposals to present and with no detailed instructions except to report back. Once in London, its members were probably too timid to make any recommendations or even to ask for new instructions, and in Moscow the few people who were qualified to handle a question of this kind were too busy with matters of direct Soviet interest, such as transforming the Lublin Committee into the government of Poland or negotiating the Soviet terms for the armistice with Rumania, to bother their heads or Stalin's head about EITO.

What could be done about this impasse? In relations between "western" countries questions could be asked informally between middle-ranking members of an embassy and members of the foreign office; within a few days intentions could be clarified and decisions taken. Since the Soviet system permits of communication only at the top and since the "top-level" channels of communication were badly overloaded with more urgent military and political questions, the negotiators for EITO had to find some way to "muddle through."

My own analysis of the situation was that the Soviet delegation would report to its own government only when it had firm American and British proposals to transmit. Instead of devoting their full effort to persuading the Soviet delegation to take a position, which it was not empowered to do, the two western delegations should now work out their differences and arrive at an agreed draft. But they should do this in front of the Russians, since otherwise the latter would regard Anglo-American consensus as a conspiracy against themselves. In arriving at a single draft the two delegations should take reasonable account of the various general Soviet objections and should point out to the Soviet delegation that they were doing so. The agreed draft should provide fully for Soviet adherence, then or in the future, to EITO, but it should provide for its coming into force without Soviet participation after a waiting-period. If it required Soviet participation in order to come into force, and if the Soviet government saw no direct benefit for itself in joining it, it would block the entire agreement merely by not answering various notes and *démarches*. On the other hand, every effort should be made to secure Soviet participation since Soviet refusal would also mean that the Soviet zone in Germany and the countries occupied by the Soviet armies would also refrain from joining this useful cooperative effort. However, on balance it seemed that the Soviet government would be more likely to join EITO if it saw that the other allies were prepared, eventually, to go ahead without it, after taking every precaution to keep the Soviet government informed at each point in the negotiation.

Neither the full hopes nor the entire fears which inspired the EITO negotiators were fulfilled. The question of Soviet participation dragged along until the Potsdam Conference of July 1945. Then, in one of the occasional moments of good feeling between the storms, the British delegation raised the question and urged Soviet participation in EITO. After some whispered consultations, in which Mr. Vyshinsky was seen to shake his head with some vigor despite an effort at impassivity, Generalissimo Stalin turned back to the table and without further discussion or questions announced that the Soviet Government would join EITO. This step, however, did not result in the Soviet Government relaxing its demands for rolling-stock, equipment, barges, tugs, cranes, repair tools, and so forth, in countries occupied or "liberated" by it; it also contributed nothing in the question of whether Germany would be treated as an economic unit or whether the Soviet zone would, as turned out to be the case, be regarded solely as a Soviet appendage.

II

By far the most frequent situation is one in which the Soviet negotiators are bound by detailed instructions rigidly pressed. Each point at issue, large or small, then becomes a test of will and nerves. Instead of striving to reduce the number of points of friction and to isolate and diminish the major conflicts of interest, the Soviet negotiator often appears to his exasperated "western" colleague to take pride in finding the maximum number of disputes and in dwelling on each of them to the full. Even during the wartime period of relative cooperation it was noticeable that each decision to convene a three-power conference was followed by the piling up of disputes and grievances, as well as by the rapid fabrication of Soviet accomplished facts. Thus the decision to hold the Yalta Conference was followed swiftly by the unilateral Soviet recognition of the Lublin Committee as the legitimate government of Poland. While arrangements were being made to hold the Potsdam Conference, at which Poland's territorial gains in the west would presumably be determined by three-power decision, the Soviet government proceeded to turn over to Polish administration a large part of the Soviet zone. This action was, of course, an assertion of the Soviet Union's exclusive role in eastern Europe, in disregard of a political agreement to determine the western boundary of Poland jointly, and in violation of the three-power agreement defining the zones of occupation in Germany.

The closely related technique of playing up grievances was also well illustrated at Potsdam. Bitter and prolonged Soviet attacks upon the presence of British troops in Greece, the Dodecanese, Syria and Lebanon took up much time and energy. When the western negotiators had been worn down by these wrangles the Soviet negotiators could face with greater equanimity the American and especially the British protests against the brutal assertion of Soviet hegemony in Hungary, Rumania and Bulgaria. By their tactics the Soviet leaders had encouraged their militant supporters in Greece, had upheld their reputation for hostility to "colonialism" in the Middle East, and had fought off any coordinated western program for loosening their grip on the three satellites.

At the same time, without fanfare, they secured what at the time promised to be a long extension of the occupation of Iranian Azerbaijan. In 1942, when the Soviet Union and Britain had promised Iran to withdraw their troops from Iranian soil "six months after the conclusion of hostilities," the Soviet Union had been at war with Germany and not with Japan. At Potsdam, when the Soviet Union was still not at war with Japan, it rejected the British assumption that the six months' period should be counted from the surrender of Germany and insisted, against western objections, that the period should be counted from the surrender of Japan! The best military advice at the time was that the war with Japan might end late in 1946 or in 1947. By occupying Iranian Azerbaijan for so many additional months, the Soviet forces, which had already cut it off from control by Teheran, could expect to complete the assimilation of this area into the ranks of the "people's democracies." Thus the wrangles over the role of British troops in the eastern Mediterranean had effectively covered up a drastic and unreasonable reinterpretation of an international agreement, made without even consulting Iran, which was a signatory to it.

The treasuring of grievances, real or imaginary, within a cycle of themes for negotiation is paralleled within the individual negotiation by the use of disconcerting ripostes and of accusations of bad-faith. One of the most important issues which confronted the Moscow Conference of Foreign Ministers in October 1943 was whether the Czechoslovak Government-in-Exile should conclude a twenty-year defensive alliance with the

Soviet Union alone, or whether the building of any regional systems of postwar guarantees against a revival of German aggression should be postponed until the three major allies could resolve the problem by joint decision. As early as February 1942 the Soviet Government had proposed twenty-year bilateral treaties of mutual defense against Germany to the Polish, Czechoslovak and Yugoslav Governments-in-Exile. Only the Beneš Government had accepted the proposal, and of the three governments concerned it alone was allowed by the Soviet government to return to its homeland, only to be overthrown in its turn by a Communist seizure of power in February 1948. The British and American viewpoint was that this and similar regional problems should be postponed until after the defeat of Germany, until the governments-in-exile had returned to their countries and had received a direct mandate from their peoples to undertake long-range commitments, and until the postwar system of international security could be worked out on the basis of the contemplated organization of the United Nations.

The Czechoslovak government was eager to cooperate with both east and west and hoped to have the support of both. However, in accordance with military prospects, it looked to the Soviet forces to enable it to return to its country and it had a mandate from the underground at home to accept Soviet support for its postwar security. Enthusiasm for Slav solidarity, Russia's ambiguously encouraging support of Czechoslovakia at the Munich crisis, in contrast to its abandonment by Britain and France, the desire to dissociate itself from the Polish-Soviet territorial dispute and to avoid the kind of internecine struggle which was tearing Yugoslavia apart were factors which encouraged the Beneš government to sign the Soviet alliance, which had been ready in draft form for many months, but it wished to do so only with the approval of the British and American governments, or at least with their express acquiescence.

It was against this background that the issue was taken up by the conference of foreign ministers, but the issues were not threshed out in detail. Early in the discussion a concrete issue of fact arose between Eden and Molotov. In a conciliatory fashion Eden began by saying, "I may be mistaken, but . . ." Before he could complete his sentence Molotov broke in harshly, "You *are* mistaken." His abrupt riposte was effective. Eden's presentation was disrupted. By this tactic, and by constant accusations that the western powers were trying to rebuild a *cordon sanitaire* in Eastern Europe, Molotov succeeded in evading any probing discussion of the nature and purpose of the Soviet program of building up a security belt of its own and won British approval and American acquiescence for the first step, the conclusion of the Soviet-Czechoslovak alliance, which was signed at Moscow two months later.

A similar attempt to use accusations of evil intentions to gain a Soviet point occurred during the negotiations of April–July 1945 over the arrangements for the occupation and control of Austria. In planning the zones of occupation the American, British and French delegations maintained that, as had been arranged in the agreement on zones of occupation in Germany, zonal boundaries should follow existing provincial or *Länder* frontiers. Any other procedure would involve complicated and detailed reshufflings of administrative, police, rationing, housing and other arrangements. The Soviet delegation, however, refused to follow the precedent which had been applied in the drawing of the German zones and insisted on cancelling all changes in administrative boundaries which had been made since the annexation by Germany in 1938.

The reason was simple enough. The *Land* of Vienna had undergone a long overdue expansion after the *Anschluss*. If the more extended post-1938 *Land* of Vienna were placed under four-power control, the province of Lower Austria, which was to be under Soviet occupation, would be reduced by that much in area, population and resources. It must be said, in all fairness, that the western position was genuinely based on the factor of administrative convenience and was not motivated directly by a desire to constrict the area of Soviet control. However, this was probably not appreciated by the Soviet negotiators, as the Western delegations were also insisting, and insisted successfully after many weeks of heated discussions, on rejecting the Soviet demand to occupy large parts of Styria and Carinthia and on limiting the Soviet zone to Lower Austria and Burgenland.

During the long and tedious debates over the question of adopting the pre-1938 or post-1938 boundaries of the *Land* of Vienna the favored argument of the Soviet delegation was that by urging the use of the post-1938 provincial boundary the

United States representative "was promoting Fascism." After hearing the changes rung on this charge for several sessions and many hours I calmly pointed out that, unlike certain other governments, my government had not given political recognition to the Nazi seizure of Austria, that the allied authorities in Austria would have enough to do in effecting the separation of Austria from Germany and in eradicating Nazism without wasting time in reshuffling minor administrative boundaries, and that I was unmoved by the charge of "promoting Fascism" since I was on record as having pointed out the warlike and aggressive dangers of German Fascism as early as 1930. This particular argument was thereupon dropped by the Soviet delegation, a factor which helped to improve the tone and quality of later deliberations on the arrangements for Austria. In the end the agreement established the *Land* of Vienna within its narrower pre-1938 boundaries, but it did so only in return for numerous concessions which were made by the Soviet delegation from its original and hard-fought demands.

III

During the course of negotiation it is often clear that the Soviet negotiators are under compulsion to try for a certain number of times to secure each Soviet point, no matter how minor. After trying up to a certain point and finding that the demand cannot be put through the Soviet representative has often given in, only to turn to the next item in dispute, over which a similarly prolonged period of deadlock ensues. What is not clear, however, is whether the number or duration of these tries has been prescribed in advance by instruction or whether it is left to the judgment of the individual Soviet negotiator to decide when he has built up a sufficiently impressive and protective record of having beat his head against a stone wall.

A good example of the "head-against-stone-wall" technique developed rather early in the negotiations of 1945–46 over the Yugoslav-Italian boundary. At the first meeting of the Council of Foreign Ministers, held at London in September 1945, almost the only item of agreement was a brief instruction to the Deputies to the effect that the boundary "should be in the main the ethnic line leaving a minimum under alien rule." When the

Deputies began their work at Lancaster House, in January 1946, the Soviet delegation began a strong campaign, lasting for some six weeks of almost daily argument, to remove the words, "in the main." The issue was fought over in long meetings of the four-power Commission for the Investigation of the Yugoslav-Italian Boundary, and from there it was carried into long, numerous and even more tense meetings of the Deputies.

The three words which aroused Soviet ire were extremely important. If the boundary was to follow "the ethnic line" it would reach the sea between Monfalcone and Trieste, leaving Trieste with its large Italian majority and the coastal strip of Western Istria within Yugoslavia. In the triangle Monfalcone-Gorizia-Trieste the ethnic boundary between Italian and Slovene villages is clearly marked and has hardly varied in several hundreds of years. On the other hand, if the boundary was to be "in the main the ethnic line," the Commission would have to give considerable weight to the claims of the Italian majorities in Trieste and in the coastal strip of Istria, offsetting against them the Slovene national character of several small villages in the coastal strip between Monfalcone and Trieste. If the words "in the main" were omitted it was hardly necessary to send out an investigating commission at all, with its attendant wave of turbulence, terrorization, kidnappings and murders, and the "ethnic line", pure-and-simple, could be drawn in Lancaster House.

During the weeks of intensive debate tension mounted around the green-topped table. As usual, Soviet intransigence turned the dispute into a test of staying-power. In view of the fact that public opinion still continued to regard any failure to reach speedy agreement with the Soviet government as primarily the fault of American or British "reactionaries," rather than attributing any part of it to the "all-or-nothing" Soviet attitude, it was not clear how long the western delegations would hold out against the Soviet demand that the boundary issue be prejudged one-hundred-percent in favor of the Soviet position. In an effort to win the Soviet delegation over to a compromise the Western delegations offered to remove from the purview of the boundary commission Fiume, the islands of the Quarnero and the primarily Yugoslav-inhabited parts of Venezia Giulia; they did insist that the formula "in the main" be retained and that the commission be free to investigate the Italian and mixed areas within the region. Finally, "enough was enough," even for Soviet negotiators enamored of indefinite repetition, and the Deputies suspended their meetings without agreement on the terms of reference.

Now, at last, the Soviet delegation had, reluctantly, to inform Moscow that the Western Deputies refused to budge on this basic issue of rewriting the formula which had been approved by the Council of Foreign Ministers. This put up to the Soviet government the question of taking the responsibility for an indefinite deadlock in the negotiation of the peace treaties. After two days of marking time the Soviet delegation asked to have a meeting of the Deputies and proceeded, without outward resentment, to approve the final western-backed version of the commission's terms of reference, retaining the key words, "in the main the ethnic line." One basic factor in the Soviet decision to recede from its stubbornly pressed demand must have been that Anglo-American forces were stationed in Trieste, Pola and the Isonzo valley. If Yugoslav or Soviet forces had been in possession the deadlock would probably have been allowed to continue indefinitely.

While western representatives are usually given some leeway to negotiate and always may refer back to their governments with recommendations and suggestions which, they believe, may advance their task, they can sometimes arouse a sympathetic response, on minor matters, in their Soviet colleagues by making it clear that there are certain points on which they cannot budge. A situation of this kind arose during the discussions of 1944 in London concerning the terms of the armistice with Bulgaria. After the Soviet Union had declared war on Bulgaria and its troops had occupied the country, the initiative in drafting the terms of the armistice passed to the Soviet delegation to the European Advisory Commission. The Russian representatives now argued for extremely favorable terms for the Bulgarians, although the latter had inflicted great and needless sufferings on both Greece and Yugoslavia. It was clear that the Soviet negotiators regarded every gain for Bulgaria, which they now regarded as a Soviet client, as a gain for the Soviet Union.

In particular, the Soviet representatives strongly opposed any

suggestion that the Bulgarians, who were then eating very well
and had, over the last few months, accumulated large supplies
of foodstuffs which could no longer be shipped to Germany because of the breakdown in transportation, should be required
to deliver reparations. On the other hand, all of Greece was
suffering severely from lack of foodstuffs and some parts were
on the verge of acute starvation, while the situation was serious
in many parts of Yugoslavia. In order to provide a bare minimum
of food, very tight Allied supplies and shipping were being
diverted to Greece, and of course American, British and Canadian tax-payers were meeting the bill for this aid. The Soviet
negotiators brushed aside all these considerations, based on the
community of the Allied war effort, and argued that since Bulgaria had declared war on Germany and was now fighting on
the side of the Allies, it was wrong to discourage its new-found
zeal by requiring the payment of reparations even through deliveries in kind. No such consideration had prevented the Soviet
government, a few weeks before, from imposing vast and indefinite obligations of reparation and restitution upon Rumania,
whose defection to the Allied side was a genuinely important
contribution to the war against Germany.

Finding that debate around the table failed to budge the Soviet representatives, I sought them out for a private talk. I explained that if Bulgaria escaped the payment of all reparations
in kind the burdens of the American government would be increased by just that much, that approval and review by the Congress of all appropriations was a basic part of our governmental
procedure, that failure to impose on Bulgaria the payment of
reparations might lead to an investigation, and that I might
then be punished. At the word, "punished," a sympathetic
gleam of understanding came into the eyes of my Soviet colleagues, and on the following day they agreed to insert the provision for payment of reparation in kind into the terms of the
armistice. It is hardly necessary to record that, in any case, the
enforcement of the terms of the armistice lay primarily in the
hands of "the Allied (Soviet) High Command" in Bulgaria, and
that, according to one report, for the authenticity of which I
cannot vouch, Bulgarian deliveries to Greece under the terms
of the armistice amounted to one broken-down wagon and two
slat-ribbed cows!

IV

One of the main pitfalls in wartime Anglo-American negotiations with the Soviet Union was the tendency to rely upon reaching an "agreement in principle," without spelling out in sufficient detail all the steps in its execution. After long and strenuous debates, studded with charges, accusations and suspicions, it was undoubtedly a great relief to reach a somewhat generally worded agreement and to go home. Prodded by manifold public and party duties, anxious to prove to themselves and to their people that current agreements and postwar cooperation with the Soviet Government were genuinely possible, facing "deadlines" with respect to the expectations of legislatures and of public opinion, the western leaders often approached these negotiations under serious disadvantages. Wooed rather than the wooer, able to deal at leisure with the manipulation of their public opinion at home, facing no dead-lines, the Soviet leaders had many advantages. In this situation the western powers sometimes gained the "principle" of their hopes, only to find that "in practice" the Soviet government continued to pursue its original aims.

At Yalta the Soviet Government agreed, after very lengthy argument and stubborn resistance, to participate in a reconstruction of the Polish Government which would, it appeared, permit the survival of some political freedom for the great non-Communist majority of the people. By delays and quibblings over the execution of the "agreement in principle" during the next few months, the Soviet Government secured about ninety percent of the original position with which it had come to Yalta and thus strengthened beyond challenge the small Communist minority in its dominant control of the country. At Yalta the Soviet Government also agreed, in return for sweeping territorial and other concessions, to deal only with the Chinese National Government as the representative of China. By turning over territory, administration and Japanese arms to Chinese Communist forces, the Russians nullified, in the areas where their forces were dominant, the principal and vital *quid pro quo* which they had promised at Yalta. When British, Canadian and American negotiators come to an "agreement in principle" they often haggle to a fare-thee-well over the implementation of an arrangement which may still be distasteful to each of them. However, they remain within the framework of the principle to which they have agreed, or else they frankly ask to reopen the agreement in principle and to renegotiate it on the grounds that further consideration has shown that they cannot carry it out. It has remained for the Soviet representatives to assert that they are carrying out "an agreement in principle" by doing just the reverse "in practice."

Except for a scant handful of legal consultants who were trained in general jurisprudence and international law prior to the great revolution of 1927–29 in Soviet academic life, Soviet representatives usually show little comprehension of the legal problems which arise in seeking agreements among nations, or in meeting the constitutional requirements of democratic states, and special obstacles have arisen not infrequently from this cause. During the Paris sessions of the Council of Foreign Ministers there was one amusing instance of this difficulty. The Soviet delegation appeared rather puzzled over the presence of Senator Tom Connally and the late Senator Arthur H. Vandenberg among the American delegation. Senator Vandenberg upset them particularly. After some especially outrageous tirade by Molotov he would take his unsmoked cigar from his mouth and grin across the table most engagingly, as if to say, "Well, well, that *is* a new angle!"

One afternoon, as we were leaving the conference hall for tea, a member of the Soviet delegation, taking me by the arm, asked, after one or two hurried preliminaries, why the Senators were there. I quickly gave him a three-minute sketch of the background and working of the bi-partisan foreign policy and explained that the peace treaties, on which the Council was working, could be ratified by the President only upon the advice and consent of the Senate, and of two-thirds of the Senate, at that. And since (using Soviet terms for clarity) American parties were "undisciplined" affirmative action by the Senate would require approval and support by influential leaders of both parties. My Soviet colleague was frankly amazed to learn of this responsibility of the Senate. "You don't mean that the Senate would refuse to ratify a treaty that your government had signed?" he asked. To that I could only reply that the Senate had often refused to act at all or had acted negatively on treaties negotiated and submitted to it by the executive.

In 1944, in the work of the European Advisory Commission, a difficult legal problem arose during the preparation of the Instrument of Unconditional Surrender which was to be imposed by the three, later four, powers at the time of the final surrender of the German government and the German High Command. Should those forces which would be surrendered in this final act, in distinction from those who surrendered or were captured during hostilities, be declared prisoners-of-war, or not? After detailed discussions with military and legal experts the American and British delegations were instructed to oppose declaring such German and other enemy personnel to be prisoners-of-war, while the Soviet Government insisted that they be so declared.

From the American and British viewpoint there was a whole series of difficulties involved in this. The final surrender might suddenly place from three to six million German armed personnel in their custody, with the legal requirement to furnish them with food, housing, clothing and medical care according to the respective standards applied by the American and British armies to their own troops on a garrison footing. This was not physically, financially, or politically feasible. Furthermore, in the unprecedented situation in which Germany would cease to be a sovereign state there was no way of knowing how long this tremendous burden might continue. It would also mean that the legally necessary provision for the German forces would place them in a greatly favored position as against the liberated populations of our own allies in Europe. Finally, there was considerable legal doubt as to whether a prisoner-of-war could be tried for war crimes aside from the previously established crimes of war. It was clear that the Soviet Union was faced by no such difficulties. Its personnel had been subjected by the Nazis to great cruelty and even to mass extermination, and it was not bound by any international conventions in its treatment of German prisoners taken during or at the close of hostilities.

For some five months this problem was a serious block in the way of completing an agreed Instrument of Unconditional Surrender. The Soviet delegation insisted day after day that the German forces must be declared prisoners-of-war. The American and British delegations explained over and over again why they were unwilling to do this, though they were willing, and proposed fairly early in the negotiation, that provision be made that each of the three, later four, commanders-in-chief be free to declare or not to declare prisoners-of-war those German forces which came under his control at the final surrender. In attacking both the position of the two western delegations and the compromise which they had offered, the Soviet representatives continually accused the latter of "promoting German militarism," "fostering Nazism," and so forth.

Finally, Soviet consent to the proposed compromise formula was secured by drawing up a fairly detailed statement of the difficulties which the Soviet proposal raised, translating it into Russian and persuading the Soviet delegation to send it to Moscow, despite the reluctance of the Soviet negotiators to appear even to question the correctness of their original instructions to which they had held so stubbornly. Even at the very end the Soviet delegation remained unconvinced that there was any real legal difficulty involved for the Western powers but were persuaded finally that there was "nothing bad" in this final compromise for the Soviet position.

V

In this as in numerous other instances Soviet negotiators, even when under some pressure to reach agreement, have shown that they are in mortal terror of violating any part, minor or major, of their instructions, and are extremely reluctant to report to Moscow that they cannot get every point and every wording in their own drafts. Making recommendations for even slight changes in their instructions exposes them to serious risks. It means that they consider their own superiors slightly less than omniscient. It may mean that they can be accused of giving undue weight to the viewpoint of another government and thus of "falling captive to imperialist insinuations." The result is that, even when, in a given question, the Soviet negotiator is committed to the desirability of achieving agreement, he is unable to take any initiative in finding a reasonable meeting ground of viewpoints and he is usually extremely reluctant even to present to his own government suggestions for compromise or reconciliation of differences which originate in other delegations.

A widespread lack of ease in using English or French commonly adds a good deal to the difficulties of the Soviet negotiator. Russian linguists have done pioneer work in the development of effective teaching of languages. Most of the newer methods which have been developed in the United States during and since the war for the intensive teaching of languages were familiar twenty years ago in the best Soviet institutes. But relatively few Soviet representatives abroad have received adequate training in languages at a sufficiently early age, and almost none have had the experience of living informally in a foreign culture at an impressionable period of their development. Since the great purge of the Soviet foreign service at the end of the 1930's the staff has been recruited primarily from among administrators and engineers, with a sprinkling of professors. Until they entered upon their new careers the newer Soviet diplomats had no need or incentive to learn a foreign language effectively, and once entered upon it they have no time or permission to relax and absorb not only a language but the culture or way of thought which is expressed in mastering it. This places a special burden on foreign negotiators to phrase their proposals and texts in a form which can be rendered exactly into Russian, if they wish their own positions to be understood.

Russian, particularly in its Soviet usage, lends itself even less readily than English to the disciplined clarity of French, the unequalled language of diplomacy. Dictionary renditions are often downright misleading. According to dictionaries and pre-Soviet usage, "predlagat' " means "to propose"; in Soviet usage, carried over from Communist Party practice, it means "to direct," to give an instruction which cannot be disobeyed. On occasion I have seen a Soviet negotiator fall into a rage because an inoffensive "propose" was turned into "predlagat' " in the translation. The word "soyuz" in Russian means both an "alliance" between two independent states and a complete "union" into a single state. "Blagorazumnyi" is as near as Russian comes to "reasonable," and the Russian word has none of the overtones or undertones of its English meaning.

The Russian word "vlast' " is usually rendered as "authority," but "vlast' " connotes a complete power of disposal, not a limited "authority." This difficulty was illustrated in an abortive attempt, in April 1945, to negotiate an agreement concerning the future status of allied newspaper and radio correspondents in Germany. The key provision of a draft agreement, which had been drawn up in the War Department for negotiation in the European Advisory Commission, was that the correspondent was to be subject "to the full authority" of the Commander-in-Chief who issued credentials to him in his own zone. When I received this draft, with the instruction to begin negotiations at once for its acceptance by the four governments, I pointed out to Washington that in the Soviet interpretation of this provision an American correspondent who entered the Soviet zone could be tried by a secret Soviet court and sentenced by purely administrative procedure to a term in a concentration camp because some article which he had written ten years earlier in America was regarded as "inimical to the security and strength" of the Soviet Union. My objections were overruled and my suggested redraftings, designed to avoid this risk, were brushed aside. I received a peremptory instruction to circulate the draft agreement and to urge its adoption.

For more than fifteen months the Soviet delegation had, time and again, been extremely slow in responding to American and British proposals, and it was usually unable to give any indication of whether it would ever be able to negotiate. In this case, however, Moscow acted with great alacrity. Within less than a week the Soviet delegation indicated that it wished to begin negotiations on the following day on the American draft agreement. It was clear that the Soviet foreign office liked the War Department's draft and that it was ready to accept it with minor changes. With no time for further argument with Washington about the dangerous draft, I wired that I expected to be asked to clarify some of the wording of the draft. If, for example, I should be asked to define "full authority," I proposed to state that its meaning was that the commander-in-chief had "full authority in matters of accrediting and disaccrediting" foreign correspondents in his zone.

A few hours later the European Advisory Commission began its first and only session on the draft agreement. The Soviet representative offered a few minor textual improvements in the American draft and then declared that he was prepared to conclude it at once. It was now my turn to explain that by "full authority" the draft meant only "full authority in matters of accrediting and disaccrediting" correspondents. After this the Soviet representative rapidly lost interest in the draft, and the subject was not discussed again in the Commission, which had many other urgent matters to struggle with.

One of the difficulties of Soviet-Russian vocabulary is that the word "compromise" is not of native origin and carries with it no favorable empathy. It is habitually used only in combination with the adjective "putrid." "Compromise for the sake of getting on with the job" is natural to American and British people, but it is alien to the Bolshevist way of thinking and to the discipline which the Communist Party has striven to inculcate in its members. To give up a demand once presented, even a very minor or formalistic point, makes a Bolshevik-trained negotiator feel that he is losing control of his own will and is becoming subject to an alien will. Therefore any point which has finally to be abandoned must be given up only after a most terrific struggle. The Soviet negotiator must first prove to himself and his superiors that he is up against an immovable force. Only then is he justified in abandoning a point which plainly cannot be gained and in moving on to the next item, which will again be debated in an equally bitter tug-of-wills.

The Soviet negotiator must try to force the acceptance of his entire proposal. Hence he regards each provision and phrase as equally important. The Bolshevik is trained to feel that ideology must be "monolithic" at any given time, even though it may change from time to time. In one period it may be wrong for a "good Bolshevik" to shave every day and to wear a neck-tie; at another time he will be reprimanded for neglecting these amenities. The important thing is to have a complete answer to past, present and future and to insist, against all contrary evidence, that this answer is, always has been, and must ever be, the same. This attitude gives rise to a, to the westerner absurd, insistence upon periodically rewriting the history of the Party, of Russia and of the world and of rewriting it each time to uphold some new "infallible" dogma.

The western negotiator is usually able to envisage a series of minor shifts in his own and other positions. He is "pluralistic" in his approach to a solution, in the adjustments of democratic decision-making at home and in seeking adjustments of interests and views among nations. The Soviet negotiator is worried, puzzled, scornful, and suspicious when the western negotiator tries out a series of minor variations to see if the opposing positions cannot be brought closer together. To him it means only that the western representative was "not serious" in the first place. If he is willing to shift so quickly from his origial position it must mean that he did not hold it in earnest to begin with and that he can eventually be forced all the way over to the Soviet position, provided the Soviet negotiator will only display "principled steadfastness" long enough and vigorously enough.

The western representative tends to assume that a minor concession here or there will facilitate achieving the common aim of cooperative action. He does not necessarily look for an immediate *quid pro quo* for each minor concession. At a later stage in the negotiation his partner will remember the facilitating concession and will yield something in turn. To him "goodwill" is both a lubricant of the negotiating process and a valuable intangible by-product. The Soviet negotiator takes a minor concession as a sign that his principles are stronger and his will is firmer than those of his opponent. He does not believe in "goodwill." He is trained to assume the ill-will of the "capitalist environment." If an "imperialist" negotiator asserts his will for peace, it means, at the best, that he is consciously in favor of peace but is unconsciously a tool of uncontrollable forces which work for war and for the final clash between "two worlds." At the worst, it means that he is trying to deceive and gain time while mouthing words of "peace." To a Bolshevik even a momentary "loss of vigilance" may have fatal consequences. The Soviet diplomat feels himself like a traveler by night in the forest who must be constantly on the watch for the smallest sound or sight of treachery. He must be unceasingly on guard against his own human tendency to "fall into complacency" and thus to underestimate the dangers which surround both him and the regime which he serves.

Soviet diplomacy is also monolithic in its method of operation and in its reactions to outside events or internal changes of stress. The American practice is to subdivide authority extensively, both at home and in foreign dealings. A military mission in Moscow, trying to work out plans for military coordination, would have nothing to say about the arrangements or conditions for lend-lease. A political negotiation, aiming to preserve the freedom of choice for an East European nation, would have no relation to another mission which might be deciding which German ships should be transferred to the Soviet Union, and all of them would have no relation to a decision concerning military and economic aid to China. No such autonomy or fragmentation of authority is felt in the Soviet conduct of its foreign policy. While it is probable that little background information on policy is communicated by Moscow to its representatives abroad, beyond that which they need individually in order to carry out their instructions, it is pretty clear that underlying attitudes are communicated rapidly to them. Thus, a negotiation over the statute of Tangier bogs down in Paris; this may be a repercussion of a crisis which has arisen in Vienna or of a note delivered in Warsaw. Bolshevist mythology is full of "chain-reaction" concepts of causality. With the clumsy force of centralized wisdom it attempts to meet this assumed universal causal interdependence ("nothing is accidental") with its confidence in its own ability to manipulate events in accordance with its own Leninist-Stalinist dialectic, which it regards as a unique instrument for both foreseeing and bringing about the future.

VI

This is a grim picture. The Soviet negotiator is tight as a spring, deeply suspicious, always trying to exert the Soviet will-power outward and to avoid reflecting non-Soviet facts and aspirations inward, a rigid agent knowing only the segment of policy which he must carry out with mechanical precision. Does this mean that "negotiation" in any real sense of the term is impossible? Admitting that negotiation under these conditions is a very limited affair and very difficult and unrewarding, it may still be both possible and essential. But it requires a special approach. Naturally, a knowledge of Russian in its Soviet nuances is important. It is equally important to understand the role of the Soviet negotiator in relation to his own government and to its ideology. The Department of State has carried on a far-sighted policy of equipping a substantial number of its representatives through language and area training and through service in mis-

sions in the Soviet-dominated areas to deal with Soviet problems, and as these young men mature in experience they will
fill an important need. The Army and Air Force have also done
a good deal along this line.

In the absence of informal channels of communication with
Soviet representatives it is important for an American delegation to be able to determine whether the Soviet negotiators have
no instructions, have definite instructions, or merely have instructions to build up a propaganda position. A well equipped
negotiator can go much more thoroughly into the range of Soviet intentions if he follows the discussion in the original, without being handicapped by the opaque veil of translation. In addition he should review each document exchanged or each statement made in the light of its clear rendering into Russian. It is
unfortunate, for example, that many American public figures
continually speak of the need for an "aggressive policy" to coun-
teract Soviet pressures, when they mean an "energetic" or "vigorous" policy. In Russian "aggressive" means only "intending
to commit or engaged in committing aggression," and the collo-
quial American use of "aggressive" inevitably receives a sinister
meaning in Russian translation, which is the form in which
documents must be utilized by all but a handful of Soviet negotiators and policy-makers.

In conducting negotiations with Soviet representatives it is
important to adopt in the beginning a single clear position, one
which can be upheld logically and politically during long discussions. The Soviet delegation will not report this position as
the final and strongly held one until they have had a chance
to attack it from all sides. Indefinite repetition of arguments
must be accepted as an inevitable preparation to negotiate. The
American negotiator is inclined to make a single presentation
and then to become impatient when the Soviet response makes
it plain that the Soviet representative either has not understood
it or does not believe it. The Soviet negotiator, of course, does
not believe what he hears, but he listens for undertones of firmness or uncertainty which tell him whether or not he is shaking
the determination of his adversary. Strong but controlled feeling, rather than impatience or anger, is an effective way of giving him his answer to this question. When a position is firmly
established it is often advantageous to prepare a special memo-

randum, accompanied by a clear and idiomatic translation into Russian, in order to be sure that one's own position is adequately reported to Moscow, the only spot at which new instructions are likely to be initiated. Oral statements of position may or may not be reported, but it is probable that every bit of written material is carefully transmitted. If some part of the English memorandum does not lend itself to clear rendering into Russian, it is useful to rewrite the English version until it can be rendered without ambiguity, for while Russian can express any thought, it does not lend itself flexibly to a literal rendering of an English concept or phrase.

Once a position has been worked out, the non-Soviet negotiator must be prepared to uphold it in detail, and for a long time. The technique of constantly trying out variant versions, which works well in the western style of negotiation, only confuses the Soviet representative, who suspects some new trick in each new variant and must subject each in turn to exhaustive interpretation. Constantly modifying one's position or the way in which it is expressed means also that the Soviet negotiator is at a loss to know what version is based on bed-rock and should therefore be reported to Moscow. Even slight shifts in position or wording increase his belief that the adversary's position is a shaky one and thus encourage him to hold out that much longer for the full Soviet position. Western negotiators are usually in a position to accept slight adaptations, but even the slightest variation must be reported back to Moscow for decision there.

Since western negotiators are generally free, in the light of previous instructions and their knowledge of their governments' overall policies, to comment at once on new proposals or statements made during the course of negotiation, they often assume that Soviet negotiators have a similar latitude and accordingly press them to express their views. When so pressed, the Soviet negotiator is always free to raise innumerable objections and criticisms. He is not free to express concordance with any part of a proposal on which he has not received instructions from Moscow. Even the "program statements" of Soviet negotiators must be reviewed or written in Moscow before they can be delivered, and therefore Soviet statements at conferences often seem to have little relation to the immediately preceding statements of other delegations.

When a negotiation is actually under way, it is useful to avoid pressing the Soviet delegation to commit itself on a new proposal or draft. During the active negotiations carried on in the European Advisory Commission, whenever a new proposal or even a redraft was first presented, it was my habit to ask questions which would clarify its meaning and implications and then to take the initiative, even if I had adequate instructions, in saying that I would have to consult my government before commenting on it, thus relieving the Soviet delegation of the onus of either declining to comment on it or else of building up a whole series of negative statements against the proposal. Then, on occasions when I had instructions on the new point at issue, I would go at once to the Soviet delegation and inform its members in detail of the American position. This meant that Moscow had before it, at the same time, the proposal and the American position on it. When there was a certain underlying desire to reach agreements, this procedure was often effective, or so it seemed, in reducing the number of divergences by providing full background on the problem before Moscow had taken a firm position, which could later be modified only by a long and exhausting tug-of-wills. Such informal discussions, conducted in Russian, also offered an occasion for learning or sensing the often unforeseen Russian objections and suspicions and for attempting to remove or alleviate them at an early stage.

When stating a position it is well to be sparing in the use of general or broadly stated principles, and when such principles are an essential part of the position it is necessary to remember that they are not shared by the Soviet negotiator. Broad statements of principle can, however, be effectively anchored in the historic experience of one's own people and, explained in that setting, they can have a certain impact on Soviet thinking. Soviet policy-makers may then accept them as a fact which must be taken into account, even though they do not believe in them or share them.

Wherever possible it is more useful to state one's position in terms of a definite material interest, as in the case of the question of Bulgaria's obligation to provide reparation to Greece and Yugoslavia. Soviet-trained negotiators pride themselves on identifying material interests and can therefore more readily visualize them as facts to which a certain adjustment can be made.

This can be illustrated from the problem of the Soviet treatment of American prisoners-of-war who were overrun in the Soviet advance into eastern Germany. Despite the agreement for mutual assistance in collecting, caring for and repatriating each other's prisoners-of-war, the agreement never received halfway adequate implementation on the Soviet side, and great and unnecessary hardships were inflicted by the Soviet attitude on American and other western prisoners. The Soviet authorities could not understand that it was a normal and automatic principle, for Americans, to give every possible care, on an American standard, to fellow-countrymen who had been taken captive. Soviet prisoners, over-run by their own armies, were given only the meager standard of care which falls to the lot of the ordinary Soviet population, and in addition they were subjected to special disabilities until they could prove that they had not, in some measure, surrendered voluntarily to the Germans. If the American authorities had emphasized that liberated American prisoners must be well cared for because they were needed immediately in the war against Japan—which was not the case—the Soviet authorities would probably have given much better co-operation in caring for and transporting them, as they would have been impressed by the direct material interest involved.

Is it worthwhile to dwell on these experiences or to talk about negotiating at all? Even during the wartime alliance against the common menaces of Germany and Japan negotiations with the Soviet government were extremely difficult and frustrating, and, aside from the advantage of having established the United Nations, even before the end of the war, as a "forum for the opinions of mankind," none of the wartime agreements on postwar co-operation has worked out as was hoped, even against hope. Since the war the Soviet government has striven by all the means in its extensive arsenal to gain and retain every advantage for its side, regardless of the fact that thereby it quickly dissipated a very large reservoir of good-will and aroused the deep alarm of all nations which lay beyond its direct control. In a period of Soviet expansion and of hope for further expansion, negotiation could have only the purpose of confusing and dividing the nations which opposed its pressure, and since the war the Soviet purpose in negotiating has not been to reach agreements with strong opponents but to intimidate weaker and adjacent countries and to undermine the stamina of its principal potential adversaries.

Protected by two oceans and remote from the direct origins of previous world wars, Americans have been accustomed to ignore the rising storm and then, once it had burst upon them, to work solely for victory over the immediate menace. Thus, they tend to feel a sharp dichotomy between "war" and "peace." When at peace they are reluctant to think of the possibility of war. When at war they concentrate solely on winning the war, as if it were a grim football match, and refuse to worry about the peace which is the goal of war. Through Lenin and Stalin Soviet thinking has fully absorbed the Clausewitz maxims that national strength and strong alliances determine the effectiveness of national policy in peace, and that in war one must never lose sight of the aims of policy for which it is waged. To the Soviet way of thinking, conflict is inherent in the development of "capitalist" society, and cannot be wished out of existence by "subjective good-will."

Within this ongoing history of conflict, however, Soviet tactics and techniques are not inflexible. Soviet policy towards the outside world has varied markedly during the past thirty-four years. True, the outward pressure of Soviet power has marked and seared the post-1945 years and the building of a reliable counterforce is only now under way in Europe. The outline of a similar counterforce cannot yet be discerned in Asia. In western policy the building of "positions of strength" and the use of negotiation must go hand-in-hand. Building of strength and negotiating cannot be regarded as alternatives or as opposites. They must be teamed. Negotiation without strength and determination behind it is frustrating, dangerous and may be suicidal. On the other hand, when strength has been built, refusal to negotiate may precipitate a colossal struggle, which would be fought as a cruel civil war in many parts of the world,—the very conflict which western strength is being fashioned to avert.

For the time being negotiation of those issues which are negotiable between the Soviet Union and the west is, generally speaking, in abeyance. But the art of policy will be to recognize, from a position of strength, future potentialities of negotiation, not with an expectation of bringing about a lasting or worldwide relaxation of Soviet ambitions, but as a means of alleviating individual sources of tension and thus of strengthening the free world. And if negotiation must go in harness with consistent and purposeful building of strength, the art and technique of international dealings must also be broadened to take full account of the peculiar character of the Soviet approach to negotiation.

Index

Date Due

NOV 11 1976		

CAT. NO. 23 233   PRINTED IN U.S.A.

Lightning Source UK Ltd.
Milton Keynes UK
UKHW022031150223
417099UK00008B/148